PMI Risk M Professional (PMI-RMP)®

PMI-RMP®
Exam Prep
Study Guide

PMI-RMP®
Exam Prep
Study Guide
5th Edition

Aligned with:
- *PMI-RMP® Examination Content Outline*
- *Practice Standard for Project Risk Management*
- *PMBOK® Guide - Fifth Edition*

Belinda S. Fremouw
PMP, PMI-SP, PMI-RMP, PgMP, CAPM, PMI-ACP

PMI-RMP® Exam Prep Study Guide - Fifth Edition
by Belinda Fremouw

Editor: Kathryn Gunn
Cover Designer: Devin Fremouw
Interior Designer: Devin Fremouw

Printing History:

April 2017:	Fifth Edition
April 2014:	Fourth Edition
November 2013:	Third Edition
November 2011:	Second Edition
April 2010:	First Edition

Version 5.6

ISBN: 978-0-9975983-5-3

Goodrich Fremaux Publishing
Peoria, AZ 85383
PassionatePM.com

Ordering Information:
Special discounts are available on quantity purchases by corporations, associations, educators, etc. For details, contact the publisher at the above address.

Using this material as an instructor? Contact us at Info@PassionatePM.com to order the accompanying PowerPoint slides.

About the Author

Belinda Fremouw, PMP, CAPM, PgMP, PMI-SP, PMI-RMP, PMI-ACP, is an internationally recognized project management consultant, author, and public speaker. With three decades of project management experience, Belinda has worked across multiple industries, including finance, healthcare, IT, engineering, and government.

She has provided training and consultation to thousands of project

managers and organizations globally. The first woman in the world to achieve the original five PMI® credentials, she has developed multiple successful project management exam preparation programs, including Project Management Professional (PMP)®, Certified Associate in Project Management (CAPM)®, PMI Agile Certified Practitioner (PMI-ACP)®, and PMI® Risk Management Professional (PMI-RMP)® boot camps.

Her robust exam prep courseware is utilized by hundreds of training companies internationally.

Belinda is the Founder of Passionate Project Management, a learning and development firm located in Phoenix, Arizona.

PassionatePM.com

BelindaFremouw.com

Table of Contents

List of Figures

Foreword

Risk is a small but powerful word that means something different to everyone who considers it. Risk is simultaneously simple and complex. It is what might happen five minutes from now or five years. Your personal true meaning of risk is dependent only on you. Believe me; you already know more about risk than you think you do! Risk is any uncertainty, good or bad.

For example, you might believe that jumping from an airplane in the middle of the night from 18,000 feet and with 200 pounds of equipment to be near or total insanity. Yet when I did just that, multiple times in my military career, it was a calculated risk. To those untrained in the required skill sets, I can easily understand how it would not seem like something to stand in line to try. I am happy to report that my parachutes always opened!

You might also consider driving 2500 miles across the United States with young children into a very uncertain job market to be an unwise decision. But when the author of this book and my dear friend Belinda Fremouw did that 20 years ago, it was also a calculated risk. The fact that you are reading this is a testament to her professional success since making that decision. In both this and the previous example, we are talking about risk tolerance, and this book will explain this concept and many others in great detail.

Now let us go back to my previous statement that you already know more about risk than you think you do. Have you ever purchased a lottery ticket with dreams of sailing away? Or perhaps sped through a yellow light, hoping to make it to work on time without getting a ticket? How many people willingly park in the most dimly lit area of the parking garage without looking over their shoulder once or twice? The list of daily risks we encounter goes on and on.

This book is an excellent resource, and I was honored when Belinda asked me to contribute. If you patiently and studiously seek to understand the content within, there is a very high probability that you will achieve your PMI-RMP certification. As I have taught from this content many times, I can personally guarantee the alignment of the material with the exam content. You will also gain the added benefit of understanding your own perception of risk in your personal and professional life. Why does the hair stand up on the back of your neck sometimes? Are you just cold heading to that project review meeting, or is some internal risk trigger warning you to take notice of a threat or an opportunity?

The last piece of advice I will offer is simple: study every day and stay focused. There can be no achievement without focus. And, as always, Passionate Project Management will "rock your face off!"

Bob Mahler, PMI-RMP, PMP

Acknowledgements

This book has been a long time in the making, and I am so pleased that it is now published.

As a project manager, I learned quickly that the one skill that differentiates an average project manager from an exceptional one is risk management. The ability to recognize the uncertainties facing your project, to educate and inform your stakeholders without sounding like Henny Penny, and to be ready when things don't go as expected (as always happens) takes a special knack. These challenges just happened to be my favorite part of managing a project. The messier, more complex, and less certain it was, the better I liked it.

When the Project Management Institute (PMI)® launched the PMI Risk Management Professional (PMI-RMP)® credential, I was thrilled. I successfully completed my PMI-RMP credential exam on June 2, 2010, scoring proficient in the four domains, Risk Communication, Risk Analysis, Risk Response Planning, and Risk Governance, just five weeks after completing my PMI Scheduling Professional (PMI-SP)®.

Later that year, I added a PMI-RMP exam prep class to our training offerings.

Since 2010, not only has our environment changed in the ways that project managers are able to learn and prepare for the exam, but the exam itself has also changed. I receive consistent feedback that the exam is much more challenging, requiring a greater depth and breadth of knowledge. I also know that many project managers are not able to afford to take an exam prep course and must rely on self-study.

For that reason, this book is very near and dear to my heart. I wanted to provide just the right amount of information, not too much and not too little, in order to ensure that candidates have what they need to prepare for and pass the exam as efficiently as possible.

I want to thank all of my students who successfully completed their PMI-RMP exams for giving me exceptional feedback. That feedback is woven into the chapters and the practice questions you will find in this book.

A special shout-out needs to go to my latest PMI-RMP Exam Prep students, who worked through this book in its final draft format. I am completely confident that they will soon be honored with the PMI-RMP credential. Thank you, Dorothy Wan, Levi McVay, and Douglas DiPiero of the Passionate Project Management's PMI-RMP Exam Prep Class (January 2017).

Getting this book "just right" took a lot of time and effort. There were many days, including evenings and weekends, when my daughters and grandchildren took a back seat, always recognizing the importance of this book.

And last, but certainly not least, I have to give a big shout out to my husband, Devin. He is always behind the scenes, fastidious about every detail, taking a microscope to margins and indents and shading and fonts. I explain my dreams to him, and he helps me make them a reality. None of this would be possible without him. #LightningTeamGo!

Chapter 1

The PMI-RMP® Exam

Introduction

Congratulations on your decision to pursue the Project Management Institute (PMI) Risk Management Professional (PMI-RMP)® credential! Being a credentialed (and possibly multi-credentialed) project manager can greatly enhance your career opportunities and salary.

One of the most critical aspects of managing projects is managing uncertainty. Uncertainty is risk. The ability to accurately identify, address, and respond to that uncertainty is the hallmark of a strong and experienced project manager. Because of that, I personally believe that the PMI-RMP credential is a natural progression for any seasoned project manager.

I earned my PMI-RMP on June 2, 2010. At that time, I found the exam surprisingly straightforward and relatively easy, compared to the Project Management Professional (PMP)® exam. I have since taught PMI-RMP exam prep to a few hundred professionals, and based on their feedback and experiences, the exam has changed over time. Candidates may experience difficulty with the exam's specialized risk analyses, especially if they lack professional experience in that aspect.

This book is intended to give you a robust study and preparation program in order to ensure your success on the exam, and to do so, it includes comprehensive yet straightforward information on the specialized risk analysis techniques. PMI's credentialing exams are notoriously difficult, and the PMI-RMP exam is no different. However, with the appropriate focus and study, I have found that many professional project managers are able to pass on their first attempt.

PMP® Certification

While there is no requirement that you have your PMP prior to pursuing your PMI-RMP, a majority of PMI-RMP aspirants have already earned their PMP.

If you are PMP-certified, you will be familiar with the PMI approach to testing and question formats. In addition, you will have some knowledge of *A Guide to the Project Management Body of Knowledge (PMBOK® Guide)*. Keep in mind that the current PMI-RMP exam is based on the *PMBOK® Guide*, 5th Edition. If you tested for your PMP on the 5th Edition, you will find that some aspects of this material provide a review of your PMP exam preparation, but it will also offer much deeper dive into the project risk management components.

If you tested for your PMP prior to the release of the 5th Edition, it may be beneficial to review the differences. If you are not PMP-certified, it is still possible to successfully complete the PMI-RMP exam on your first attempt, but it may take slightly more effort. For either situation, I will be highlighting the key aspects and components of information within the *PMBOK® Guide* that are applicable to the current PMI-RMP exam throughout this book.

An important step toward completing your PMI-RMP exam is committing to and following through with a dedicated study plan and approach. I recommend pinpointing a date by which you want to complete the exam and building your study plan accordingly. Commit to your date below.

I, _____, **commit to completing my PMI-RMP exam by** _____.

Using This Book

Each of the nine chapters in this book includes review questions covering its sections. Ideally, you should be scoring at least 80-85% on the review questions. If you are scoring less than that, be sure to identify your gaps and go back to the related sections.

You will also find that each chapter includes a vocabulary review exercise. Because one of the goals of PMI is to formalize a common project management vernacular, it is important to be very strong in your knowledge of these terms and definitions. It is possible that you will find a difference between a term you have used in practice and PMI's definition of that term. Always align with the PMI definition!

Finally, this book includes a full-length PMI-RMP practice exam, which aligns with the PMI exam blueprint, its allocation of questions, and its timing. Approach this practice exam as though it were the actual exam. Ideally, you should score at least 75 -80% on the practice test to indicate readiness for the actual exam.

Project Management Institute (PMI)®

Founded in 1969, the Project Management Institute (PMI) has a primary focus on advancing the practice of project management. A not-for-profit organization, PMI develops and publishes project management standards, manages an extensive research program, and offers professional development opportunities to project managers working in all industries.

PMI has more than 250 chapters around the world and 30 industry- or interest-based communities of practice.

As of January 2017, PMI's annual membership fees are:

- Individual – $139 to join, $129 to renew
- Student – $32 to join, $32 to renew
- Retiree – $65 to renew

Benefits of membership include:

- Access to members-only information and resources on PMI.org
- Discounts on the PMI credential exams
- Access to PMI's career framework
- A digital copy of all of the PMI practice standards, including the *PMBOK® Guide*, 5th Edition
- Leadership and volunteer opportunities
- Publications including *PM Network®*, *PMI Today®*, and *Project Management Journal®*
- Up to a 20% discount on PMI store purchases

The PMI-RMP® Credential

Launched by PMI in 2008, the first PMI-RMP credential was granted on June 2, 2008, and 63 additional project risk management practitioners achieved the credential by the end of 2008. As of October 31, 2016, there are 3,783 PMI-RMP credential holders globally.

The specialized PMI-RMP credential is intended for professionals who not only demonstrate knowledge and experience in general project management practices but also demonstrate significant experience and expertise in the practice of project risk management.

Project risk management involves not only the ability to identify and assess project risks but also the ability to manage negative risks (threats) and capitalize on positive risks (opportunities). This may be the first time you have seen risk referred to as potentially positive. On the exam and from a PMI-perspective, it is important to recognize that risk can be both positive and negative. I will address this in more detail later in this book.

According to PMI, 83% of organizations that are high performers in project management practice risk management frequently, while just 49% of low performers do so.

PMI-RMP Credential Snapshot

	PMI-RMP®	
Credential Name	PMI Risk Management Professional®	
Project Role	Assesses and identifies risks, mitigates threats, and capitalizes opportunities	
Eligibility	HS diploma: 4,500 hours of project risk management experience within the last five consecutive years and 40 hours of project risk management education OR Bachelor's degree: 3,000 hours of project risk management experience within the last five consecutive years and 30 hours of project risk management education	
Exam Information	3.5 hours 170 questions	
Fees	Member $520 Non-Member $670	
Credential Maintenance	3 years; 30 PDUs	

PMI-RMP Requirements

To qualify to apply for the PMI-RMP credential, you must meet the following criteria:

- With a high school diploma or global equivalent:
  - At least 4,500 hours of experience in professional project risk management within the last five consecutive years *and*
  - 40 contact hours of formal education in the specialized area of project risk management
- With a bachelor's degree or global equivalent:
  - At least 3,000 hours of experience in professional project risk management within the last five consecutive years *and*
  - 30 contact hours of formal education in the specialized area of project risk management

PMI-RMP Application

If you have your PMP credential, the application process for the PMI-RMP will be similar. To complete your PMI-RMP application:

1. Create a profile on www.PMI.org.

2. From the PMI home page: Home > Certification > PMI Risk Management Professional (PMI-RMP).

3. Select "Ready to Apply?"

4. You will be guided through the application process and asked to provide your educational history and your project risk management experience.

   • Project risk management experience must date back at least three years from the application submission date but must begin no earlier than five years prior to the application submission date.

   • Project risk management experience is required in each of the five areas: risk strategy/planning, stakeholder engagement, risk process facilitation, risk monitoring/reporting, and specialized risk analyses, although you do not need experience in all domains for all projects.

5. Once you submit your application to PMI, it will take approximately five business days to be reviewed and approved.

6. You will receive a notification that your application has been approved, and you will be directed to pay your credential fees.

   • If you are a PMI member, the exam fees are $520. For non-members, the fees are $670.

7. Upon payment of the exam fees, you will be provided with either:

   • A payment receipt containing your eligibility ID, which will be used to schedule your exam, *or*

   • A payment receipt with audit notification.

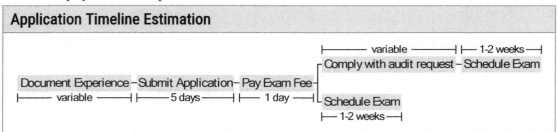

Audit

PMI randomly selects approximately 25% of applications for audit upon payment of the exam fees. If you are audited, verification of your experience and education must be provided to PMI before they will issue your eligibility ID, which you will need to schedule your exam.

You will complete your experience verification using forms that are pre-printed with your submitted experience. You will need to have these forms physically, not electronically, signed by the contact person for the organization you identified on your application. The signed forms need to be placed into an envelope and sealed with the contact's signature across the flap.

These experience forms, your training transcripts, and proof of your education (a photocopy of a diploma or an unofficial transcript) should be sent to PMI in one envelope. It typically takes less than a week from the receipt of the materials for PMI to clear a candidate from audit.

I advise my students to assume that they are going to get audited. It's better to have a good surprise than a bad surprise from PMI. Be certain that the information you are submitting is factual. I also recommend giving the organization contact you list (manager, supervisor, etc) a heads-up as to what you will be submitting on the application and advise them that you may need them to sign off on the work.

The PMI-RMP Exam

Once you have your Eligibility ID, you will be able to schedule your PMI-RMP exam online at www.Prometric.com/PMI. PMI-RMP exams are offered year-round at designated Prometric sites, and in most U.S. regions, candidates can secure a seat within a few weeks. For other global areas, it can be more challenging to schedule the test.

If you need to reschedule or cancel your exam, do so more than 30 days prior for no cost. If you must cancel or reschedule within 30 days prior to your exam, there will be a $70 fee. If you cancel or reschedule within 48 hours prior to your exam, you will forfeit your entire exam fee.

There are 170 questions on the PMI-RMP exam, and you will have 3.5 hours to complete the test. Of the 170 questions, 150 are scored and 20 are considered "pre-test" or unscored questions. These are questions that PMI is evaluating for future inclusion in their testing bank. There will be no indication of whether a question will be scored or unscored, so assume that every question counts and never leave a question blank.

The Exam Experience

There are Prometric locations globally, and many of them are located in educational centers such as Sylvan Learning Centers. These test centers provide exams on a multitude of topics, not just the PMI credentials.

You will be asked to provide your government-issued ID, and the name on your ID must match the name on your PMI application. Each testing candidate is provided with a locker, and everything you bring must go into that locker, including your phone, wallet, purse, jacket, etc. Given the introduction of smart watches, do not be surprised if they ask you to leave your watch in your locker as well.

If you cannot go through the exam without a drink or a snack, be sure to leave those items outside of your locker on the designated shelf. Food, drinks, and gum are not allowed within the testing room, and you will not be able to open your locker once the exam has started.

Before you are escorted to your testing seat, it is very likely that you will be searched, asked to turn your pockets inside-out, and/or checked with a security wand. There is no need to be offended by these actions, as they are to protect the integrity of the testing site, the various exams, and the test-takers.

Additional security measures include cameras in the testing room and a camera over your test station. The proctor will also walk through the room periodically. The testing centers are used to administer a number of different exams, and their seating times may vary. Because of this, you may notice that there are people coming in and leaving throughout your exam. If you are worried that this may be distracting to you, the test centers do offer headphones that you can use.

According to the PMI testing guidelines, candidates must use the calculator that is built into the testing module on the computer. However, when asked, some test centers will provide candidates with a single-function calculator. If you prefer the hand-held calculator to the system calculator, it does not hurt to ask for it. The worst that they can say is "no."

The testing system is relatively straightforward. Once seated at your test station, you will be allowed 15 minutes to complete a system tutorial. This tutorial will show you the features of the exam system, and it typically does not take more than a few minutes to complete.

Once you are done with the tutorial, you can choose either to wait for the remaining time to run down or to start the actual exam, starting your 3.5-hour clock. You will be provided with either scratch paper and pencils or a dry-erase board with markers. Many of the test centers are moving to the dry-erase boards.

Some candidates choose to start by doing a memorization "dump sheet," including formulas, key concepts, etc. I would recommend assuming that you are going to be provided with a dry-erase board rather than a packet of paper and being cognizant of the amount of space required for your dump sheet. Ensure that you leave room for any notes and equations that you will need to work through during the exam. While most of my PMP students leverage a dump sheet, it is not as common for the PMI-RMP exam.

On the testing screen, you will be shown one question at a time, with a clock in one corner and a question counter in the other. For each question presented, you will have the opportunity to answer it, answer it and mark it, or leave it blank. In addition, there are now options to strike through answers that you believe are incorrect and highlight pieces of information that you believe are important.

Exam Anxiety

Exam anxiety is one of the most concerning aspects of these tests and can be particularly harmful. It is important to recognize the symptoms of our "fight-or-flight" response to testing. When we are nervous, our body is getting ready to either fight the threat or run from the threat, which means that our blood flow is redirected from the logical processing part of our brain to our large muscles. Unfortunately, those large muscles are not very helpful for reading complex questions.

My recommendation is to cycle through the questions, answering short or easy ones first. This will help you burn down your adrenaline to a more helpful level while also dispelling your fear of the unknown. You can cycle through the questions as many times as you need to within the 3.5 hours. Do not sit on one question for an extended period of time. It will not only waste time, but it can potentially increase your anxiety.

Once you finish a pass of the 170 questions, you will have the option to review all the questions or just the questions you left blank and/or marked. Go to the questions you left blank and/or marked, answering as many as you can easily, and repeat.

Exam Strategy

I strongly discourage reviewing questions you already answered. Generally speaking, your first gut instinct is going to be correct. The exception to that are math questions involving some calculations. It is never a bad idea to run through the calculations again to be sure you answered correctly. Because of this, I suggest marking any math questions to be sure you double-check your math. Another exception would be if another question prompted you to remember something applicable to a previous question.

It is very possible that you will have questions on the exam that contain typographical, punctuation, or grammatical errors. It happens. Do not allow that to distract or discourage you as you work through the questions.

For example, on my exam, I had a question that referenced my "high rise" project, so I envisioned building a high-rise building. After reading it through a few times, I realized that it was actually a "high-risk" project, not a "high rise" project.

Submitting Your Exam

Once you complete all 170 questions, you can submit your exam. Be sure that you have not left any questions blank, as they will count against you. It is more likely than not that you will feel a bit unsure when you submit your exam. This is due to the fact that, for many of the questions, you will have answered from the PMI's perspective rather than your own. Do not use that as an excuse to go back through the exam and change your answers. Usually your first response to a question is the correct one.

Upon submission, you will be prompted to complete a brief survey that will ask questions about your exam preparation and experience. After you submit the survey, you will be shown your pass or fail result on the screen. Acknowledge your result on the computer and collect your printed score report from the front desk.

Your score report will show your results and proficiency ratings (Proficient, Moderately Proficient or Below Proficient) in the following domains:

- Risk strategy and planning – 19-20% of the exam questions
- Stakeholder engagement – 19-20% of the exam questions
- Risk process facilitation – 25-28% of the exam questions
- Risk monitoring and reporting – 19-20% of the exam questions
- Performing specialized risk analyses – 14-16% of the exam questions

Passing the PMI-RMP Exam

"What is the passing score?" is the most common question I receive related to the PMI exams. And the unwelcome response is "I don't know." A few years ago, PMI stopped publishing the passing score for the exams. PMI employs a robust psychometric analysis model. Each exam question is evaluated and scored by a test population of project risk managers, and an appropriate weighting is applied. Depending on your particular pool of questions and their associated weights, the score to pass can vary.

Candidates can pass the exam without being "proficient" in any one domain but must have multiple domains in which they are "moderately proficient." A frustration associated with PMI exams is its inability to identify and address gaps beyond a simple proficiency rating in a domain. You will not receive a copy of your exam, nor will you know how many questions you answered correctly.

In the event that you do not pass your exam, you have the option to repeat the exam up to two more times during your eligibility year. Your eligibility year begins the day your application is approved by PMI. To repeat the exam, you will be responsible for paying the re-examination fee. The fee is $335 for PMI members and $435 for non-PMI members.

As I mentioned previously, I suggest that you score at least an 80% on the practice test given in this book to indicate readiness for the actual exam.

Maintain Your PMI-RMP Credential

Once you pass your exam, your PMI-RMP credential will be valid for a period of three years from the exam date. During these three years, you must achieve no less than 30 professional development units (PDUs) of continuing education in order to maintain your credential.

PMI recently launched the Talent Triangle®, requiring credential holders to earn PDUs in the following categories: Technical, Leadership, and Strategic and Business. PMI-RMP credential maintenance requires:

- Technical education – a minimum of 4 PDUs
- Leadership education – a minimum of 4 PDUs
- Strategic and business education – a minimum of 4 PDUs

In addition to education, PDUs can be earned through your experience and activities, up to a maximum of 12 PDUs.

- Working as a practitioner – a maximum of 4 PDUs.
- Other giving back, such as creating content, giving presentations, sharing knowledge, and volunteering – a maximum of 12 PDUs (including those you have earned working as a practitioner)

All PDUs you earn are reported through PMI's Continuing Certification Requirements (CCR) system. Any PDUs earned to maintain your PMI-RMP will also be credited toward maintaining your PMP credential.

Project Risk Management

A project risk is defined as an uncertain event that, if it occurs, will have an impact on the project objectives. That impact may be positive (an opportunity) or negative (a threat).

Project risk management is a key component of project management and is identified as a knowledge area within the *PMBOK® Guide* Framework. According to PMI, a project is defined as a "temporary endeavor undertaken to create a unique product, service, or result." Leveraging that definition, the idea of risk (or uncertainty) is evident and unavoidable. Creating, developing, or building something unique within a time-bound period presents an inherent level of uncertainty.

There are a number of factors that affect that level of uncertainty. These factors can be internal, such as available resources, skill levels of human resources, funding availability, management approach, time constraints, etc. In addition, there are a number of external factors that can also influence the level of uncertainty, such as economic conditions, industry implications, global considerations, and legal regulations, laws, or controls.

Experienced project managers should have the ability to identify the areas of uncertainty, evaluate the impact of those uncertainties, and develop plans and approaches to respond to them. In addition, experienced project managers should be able to report and leverage data and metrics while the project is underway to identify trends that could indicate a changing risk environment.

Risk Taxonomy

An organization's risk taxonomy is the language the organization uses to talk about risk. Successful project risk management is dependent upon organizational agreement on the key aspects of and approach to risk management. Consistently applied definitions and structure lend to a credible and repeatable approach that can then be used to continually improve project risk management for the organization.

Risk taxonomy can include defining:

- Risk – How does the organization define risk, and will it consider both negative risks (threats) and positive risks (opportunities)?
- Risk categories – How does the organization categorize risks? Are there standard categories across the organization that can be presented within an organizational risk breakdown structure (RBS)?
- Risk rating scales – How does the organization rank and rate risk impact and risk probability? Is there a standard numerical scale that corresponds to a low-medium-high or green-yellow-red scale?
- Risk assessment and analysis – What methods are used to assess risk? Do these include qualitative and quantitative methods? When is it acceptable to use each method? Other than probability and impact, are there other factors that will be evaluated, such as frequency, controllability, and urgency? How are the assessments documented?

- Risk appetite and tolerance – How is risk appetite and tolerance defined for the organization? Is risk appetite or tolerance dependent on any internal or external variables? How are risk decisions handled, based on the organization's risk appetite and tolerance?

The PM's Role in Risk Management

Project management and project risk management are inextricably linked. In many circumstances, the project manager owns project risk management, rather than someone having the sole role of managing the risk of the project. From an exam perspective, you will find that some questions will ask you to think "as project manager," and some will ask you to think "as project risk manager." Regardless of this differentiation, your position and answers will be the same.

The project manager's role for project risk management typically involves stakeholder management, oversight of the risk processes, and leadership and decision-making.

Stakeholder Management

Stakeholder management from a project risk perspective includes:

- Working with stakeholders to determine the acceptable level of risk exposure for the project, including ongoing dialogue in the event of changes in risk tolerance
- Reporting risk status to the key stakeholders on a regular and consistent basis. This will include recommendations regarding any type of decision or action necessary to ensure the appropriate level of risk exposure for the project
- Working with senior management to ensure that there is ongoing and continual support for the project risk management approach
- Maximizing open and honest communication with stakeholders, leadership, and the project team surrounding the project risk exposure and actions suggested or taken

Risk Process Oversight

As the project manager, you have ownership of and accountability for the project risk management processes, approach, actions, and control. This includes:

- Participating in the project risk management processes with the project team, experts, and stakeholders
- Developing and approving the project risk management plan
- Ensuring that contractors, vendors, and suppliers are properly applying risk management
- Monitoring the effectiveness of the project risk management approach, including auditing risk responses for effectiveness
- Continually capturing, documenting, and sharing lessons learned as they relate to project risk management

Leadership and Decision-Making

While the authority of a project manager can vary greatly depending on the environment and the organization, generally speaking, the project manager will have some type of decision-making authority in areas that relate to project risk management. The level of authority and decision-making should be determined and documented explicitly within the project risk management plan.

Leadership and decision-making responsibilities may include:

- Approving risk responses and the associated actions, tasks, and anticipated impacts
- Identifying and applying the project contingency funding to risks that occur
- Escalating identified risks to senior management when necessary. Escalation should occur when the risk impact or required action is outside of the authority of the project manager, when a decision requires input from outside the project, and/or when there is a need to access management reserve funds

PM Skills and Knowledge

Being an effective project manager and project risk manager is highly dependent upon a number of management and leadership skills and techniques. The project manager is often required to influence members of the organization without any type of formal authority. These may include project team members, stakeholders, and the organization's leadership.

Communication

It is estimated that 90% of a project manager's job is communication. The project manager is responsible for communicating effectively and efficiently with project team members, stakeholders, the project sponsor, the steering committee, and other organizational leaders. The ability to recognize various communication needs and approaches based on the audience and situation is critical. While we often listen to respond, it is more important to listen to understand.

Communication Model

A communication model includes the following components:

- Sender – the individual who needs to convey a message
- Receiver – the intended recipient of that message
- The message – what the sender intends to convey
- Encoding and decoding – the interpretation of the message (the sender encodes the message and the receiver decodes the message)
- Medium – the method in which the message is conveyed, such as verbal discourse, email, etc.

- Noise – biases, perspectives, and conditions that may impact the receiver's decoding of the message

- Acknowledgement – a signal that the message has been received, which does not necessarily mean it has been comprehended or agreed with

- Feedback/response – a new encoded message sent from the receiver to the sender after the original message has been decoded and understood

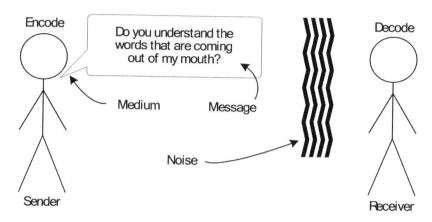

Communication Categories

There are three general categories of communication: interactive, push, and pull.

Interactive communication is in real time, allowing for the most efficient flow of information between parties. Interactive communication allows both the sender and receiver to interpret not only each message, but also its tone, inflection, and delivery. Face-to-face meetings, web-based meetings, and phone conversations are all considered interactive communication.

Push communication involves the sender delivering the message to the receiver. The sender may know that the message was delivered but cannot know how it was interpreted or understood. As communication technology has advanced, push communication has become a standard form of communication, and a primary example is email. While convenient, it should not be used to relay information that is sensitive, urgent, or likely to be misunderstood or misinterpreted.

Pull communication occurs when the receiver must proactively seek out the information to receive it. Pull communication is often used for information that is FYI only, for large volumes of information, and for large distributions. Shared directories, bulletin boards, and web interfaces are examples of platforms for pull communication.

Communication Channels

Another aspect of communication management is identifying and understanding the number of communication channels or paths in your project and the implications of that number. The more people involved in the project, the larger the number of channels or paths. A high number of communication channels in the project may indicate an increased risk of misunderstandings or misinformation.

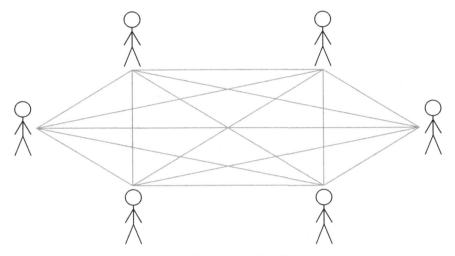

Figure 1-1: Communication Channels

To calculate the communication channels on your project, use the formula: $n(n-1)/2$, where "n" represents the number of project team members and stakeholders, including you as the project manager.

For example, for a project with 32 stakeholders, there are 496 communication channels, representing each member talking directly with every other member. If the project size increases to 34 stakeholders, the number of channels increases to 561.

For large projects involving a high number of stakeholders, this concept should be considered and factored into the communication plan.

While I personally have never felt the need to actually calculate the number of communication channels in my projects, the concept is an important one from a communication and risk perspective. I compare it to kids playing a game of telephone. I whisper something in the first person's ear; they whisper it to the next person, and so on until, at the end of the chain, the last listener states what they heard. Typically, laughter ensues at how messed up the original message has become along the chain. This is not unlike a lot of project conversations!

Regardless of the fact that most project managers will not run the actual calculation, it is possible that you will receive a question on communication channels and the formula for calculating the number of them in a project on the PMI-RMP exam.

Exercise: Communication Channels

1. You are the project manager for a multi-year, global project. Upon completion of the analysis phase, the team increased from 28 members to 38 members. As such, the number of communication channels increased by:

   A. 10
   B. 325
   C. 76
   D. 252

2. The Widget Futura project is leveraging a vendor to provide contract resources. The vendor has provided 17 individuals, all in a part-time capacity. Other than the project manager, the remainder of the organization's core team is made up of 72 engineers, analysts, and developers. The best estimate of the number of communication channels in this project would be:

   A. 3,916
   B. 2,556
   C. 2,628
   D. 4,005

Facilitation

Project meetings tend to be the primary format for sharing project information, receiving project updates, and working through project risks and issues. Aside from team meetings, project managers often find themselves serving as facilitators of other related meetings with change control boards, steering committees, or other audiences.

There are three general principles of project meeting facilitation: demonstrate a respect for others, plan for the meeting appropriately, and stay focused on the desired outcomes.

General facilitation rules:

- Prepare an agenda – Prior to the meeting, prepare and distribute a specific agenda with time allocations for each topic.
- Start on time – Meetings should always start at the time they were planned. Delaying the start of a meeting is disrespectful to attendees who are on time.
- Review agenda and desired outcomes – Start the meeting by briefly reviewing with the group the agenda and the desired outcomes for the planned topics, such as making a decision, gathering information, or assigning ownership.
- Create a parking lot and identify owners – Capture items that do not fit within the planned topics as "parking lot" items, and immediately identify an owner for each topic.

- Keep the meeting on track – Facilitate firmly by maintaining control over both the discussions and the time. Ask pointed questions, redirect conversation, and remind the participants of the time allocations.

- Summarize decisions and actions – Always allow time at the end of the meeting to summarize the decisions that were made and the actions that were assigned. Shortly after the meeting, send out the meeting notes.

I always recommend that my project managers read "Death by Meeting" by Pat Lencioni (author of *The Five Dysfunctions of a Team*) to gain some useful facilitation advice. Pat's books are written in the form of fables and present easily digestible information in a relatively quick read.

Negotiation

In increasingly complex and competitive environments, project managers are expected to represent the project objectives and act in the best interests of those objectives. This necessitates the ability of project managers to negotiate effectively with a number of parties, including but not limited to the project sponsor, functional and operational managers, team members, stakeholders, partner organizations, and vendors.

While some may position negotiation as the attempt to achieve a win-win situation, it can often result in something that feels more like a lose-lose situation, in which each party must agree to give up something in order to come to a resolution.

Generally speaking, there are four phases involved in negotiating: pre-negotiation, conceptualization, settling the details, and follow-up.

- During the pre-negotiation phase, the project manager should assess his or her particular needs and/or concerns to address. The project manager may develop a prioritized negotiation checklist of the items in contention.

- During conceptualization, both parties work through their individual perspectives, needs, and desires in order to find places of alignment and define a shared ideal outcome.

- Once the resolution is conceptualized, the next phase is to plan how to achieve it and settle the details, reviewing the expectations and actions expected from both parties.

- After reaching and executing the agreement, the project manager should follow up on outstanding items, concerns, or lessons learned from the process.

Dr. Robert Cialdini, the Regents' Professor Emeritus of Psychology and Marketing at Arizona State University, is most well-known for his book *Influence: The Psychology of Persuasion*. This is another book that I recommend to project managers. Rather than structuring it as a "how-to" book, Dr. Cialdini gives the "why" behind individuals' decision-making processes. The understanding this book offers is incredibly powerful when it comes to negotiation.

Leadership and Organizational Theory

If you completed your PMP exam, you may remember learning about or being tested on various leadership and organizational theorists. I affectionately call these the "dead guys," though some are still alive as of the writing of this book. An understanding of these theorists and their theories can be beneficial for project management. Understanding traits of human behavior and the origins of that behavior can enable the project manager to productively modify his or her approach to leadership, change, and communication.

I would not anticipate a large number of questions on these theorists on the exam, but you may encounter one or two. As this is not an area in which I recommend extensive study, I will provide you with my silly mnemonic hints for remembering the theorists and their theory.

Abraham Maslow (1908-1970) – Hierarchy of Needs

Maslow was an American psychologist who is best known for his hierarchy of needs. As a humanistic psychologist, he believed that every person has a strong desire to realize his or her full potential and ultimately reach the level of self-actualization. He identified human needs as a hierarchy, often depicted as a pyramid, and believed that someone's lower-level needs must be met before they can concern themselves with fulfilling their higher-level needs.

From low to high:

- Basic physiological needs – breathing, food, water, sex, sleep, homeostasis
- Safety needs – security, order, stability
- Love and belonging needs – friendship, family, intimacy
- Esteem needs – self-esteem, confidence, achievement, respect for and from others
- Self-actualization needs – morality, creativity, spontaneity, problem-solving, lack of prejudice, acceptance of facts

Hint: Think opposites – Mas<u>low</u>/<u>Hi</u>erarchy (low/high)

William Ouchie (1943-   ) – Theory Z

Ouchie studied the difference between American and Japanese companies to formulate his Theory Z.

Mirroring Japanese management approaches, Theory Z focuses on increasing employee loyalty by providing a job for life with a strong emphasis on the well-being of the employee both on and off the job. Ouchie believed that a Theory Z management style promotes stable employment, high productivity, and high employee morale and satisfaction.

Hint: Attrition hurts (Ouch); providing a job until the end of an employee's career (Z is at the end of the alphabet)

Douglas McGregor (1906-1964) – Theory X and Theory Y

McGregor proposed that a manager's individual assumptions about human nature and behavior determine how he or she will manage employees.

Theory X is based on pessimistic assumptions of human behavior and assumes that average employees have little to no ambition, shy away from work or responsibilities, and are of less intelligence than the manager. As such, Theory X managers believe that these employees function best with a high level of hands-on management. Theory X management is typically applied in environments in which employees are responsible for repetitive tasks.

Theory Y managers assume that people in the workforce are internally motivated, enjoy their work, and will work to better themselves without any direct reward in return. Theory Y managers assume that employees are the most valuable company assets, and that assumption drives the internal workings of the company. Because Theory Y management sees employees as are self-driven, it gives employees minimal supervision and direction.

Hint: Think of "X" as crossing items off a list when employees are micro-managed and "Y" as the shape of open arms welcoming employees as valuable assets

Victor Vroom (1932-   ) – Expectancy Theory

Vroom's research attempted to explain why individuals choose to follow certain courses of action in organizations, particularly in decision-making and leadership. Vroom's expectancy theory proposes that an individual is motivated to select a specific behavior over other behaviors due to what he or she expects as a result of the chosen behavior.

Essentially, individuals will choose to put effort toward improving performance if they believe that the improved performance will result in a reward that will justify the effort.

Hint: You need "vroom, vroom, vroom" to the hospital when you're "expecting" a baby

David McClelland (1917-1998) – Need Theory

McClelland developed the need for achievement (n-achievement) theory, a motivational model that explains how employees' needs for achievement, power, and affiliation affect their actions.

Individuals with a high need for achievement will select tasks that are moderately difficult in order to earn a sense of accomplishment and will avoid tasks that are very low-risk or very high-risk. They prefer work in which results are based on effort, and they prefer to receive feedback on their work.

Hint: The last two letters in the name McClelland are "nd," which expands to "need" – need for achievement

Frederick Herzberg (1923-2000) – Motivator-Hygiene Theory

Herzberg is known for introducing job enrichment and the Motivator-Hygiene Theory, also known as the two-factor theory of job satisfaction. According to this theory, people are influenced by two sets of factors, hygiene factors and motivational factors.

Hygiene factors will not motivate employees, but their absence can lower motivation. These factors, extrinsic to the work itself, include appropriate office set-up and space, clean restrooms, a reasonable level of pay, vacations, and job security.

The absence of motivational factors will not necessarily lower motivation, but their presence can be responsible for increasing motivation. Motivational factors are intrinsic to the work itself, such as challenging work, job recognition, growth or advancement potential, and responsibility.

Hint: Think "H" for Herzberg and Hygiene

Statistics for Risk Management

While statistics is not generally recognized as a project management area of expertise, it is a component of many of the quantitative risk analysis techniques. Statistics, in and of itself, could comprise a complete book or class or even multiple books and classes.

For the benefit of the exam, I will provide a brief overview of statistics and some of its common terminology here. Additional details and information are included in the later section on quantitative risk analysis.

Statistics is the study of the collection, analysis, interpretation, presentation, and organization of data. Two main statistical methodologies are used in data analysis: descriptive and inferential statistics.

Descriptive Statistics

Descriptive statistics describes or summarizes the features of a collection of information. Its aim is to summarize a sample rather than to learn more about the population a sample is thought to represent.

Measures commonly used to describe a data set are measures of central tendency and measures of variability or dispersion.

Measures of central tendency include mean, median, and mode. Measures of variability include standard deviation, minimum and maximum values, and skewness.

Mean

The mean is typically the average result of the data set (the sum of the values divided by the number of values).

For example, for the data set [1, 1, 1, 3, 5, 5, 6, 6, 8], the mean would be 4.

Median

The median is the middle value in the list, the value separating the higher half of the data sample from the lower half of the sample.

For example, for the same data set, the median would be 5.

Mode

The mode is the element of the sample that occurs most often in the data set.

For example, the mode for the same data set would be 1.

Standard Deviation (σ)

Standard deviation is a measure used to quantify the amount of variation or dispersion in a set of data values. A low standard deviation indicates that the data points tend to be close to the mean, while a high standard deviation indicates that the data points are spread out over a wide range of values.

For example, for the data set [1, 1, 1, 3, 5, 5, 6, 6, 8], the mean is 4. To calculate the standard deviation, calculate the deviations of each data point from the mean and square the result of each:

$$(1 - 4)^2 = (-3)^2 = 9$$
$$(1 - 4)^2 = (-3)^2 = 9$$
$$(1 - 4)^2 = (-3)^2 = 9$$
$$(3 - 4)^2 = (-1)^2 = 1$$
$$(5 - 4)^2 = (1)^2 = 1$$
$$(5 - 4)^2 = (1)^2 = 1$$
$$(6 - 4)^2 = (2)^2 = 4$$
$$(6 - 4)^2 = (2)^2 = 4$$
$$(8 - 4)^2 = (4)^2 = 16$$

The variance is the mean of these values:

$$(9 + 9 + 9 + 1 + 1 + 1 + 4 + 4 + 16) / 9 = 6$$

The standard deviation is equal to the square root of the variance: 2.45

Minimum and Maximum Values of the Variables

These simply refer to the highest and lowest values listed in a data set. For example, in the data set used above, the minimum value is 1 and the maximum value is 8.

Skewness

Skewness is a measure of the asymmetry of the probability distribution of a real-valued random variable about its mean. Skewness can be positive or negative.

Negative skew occurs when the left tail is longer and the mass of the distribution is concentrated on the right side of the figure. This represents the fact that there are more data points or results that are higher than the mean than there are lower than the mean.

Positive skew occurs when the right tail is longer and the mass of the distribution is concentrated on the left side of the figure. This represents the fact that there are more data points or results that are lower than the mean than there are higher than the mean.

For example, in the data set [30, 31, 32], the values are evenly distributed around a central value of 31.

To create a negative skew, you would add values far below the mean. For example: [20, 30, 31, 32]

To create a positive skew, you would add values far above the mean. For example: [30, 31, 32, 40]

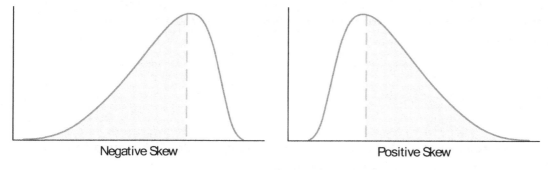

Negative Skew   Positive Skew

Figure 1-2: Probability Distribution Skew

Inferential Statistics

Inferential statistics draws conclusions from data that is subject to random variation, inferring properties about a population that is larger than a given sample. It includes testing hypotheses and deriving estimates.

The conclusion of a statistical inference is a statistical proposition. The most common statistical proposition used in quantitative risk analysis is an interval estimate, specifically a confidence level.

Confidence levels are used to state the likelihood of occurrence of a certain outcome, such as a project completion date or an amount of project spending. For example, a total project cost of $130,000 at a P30 interval would represent a 30% probability of the project cost coming in at $130,000 or below. This is discussed in more detail in the quantitative risk analysis section.

Review Questions   Chapter 1

1. **Ouchie's theory can best be described as being concerned with:**
   A. Ensuring that the employees' lower-level needs are met so that they can be more productive workers
   B. Caring for employees both in and outside of work and providing a job for life
   C. Assuming that employees are internally motivated and enjoy their jobs with little intervention from their managers
   D. Proposing that employees will be more motivated when they believe that more effort will yield better results and that better results will yield rewards

2. **You have conducted a communication channels analysis on your large, international project. You have identified 496 communication channels. You know this means that, other than you, there are ____ team members and stakeholders.**
   A. 32
   B. 31
   C. 30
   D. 20

3. **According to this theorist, there is a risk that the workforce would suffer a loss of motivation if the annual bonuses were eliminated from the compensation plan.**
   A. Herzberg
   B. McClelland
   C. Maslow
   D. Deming

4. **Consider the following dataset: [18, 20, 20, 24, 27, 29, 29, 29, 30, 35, 40]. What is the mean of the dataset?**
   A. 31
   B. 26
   C. 29
   D. 27

5. **Successful project risk management is dependent upon organizational agreement on the key aspects of and approach to risk management. Consistently applied definitions and structure lend to a credible and repeatable approach that can be used to continually improve project risk management for the organization. Which of the following statements is most accurate regarding a consistent approach to and vernacular for project risk management?**
   A. The project sponsor will provide the mandatory project lexicon that will be adhered to throughout the project.
   B. The project manager should take the initiative to develop terminology and acronyms specific to the project in order to ensure that the team has a deep understanding of the terms being used on the project.
   C. Developing and leveraging a risk taxonomy that is specific to the organization and applied consistently to its projects assists in ensuring that team members and stakeholders understand the terms being used for the project.
   D. A risk taxonomy based on ISO 31000 and the *PMBOK® Guide* will increase the chances of project success.

6. One of your team members, Ashley, had a very bad experience with one of your key stakeholders, Bob, on a previous project. At a team meeting, you notice that Ashley is not open to feedback, suggestions, or requests from Bob and that the team's communication is suffering consistent misunderstandings as a result. What is the most likely cause of the misunderstandings?

   A. Because Bob has an issue with Ashley, he is not communicating his messages in the correct manner.
   B. Ashley's preconceived notion and impression of Bob is creating unproductive "noise," which is getting in the way of effective communication.
   C. Because Bob and Ashley do not like each other, they will not be able to communicate effectively.
   D. Because Bob is a difficult stakeholder, Ashley is acting appropriately to guard her and the project.

7. You have recently noticed a team member's work slipping, and he has been repeatedly late turning in his assigned work. He has also not been joining team-building events, despite the fact that he was previously very active. Upon further investigation, you learn that his home is under foreclosure due to his wife's medical expenses. What statement is most accurate regarding this situation?

   A. According to Vroom's expectancy theory, this team member is not having his needs met at work and is therefore exploring other options.
   B. According to Ouchie's theory Z, this team member has low morale due to the fact that the job is less important than his personal life.
   C. According to McClelland's need theory, the team member needs to be provided with extra support and some leeway on finishing his assignments.
   D. According to Maslow's hierarchy of needs, the team member's lower-level needs are not being met, so he is not as concerned with his higher-level needs.

8. Which of the following data sets has a median value of 8?

   A. 2, 5, 5, 9, 9, 13, 14
   B. 3, 4, 7, 8, 12, 14, 14
   C. 3, 3, 4, 7, 9, 14, 15
   D. 1, 4, 8, 10, 10, 12, 13

9. Which statement is most accurate regarding the difference between inferential and descriptive statistics?

   A. Descriptive statistics summarizes the data from a sample to learn about the population it is thought to represent, while inferential statistics draws conclusions from data that is subject to random variation, resulting in a proposed confidence level.
   B. Inferential statistics summarizes the data from a sample to learn about the population it is thought to represent, while descriptive statistics draws conclusions from data that is subject to random variation, resulting in a proposed confidence level.
   C. Mean, median, mode, and standard deviation calculations are inferential statistics.
   D. Descriptive statistics will provide the likelihood of a certain outcome occurring.

10. The project sponsor suspects that if your product development project is delivered in the first quarter of next year, there is a possibility that your company will capture a large amount of the market share. Delivering in the first quarter will most likely lead to launching your product ahead of your competitor's launch of a similar product. This situation would be considered:

    A. A business case
    B. An opportunity
    C. A marketing positioning
    D. A benefit measurement

11. Typically, projects have a greater likelihood of coming in over the budget estimate than under it. The potential spread of costs is also greater over budget than under budget. This would be represented in:
    A. A positively skewed probability distribution
    B. A negatively skewed probability distribution
    C. An evenly skewed probability distribution
    D. Multiple positively skewed probability distributions

12. A measure used to quantify the amount of variation or dispersion in a set of data values is known as:
    A. Mean
    B. Mode
    C. Standard deviation
    D. Data variance

13. The consulting firm that you work for is experiencing rapid growth with high-value clients. Project managers who are assigned to these clients are receiving higher bonuses than the other project managers. To get assigned to these clients, project managers must demonstrate competency in a number of areas, including risk management, scheduling, budgeting, and team development. As such, some of the project managers are working longer hours, often off the clock, and are more aggressively allocating extra time to complete training and get experience in those areas. This is an example of:
    A. Maslow's hierarchy of needs
    B. Vroom's expectancy theory
    C. McClelland's need theory
    D. Herzberg's two-factor theory

14. For the first test population, the standard deviation was 3.98. For the second test population, the standard deviation was 2.1. Which statement is most accurate?
    A. The first population will have data points closer to the mean than the second population.
    B. The first population will have a positively skewed probability distribution, while the second population will have negatively skewed probability distribution.
    C. The first population will have a negatively skewed probability distribution, while the second population will have positively skewed probability distribution.
    D. The second population will have data points closer to the mean than the first population.

15. The four phases typically involved in negotiation are:
    A. Pre-negotiation, conceptualization, settling the details, and follow-up
    B. Pre-meeting preparation, design, agreement, and review
    C. Pre-negotiation, allocation of resources, discussion, and contract
    D. Preparation, analysis, meeting and discussion, and finalization

Vocabulary Review   Chapter 1

Descriptive statistics	Message	Pull communication
Herzberg	Mode	Push communication
Inferential statistics	Negative skew	Receiver
Interactive communication	Noise	Risk taxonomy
Maslow	Opportunity	Sender
McClelland	Ouchie	Standard deviation
McGregor	Positive skew	Statistics
Mean	Project	Threat
Median	Project risk	Vroom
Medium		

1. _____ A category of communication in which the recipient has to proactively retrieve the information

2. _____ An uncertain event that, if it occurs, will have an impact on the project

3. _____ A theorist who believed that people with a high need for achievement will seek out moderately challenging tasks to feel a sense of accomplishment

4. _____ A positive risk

5. _____ A theorist who believed that employees will put in more effort when they believe that the effort will lead to better results and those results will generate rewards

6. _____ Calculated as the average of a data set

7. _____ Draws conclusions from data that is subject to random variation, inferring properties about a population that is larger than the particular sample

8. _____ The right tail is longer, and the mass of the distribution is concentrated on the left of the figure

9. _____ A category of communication that involves the real-time transmission of information between at least two parties

10. _____ A theorist who believed in providing employees a job for life, increasing satisfaction and loyalty, and caring for employees both in and out of the workplace

11. _____ A temporary endeavor undertaken to create a unique product, service, or result

12. _____ The recipient of an intended message

13. _____ A theorist who believed that employees' lower-level needs must be met before they can concern themselves with their higher-level needs, a concept typically depicted in a pyramid

14. _____ Biases, perspectives, or other distractions that can impact or interfere with the decoding of a message

15. _____ The study of the collection, analysis, interpretation, presentation and organization of data

16. _____ Describes or summarizes the features of a collection of information

17. _____ A measure used to quantify the amount of variation or dispersion in a set of data values

18. _____ The left tail is longer, and the mass of the distribution is concentrated on the right of the figure

19. _____ A negative project risk

20. _____ Information or an idea that needs to be conveyed from a sender to a receiver

21. _____ A theorist who researched motivators, which are intrinsic to work, and hygiene factors, which are extrinsic to work.

22. _____ The individual conveying a message to a receiver

23. _____ A theorist who believed that a manager's assumptions about their employees determines their behavior, with Theory X leaning toward micromanagement and Theory Y allowing teams to be self-managed

24. _____ Method of transmitting information or ideas from the sender to the receiver

25. _____ A category of communication in which the information is delivered from the sender to the receiver but whether the information was interpreted or understood as anticipated cannot be confirmed

26. _____ The language the organization uses to talk about risk

27. _____ The element of the sample that occurs most often in the collection

28. _____ The value separating the higher half of the data sample from the lower half of the data sample

Answer Key   Chapter 1

Chapter Exercise Answers

Exercise: Communication Channels

1. **Answer: B**

   28 Members --- 28 x (28 - 1) ÷ 2 = 378 communication channels

   38 Members --- 38 x (38 - 1) ÷ 2 = 703 communication channels

   703 - 378 = 325 additional communication channels

2. **Answer: D**

   17 + 1 + 72 = 90 individuals

   90 x (90 - 1) ÷ 2 = 4,005 communication channels

Review Question Answers

1. **Answer: B**

   Ouchie's Theory Z focuses on providing employees with a job for life and cares for their wellbeing both inside and outside of work. Maslow's Hierarchy of Needs suggests that employees' lower-level needs must be met before they can be productive workers. McGregor's Theory Y managers believe that employees are internally motivated. Vroom believed that employees will be more motivated if they believe that more effort yields better results and better results yield rewards.

2. **Answer: B**

   With a team of 32 stakeholders, there would be 496 communication channels. Because the question asks for the number not including you, the correct answer is 31. 32 (32-1) / 2 = 496.

3. **Answer: A**

   Herzberg's theory is the dual factor theory, in which compensation/salary is considered a hygiene factor. Salary in and of itself does not provide satisfaction, but if it suffered a disruption, it could lead to dissatisfaction. McClelland created the Need for Achievement theory, stating that employees have varying levels of need for achievement. Maslow's Hierarchy of Needs states that employees' lower-level needs must be met before higher-level needs are considered. W. Edwards Deming is a quality theorist, not a motivational theorist.

4. **Answer: D**

   The mean of the data set is 27. The sum of the data set is 301. Dividing 301 by 11 gives a mean of 27.36. The closest answer available is 27.

5. **Answer: C**

   Developing and using a risk taxonomy, standardized language for discussing risk, helps to increase the risk knowledge of team members and stakeholders. There is nothing known as a mandatory project lexicon. The project manager should leverage the terminology and acronyms of the overall organization rather than develop project-specific terms. Risk taxonomy is unique to an organization. While it can be helpful to leverage or align with ISO 31000 and the *PMBOK® Guide*, doing so does not increase the chances of project success.

6. **Answer: B**

It appears that Ashley's noise is impacting her ability to decode and recode the communication. There is no indication in the question that Bob has a problem with Ashley, which eliminates answers A and C. Ashley is not acting appropriately for the benefit of herself or the project.

7. **Answer: D**

According to Maslow's Hierarchy of Needs, an employee's lower-level needs must be met before he or she becomes concerned about higher-level needs. Vroom believed that employees are more motivated if they believe that more effort yields better results and better results yield rewards. Ouchie's theory was that the organization should care for the employees' well-being and provide jobs for life. McClelland created the Need for Achievement theory, which stated that employees have varying levels of need for achievement.

8. **Answer: B**

The median is the value in the middle of the data set that separates the lower values from the higher values. The median value of A is nine. The median value of C is seven. The median value of D is ten.

9. **Answer: A**

Descriptive statistics summarizes data, whereas inferential statistics draws conclusions and provides the likelihood of an outcome occurring. Mean, median, mode, and standard deviation calculations are descriptive statistics.

10. **Answer: B**

The situation is uncertain, leading to a positive effect, so it is an opportunity. A business case is used to justify the pursuit of a particular project, typically including a cost-benefit analysis. Marketing positioning and benefit measurements are typically documented within the business case or business plan for a product and are not documented for every project.

11. **Answer: A**

Positively skewed distributions have a narrower difference between the mean and the lowest values and a wider difference between the mean and the highest values. This is typical of most projects. Negatively skewed distributions have more values below the mean than higher than the mean. An evenly skewed distribution is balanced around the mean. There should be only one distribution for a project, not multiple distributions.

12. **Answer: C**

Standard deviation measures the amount of variation or dispersion in a set of data values. The mean is the average of a data set. The mode is the value that occurs most frequently. Data variance is not a term commonly discussed in project risk management.

13. **Answer: B**

Vroom's expectancy theory states that employees put in more effort if they believe that the effort will yield better performance and that better performance will increase their rewards. In this scenario, they believe that actively and aggressively pursuing the training will allow them to be placed with the higher-value clients and will potentially allow them to receive bigger bonuses. This scenario does not relate to their lower-level needs. While the scenario does suggest that the employees are driven, it does not explicitly state that it is for personal satisfaction and does state that it is for a financial reward. Those pursuing the training could be seen as Herzberg's Theory Y employees, but there is more to this scenario than the fact they are self-directed.

14. **Answer: D**

Smaller standard deviations indicate a smaller spread of values. A standard deviation of 2.1 has a more narrow range of values than a standard deviation of 3.98. Because the data set is not provided, it is not possible to know the skewness of the results.

15. **Answer: A**

The four phases typically involved in negotiation include pre-negotiation, conceptualization, settling the details, and follow-up.

Vocabulary Review Answers

1. Pull communication
2. Project risk
3. McClelland
4. Opportunity
5. Vroom
6. Mean
7. Inferential statistics
8. Positive skew
9. Interactive communication
10. Ouchie
11. Project
12. Receiver
13. Maslow
14. Noise
15. Statistics
16. Descriptive statistics
17. Standard deviation
18. Negative skew
19. Threat
20. Message
21. Herzberg
22. Sender
23. McGregor
24. Medium
25. Push communication
26. Risk taxonomy
27. Mode
28. Median

Project Risk Management

PMI Publications

The *PMBOK® Guide* and the *Practice Standard for Project Risk Management* are the PMI publications used as the basis for the PMI-RMP exam. While the *PMBOK® Guide* offers information on standardized project management practices across ten knowledge areas, the *Practice Standard* focuses strictly on project risk management, providing a much deeper dive into risk management topics and tools.

From the aspect of reading and learning, neither publication is especially reader-friendly (read: they are boring) and there are both redundancies and slight contradictions between the two publications. I have incorporated information from both publications in this study guide in a format that is arranged more logically and makes the material easier to learn. If you wish to read either publication, you will find it easier to do so after completing this book.

If you are PMP-certified, you are likely to be at least somewhat familiar with the *PMBOK® Guide*. Keep in mind that the current version is the 5th edition. I do not recommend reviewing earlier editions, as there are considerable differences outside of the risk processes.

The *PMBOK® Guide*

A Guide to the Project Management Body of Knowledge (*PMBOK® Guide*) is the result of a collaborative effort of project managers working globally and across industries. It provides the fundamentals of project management as they apply to a wide range of projects.

As the title implies, it is a "guide" to the body of knowledge and should not be interpreted as a definitive methodology. The intention of the *PMBOK® Guide* is to provide concepts for project managers to apply as appropriate within the constraints of individual organizations' projects and needs.

Project risk management is an inherent part of project management, and vice versa. The two cannot be separated or viewed as individual approaches. PMI-RMP candidates are expected to be familiar with the project management processes, tools and techniques, and vocabulary described in the *PMBOK® Guide*. When appropriate, that information is explicitly addressed in this study guide.

The project management framework within the *PMBOK® Guide* encompasses ten knowledge areas, five process groups (or domains), and 47 project management processes. Each process is associated with a knowledge area and a process group.

Knowledge Areas	Process Groups				
	Initiating	Planning	Executing	Monitoring and Controlling	Closing
Integration	• Develop Project Charter	• Develop Project Management Plan	• Direct and Manage Project Work	• Monitor and Control Project Work • Perform Integrated Change Control	• Close Project or Phase
Scope		• Plan Scope Management • Collect Requirements • Define Scope • Create WBS		• Validate Scope • Control Scope	
Time		• Plan Schedule Management • Define Activities • Sequence Activities • Estimate Activity Resources • Estimate Activity Durations • Develop Schedule		• Control Schedule	
Cost		• Plan Cost Management • Estimate Costs • Determine Budget		• Control Costs	
Quality		• Plan Quality Management	• Perform Quality Assurance	• Control Quality	
Human Resource		• Plan Human Resource Management	• Acquire Project Team • Develop Project Team • Manage Project Team		
Communication		• Plan Communications Management	• Manage Communications	• Control Communications	
Risk		• Plan Risk Management • Identify Risks • Perform Qualitative Risk Analysis • Perform Quantitative Risk Analysis • Plan Risk Responses		• Control Risks	
Procurement		• Plan Procurement Management	• Conduct Procurements	• Control Procurements	• Close Procurements
Stakeholder	• Identify Stakeholders	• Plan Stakeholder Management	• Manage Stakeholder Engagement	• Control Stakeholder Engagement	

Figure 2-1: *PMBOK® Guide* Framework

PMBOK® Guide, page 61

Knowledge Areas

The framework contains ten knowledge areas:

1. Integration – The project integration management knowledge area encompasses the processes that identify, define, combine, unify, and coordinate the rest of the processes in the correct project management process groups. As such, they can be considered umbrella processes. You will notice that the integration knowledge area is the only one that lists processes for all five process groups. These processes produce some of the most critical outputs, such as the project charter, the project management plan, the project deliverables, and the work performance reports, etc.

2. Scope – The project scope management knowledge area encompasses the processes required to ensure that the project includes all the work required and only the work required to complete the project successfully. During the scope

processes, requirements are gathered, the scope statement is developed, and from the scope statement, the work breakdown structure (WBS) is developed. The scope baseline, a component of the project management plan, is the "frozen," approved scope of the project. The scope knowledge area also includes obtaining customer acceptance of the completed project deliverables during the process of validating the scope.

3. Time – The project time management knowledge area encompasses the processes required to manage the timely completion of the project through the identification of activities to be completed and the development of the project schedule. The schedule baseline, a component of the project management plan, is the "frozen," approved schedule for the project. Controlling the schedule may also involve conducting various analyses, including but not limited to an earned value analysis to calculate the schedule variance (SV). You will notice that all processes within the time knowledge area have either "activity" or "schedule" in their name.

4. Cost – The project cost management knowledge area encompasses the processes involved in planning, estimating, budgeting, and controlling costs so that the project can be completed within the approved budget. The cost baseline, a component of the project management plan, is the "frozen" approved budget for the project. Controlling costs on the project may also involve using a number of variance analysis and forecasting techniques, including but not limited to computing an earned value analysis to determine the cost variance (CV), forecasting the estimate to complete (ETC) and the estimate at completion (EAC), and determining the to-complete performance index (TCPI).

5. Quality – There are three processes in the project quality management knowledge area that determine, measure, and improve the quality of both the product and the project. Many of the tools and techniques that are used in the quality knowledge area also apply to project risk management.

6. Human Resource – The project human resource management knowledge area encompasses the processes of organizing, managing, and leading the project team. These include documenting roles and responsibilities, acquiring the team members from internal and/or external sources, enhancing the team's competencies and working relationships, and resolving conflicts and managing issues within the team.

7. Communications – The project communications management knowledge area encompasses the processes that are required to ensure timely and appropriate planning, collection, creation, distribution, management, and control, as well as the ultimate disposition of information. This area includes both written and verbal communication techniques, record management, and status reporting. Project communication management is integral to managing stakeholder engagement.

8. Risk – The project risk management knowledge area encompasses the processes of conducting risk management planning, identification, analysis, response planning, and risk control for the project. These six risk processes will be discussed in extensive detail in the last six chapters of this book.

9. Procurement – The project procurement management knowledge area encompasses the processes necessary for purchasing or acquiring products, services, or results needed from outside the project team. Upon conducting a make-or-buy analysis, it may be determined that certain project materials or services should or must be procured externally. Alignment with the organization's procurement policies, including vendor selection and contract utilization, is required. Risk responses may also require procurement activities for the appropriate transfer of information about risks.

10. Stakeholder – The project stakeholder management knowledge area encompasses the processes required to identify the people, groups, or organizations that could impact or be impacted by the project, to analyze stakeholder expectations and their impact on the project, and to develop appropriate management strategies for effectively engaging stakeholders in project decisions and execution. The stakeholder knowledge area was a new addition to the 5th Edition of the *PMBOK® Guide*. Previously, the stakeholder processes were considered part of the project communication management knowledge area, and because of this, there is some overlap and redundancy between the two knowledge areas.

Process Groups

The project management framework consists of five process groups: initiating, planning, executing, monitoring and controlling, and closing. Because a project is a temporary initiative, it generally starts with the initiating processes and ends with the closing processes. However, planning, executing, and monitoring and controlling processes occur concurrently and iteratively throughout the project.

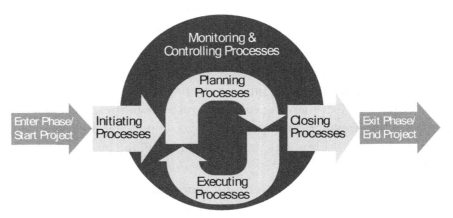

Figure 2-2: Project Management Process Groups
PMBOK® Guide, page 50

The process groups (or domains) represent groups of related processes and not project phases. These process groups may be repeated throughout multiple project phases. This can be one of the more confusing aspects the project management framework, because at first glance, the process groups misleadingly appear to reflect project phases. Figure 2-2 above is a good visual to keep in mind to understand the relationships between these domains.

1. Initiating – The initiating process group encompasses the two processes that begin to define the project and objectives. These processes may occur at the beginning of a project or the beginning of a new phase of the project. The initiating processes secure authorization for the project or phase to begin. In addition, it is during this process group that the stakeholders for the project are identified.

2. Planning – The planning process group encompasses those processes that define and refine the project objectives. The planning processes identify the project approach to achieving the objectives and scope of the project and span all ten knowledge areas. While there are 24 processes in planning (over half of the total processes), this does not represent the proportional time spent on these processes in reality. Rather, it reflects the need to ensure that all aspects of the project have undergone appropriate planning. The ultimate output of these planning processes is the project management plan. The project management plan includes the project baselines and all of the subsidiary plans. Planning processes are performed iteratively throughout the project.

3. Executing – The executing process group encompasses those processes that integrate the project resources to carry out the project management plan. There are only eight executing processes, but these processes represent the majority of the work, effort, and budget of the project. This is where the work of the project actually occurs, and as such, it should not be considered a phase. Rather, the executing processes occur throughout the project life cycle.

4. Monitoring and Controlling – The monitoring and controlling process group encompasses those processes that measure and monitor progress against the project management plan and specifically against the project baselines. These processes identify variances from those baselines and determine the actions that need to be taken to address those variances. The monitoring and controlling of the project occurs from initiation to completion.

5. Closing – The closing process group encompasses the two processes that formalize acceptance of the product, service, or result. The closing processes close out any procurements, bring the project or phase to a close, and complete the administrative closure of the project. Closing processes may be occurring throughout the project.

Though they may resemble phases, the process groups are really iterative groups of related processes.

The interactions of the process groups are based on the Plan-Do-Check-Act (PDCA) cycle as defined by Walter Shewhart. The PDCA cycle was later modified by W. Edwards Deming.

- "Plan" represents the planning process group
- "Do" represents the executing process group
- "Check" and "Act" represent the monitoring and controlling process group

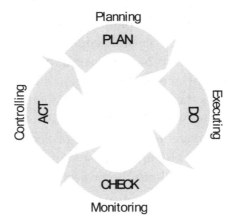

Figure 2-3: Plan-Do-Check-Act-Cycle

Note the iterative nature of the relationship, indicating that as work progresses, the results will be continuously monitored, controlled, and potentially re-planned.

The *Practice Standard for Project Risk Management*

The *Practice Standard for Project Risk Management*, published in 2009, defines the aspects of project risk management that are recognized as good practice for most projects.

While the *Practice Standard* aligns with and is a bit redundant with the risk section within the *PMBOK® Guide*, it provides more information on a number of risk tools and techniques.

There are some slight differences between the components of the risk management processes, related to the inputs, tools and techniques, and outputs. Those differences are highlighted in this book.

PMI Risk Processes

Both the *PMBOK® Guide* and the *Practice Standard for Project Risk Management* present six project risk management processes. The first five processes are in the planning process group, and the final process is in the monitoring and controlling process group:

1. Plan Risk Management
2. Identify Risks
3. Perform Qualitative Risk Analysis
4. Perform Quantitative Risk Analysis
5. Plan Risk Responses
6. Control Risks (note that in the *Practice Standard*, this process reflects the *PMBOK® Guide*, 4th Edition name "Monitor and Control Risks")

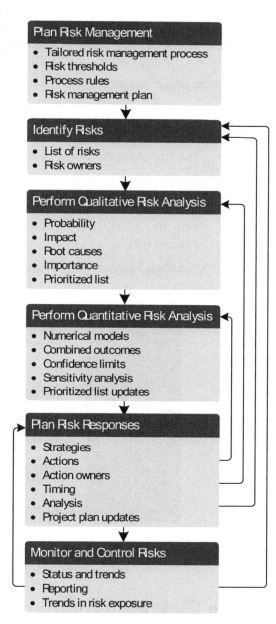

Figure 2-4: Project Risk Management Process Flow Diagram
Practice Standard for Project Risk Management, page 17

To remember the processes, use the acronym PIER-C: Plan, Identify, Evaluate (qualitatively and quantitatively), Respond, and Control.

ISO 31000 Risk Principles and Guidelines

ISO (the International Organization for Standardization) is a worldwide federation of national standards bodies. ISO 31000 is the ISO standard for risk management. PMI's *PMBOK® Guide* and the *Practice Standard for Project Risk Management* align with ISO 31000, although some of the terminology may be somewhat different. As reference, these differences are presented throughout this text.

For example, the naming of the processes differs from the *PMBOK® Guide* and the *Practice Standard* in the ISO 31000 standard:

- Plan Risk Management is known as "establishing the context"
- Identify Risks is known as "risk identification"
- Perform Qualitative Risk Analysis is known as "risk analysis"
- Perform Quantitative Risk Analysis is known as "risk analysis" and "risk evaluation"
- Plan Risk Responses is known as "risk treatment"
- Control Risks is known as "monitoring and review"

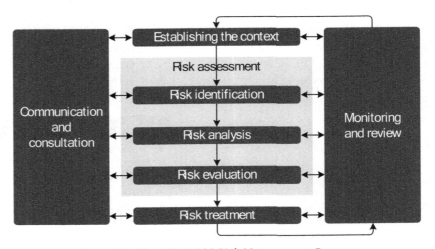

Figure 2-5: The ISO 31000 Risk Management Process

ISO 31000 - Risk Management Principles and Guidelines, page 14

Plan Risk Management

The Plan Risk Management process defines the scope and objectives of the project risk management approach, ensuring that the project risk management is fully integrated with the overall project management.

The risk management plan, a subsidiary plan to the project management plan, provides detailed information on the risk management approach, taxonomy, tools, communication, and risk analysis structure. The risk management plan is one of the more comprehensive and necessary subsidiary plans, as it provides the foundation and framework for project risk management. The risk management plan may be developed generally for an organization, but it must be modified appropriately for individual projects, as each project will require unique aspects of risk management.

Plan Risk Management: Inputs, Tools and Techniques, and Outputs

Inputs	Tools and Techniques	Outputs
1. Project management plan	1. Analytical techniques	1. Risk management plan
2. Project charter	2. Expert judgment	
3. Stakeholder register	3. Meetings	
4. Enterprise environmental factors		
5. Organizational process assets		

Figure 2-6: Plan Risk Management ITTOs

PMBOK® Guide, page 313

In ISO 31000, planning risk management is known as "establishing the context" of the project risk management approach. When the context is established, the objectives of project risk management are articulated, the internal and external parameters are defined, and the scope and risk criteria for the remaining processes are structured.

Identify Risks

The Identify Risks process, which is conducted iteratively throughout the project, seeks to identify all knowable risks of the project.

Risk identification must occur early in the project, theoretically even before the project is chartered, and must be considered an ongoing process from project conception to completion.

Identify Risks: Inputs, Tools and Techniques, and Outputs

Inputs	Tools and Techniques	Outputs
1. Risk management plan	1. Documentation reviews	1. Risk register
2. Cost management plan	2. Information gathering techniques	
3. Schedule management plan	3. Checklist analysis	
4. Quality management plan	4. Assumptions analysis	
5. HR management plan	5. Diagramming techniques	
6. Scope baseline	6. SWOT analysis	
7. Activity cost estimates	7. Expert judgment	
8. Activity duration estimates		
9. Stakeholder register		
10. Project documents		
11. Procurement documents		
12. Enterprise environmental factors		
13. Organizational process assets		

Figure 2-7: Identify Risks ITTOs

PMBOK® Guide, page 313

According to ISO 31000, "risk identification" includes identifying sources of risk, areas of impacts, and the causes and potential consequences of events. The aim of this step is to generate a comprehensive list of risks based on those events that might create, enhance, prevent, degrade, accelerate, or delay the achievement of the project objectives.

Perform Qualitative Risk Analysis

The Perform Qualitative Risk Analysis process assesses and evaluates the probability of an individual risk occurring and assesses the impact of the risk if it were to occur. This evaluation is based on a pre-defined and communicated risk assessment scale, such as 0-1 or 1-5. These risk assessment scales are documented within the project management plan.

Using the probability and impact scores, the risks are then prioritized for additional analysis or response planning as appropriate. All risks are evaluated using a qualitative risk analysis.

Perform Qualitative Risk Analysis: Inputs, Tools and Techniques, and Outputs		
Inputs	**Tools and Techniques**	**Outputs**
1. Risk management plan	1. Risk probability and impact assessment	1. Project documents updates
2. Scope baseline	2. Probability and impact matrix	
3. Risk register	3. Risk data quality assessment	
4. Enterprise environmental factors	4. Risk categorization	
5. Organizational process assets	5. Risk urgency assessment	
	6. Expert judgment	

Figure 2-8: Perform Qualitative Risk Analysis ITTOs

PMBOK® Guide, page 328

According to ISO 31000, "risk analysis" involves consideration of the causes and sources of risk, their positive and negative consequences, and the likelihood that those consequences will occur. Factors that affect consequences and their likelihoods should be identified.

Perform Quantitative Risk Analysis

The Perform Quantitative Risk Analysis process further evaluates the higher-priority risks in terms of impact on costs and/or schedule.

In a qualitative analysis, a risk may have an impact score of 3, but in quantitative analysis, that same risk may have a $3,000 or 10-day schedule delay impact.

Quantitative analysis is used to evaluate the aggregate effect of risks on the overall project objectives. Because quantitative risk analysis is more time-consuming and may require specialized tools and knowledge, not all risks are analyzed quantitatively.

Perform Quantitative Risk Analysis: Inputs, Tools and Techniques, and Outputs

Inputs	Tools and Techniques	Outputs
1. Risk management plan	1. Data gathering and representation techniques	1. Project documents updates
2. Cost management plan	2. Quantitative risk analysis and modeling techniques	
3. Schedule management plan	3. Expert judgment	
4. Risk register		
5. Enterprise environmental factors		
6. Organizational process assets		

Figure 2-9: Perform Quantitative Risk Analysis ITTOs

PMBOK® Guide, page 334

In ISO 31000, quantitative risk analysis is part of both "risk analysis" and "risk evaluation." Risk analysis can be qualitative, semi-quantitative, quantitative, or a combination of these, depending on the circumstances and the resources available to the team. Risk evaluation is used to assist in making decisions, based on the outcomes of risk analysis, about which risks need treatment and the prioritization of treatment implementation.

Plan Risk Responses

During the Plan Risk Responses process, the prioritized risks are evaluated for the most appropriate responses. Responses may be proactive strategies, which are implemented prior to the risk event occurring, or contingent response strategies, which are planned in advance but only implemented if the risk event or risk trigger occurs.

In addition to determining responses, a risk owner is also identified for each of the prioritized risks. This process identifies residual and secondary risks. Residual risks are those risks that remain after a response is taken. Secondary risks are those that arise as a result of implementing a risk response.

Plan Risk Responses: Inputs, Tools and Techniques, and Outputs

Inputs	Tools and Techniques	Outputs
1. Risk management plan	1. Strategies for negative risks or threats	1. Project management plan updates
2. Risk register	2. Strategies for positive risks or opportunities	2. Project documents updates
	3. Contingent response strategies	
	4. Expert judgment	

Figure 2-10: Plan Risk Responses ITTOs

PMBOK® Guide, page 342

In ISO 31000, risk response planning is considered "risk treatment." Risk treatment involves selecting one or more options for modifying risks and implementing those options.

Control Risks

During the Control Risks process, the identified risks are monitored and potentially reassessed as the environment or circumstances change. In addition, the risk responses and risk management approach are audited to ensure that risk is being adequately managed for the project.

Control Risks: Inputs, Tools and Techniques, and Outputs

Inputs	Tools and Techniques	Outputs
1. Project management plan	1. Risk reassessment	1. Work performance information
2. Risk register	2. Risk audits	2. Change requests
3. Work performance data	3. Variance and trend analysis	3. Project management plan updates
4. Work performance reports	4. Technical performance measurement	4. Project documents updates
	5. Reserve analysis	5. Organizational process assets updates
	6. Meetings	

Figure 2-11: Control Risks ITTOs

PMBOK® Guide, page 349

In ISO 31000, controlling risks is considered "monitoring and review." Both monitoring and review should be a planned part of the risk management process and involve regular checking or surveillance. It can be periodic or ad hoc.

Additional Tools and Techniques

There are a number of additional risk management tools and techniques that are presented in the *Practice Standard for Project Risk Management*. The table below summarizes these tools and techniques and the processes that may use them. These tools and techniques are defined in more detail later in the book.

From an exam perspective, it is not critical that you memorize this table. You will find that many of the tools and techniques can be used in a number of different ways and can apply to multiple processes.

	Identify Risks	Perform Qualitative Risk Analysis	Perform Quantitative Risk Analysis	Plan Risk Responses	Control Risks
Analytic hierarchy process (AHP)		X			
Brainstorming	X			X	
Cause and effect diagrams	X				
Checklists	X			X	
Contingency planning				X	
Contingency reserve estimation				X	
Critical chain project management (CCPM)				X	X
Decision tree analysis				X	
Delphi technique	X			X	
Estimating techniques		X			
Expected monetary value (EMV)			X	X	
FMEA / fault tree analysis	X				
Force field analysis	X			X	
Industry knowledge base	X			X	
Influence diagrams	X				
Interviews	X		X	X	
Post project reviews / lessons learned / historical information	X	X			
Prompt lists	X				
Questionnaire	X				
Risk breakdown structure (RBS)	X				
Root cause analysis	X	X			
System dynamics	X				
Work breakdown structure (WBS) review	X				

Figure 2-12: Practice Standard for Project Risk Management Tools

Practice Standard for Project Risk Management

Review Questions   Chapter 2

1. **This process evaluates the highest-priority risks in terms of the cost and/or schedule impact.**

   A. Perform Qualitative Risk Analysis
   B. Perform Quantitative Risk Analysis
   C. Plan Risk Management
   D. Plan Risk Responses

2. **All of the following are characteristics of the project management process groups except:**

   A. The process groups can be in use concurrently throughout the project.
   B. The output of one process generally becomes an input for another process or is a deliverable of the project.
   C. All of the processes are needed on all projects, and all of the interactions apply to all projects or project phases.
   D. When a project is divided into phases, the process groups are normally repeated within each phase throughout the project's life to effectively drive the project to completion.

3. **The Project Management Institute:**

   A. Is a not-for-profit organization with a primary focus on advancing the practice of project management globally
   B. Is a for-profit organization representing the interests of project managers nationally
   C. Is a global organization that administers the mandatory certification for project managers
   D. Is a government-run organization that develops and applies project auditing standards

4. **The risk management process involves:**

   A. Risk identification, qualitative risk analysis, and risk response development
   B. Risk management, risk execution, and risk controlling
   C. Planning the risk management approach, identifying and analyzing risks, determining the best responses for the risks, and ongoing risk monitoring and controlling
   D. Risk identification, risk response management, and quantitative risk analysis

5. **The project management process groups are:**

   A. Planning, checking, directing, monitoring, and recording
   B. Planning, executing, directing, closing, and delivering
   C. Initiating, executing, monitoring, evaluating, and closing
   D. Initiating, planning, executing, monitoring and controlling, and closing

6. **The difference between the *PMBOK® Guide* and ISO 31000 can best be described as:**

   A. The *PMBOK® Guide* describes best practices for project risk management, while ISO 31000 is a project management methodology.
   B. The *PMBOK® Guide* describes an approach and best practices for project management, while ISO 31000 is a risk management standard.
   C. The *PMBOK® Guide* is a mandatory project management methodology, while ISO 31000 provides techniques for project management.
   D. The *PMBOK® Guide* provides techniques for risk management, while ISO 31000 describes project management best practices.

7. **The objective of this process is to prioritize the project risks.**
    A. Identify Risks
    B. Plan Risk Management
    C. Perform Qualitative Risk Analysis
    D. Plan Risk Responses

8. **The process groups interact based on:**
    A. The plan-do-check-act cycle
    B. The risk management plan
    C. The project management plan
    D. The DACI cycle

9. **Also known as establishing the context, this process defines the scope and objectives of the project risk management approach.**
    A. Identify Risks
    B. Develop Risk Management Plan
    C. Develop Risk Taxonomy Approach
    D. Plan Risk Management

10. **The project management framework is best described as:**
    A. A defined methodology for implementing IT projects
    B. An approach that encompasses ten knowledge areas and five process groups
    C. An approach to project management with five distinct phases
    D. An approach that encompasses ten process groups and five knowledge areas

11. **Which statement is most accurate regarding the Identify Risks process?**
    A. The project must be chartered before the process can be started.
    B. The process is ongoing throughout the project.
    C. The process seeks to identify knowable and unknowable risks.
    D. The process must be complete before the project is chartered.

12. **Which statement is most accurate?**
    A. If a project is divided into phases, the process groups will only be utilized once during the project.
    B. Risk management is considered a process group.
    C. Since management of a project is a finite effort, the initiating process group processes generally begin the project and the closing process group processes generally end it.
    D. The project management framework consists of ten process groups.

13. **Which statement is least accurate regarding the Plan Risk Responses process?**
    A. During this process, the prioritized risks are evaluated for the most appropriate responses.
    B. The responses may be proactive or contingent response strategies.
    C. According to ISO 31000, the process is known as risk evaluation.
    D. The risk owners will be identified during this process.

14. **The following statements are true about the *PMBOK® Guide*, except:**

    A. The *PMBOK® Guide* provides and promotes a common vocabulary within the project management profession.
    B. The *PMBOK® Guide* is the mandatory methodology for projects.
    C. The *PMBOK® Guide* includes best practices and a modular framework rather than a methodology.
    D. The *PMBOK® Guide* identifies the subset of the project management body of knowledge generally recognized as good practice.

15. **During which process are the risk responses and risk management approach audited?**

    A. Control Risks
    B. Review Risk Process
    C. Plan Risk Responses
    D. Plan Risk Management

Vocabulary Review   Chapter 2

Closing process group   ISO   *PMBOK® Guide*
Communication knowledge area   ISO 31000   *Practice Standard for Project Risk Mgt*
Control Risks   Monitoring/controlling process group   Procurement knowledge area
Cost knowledge area   Perform Qualitative Risk Analysis   Quality knowledge area
Executing process group   Perform Quantitative Risk Analysis   Risk knowledge area
HR knowledge area   Plan Risk Management   Scope knowledge area
Identify Risks   Plan Risk Responses   Stakeholder knowledge area
Initiating process group   Planning process group   Time knowledge area
Integration knowledge area

1. _____   Conducted iteratively throughout the project, this process seeks to identify knowable risks to the project

2. _____   The processes that begin to define the project and objectives

3. _____   The processes involved in planning, estimating, budgeting, financing, funding, managing, and controlling costs so that the project can be completed within the approved budget

4. _____   The processes required to identify the people, groups, or organizations that could impact or be impacted by the project, to analyze expectations and their impact on the project, and to develop appropriate management strategies for engaging them

5. _____   A worldwide federation of national standards bodies

6. _____   The processes and activities of the performing organization that determine quality policies, objectives, and responsibilities so the project will satisfy the needs for which it was undertaken

7. _____   The process in which identified risks are monitored and potentially reassessed as the environment or circumstances change

8. _____   The process that defines the scope and objectives of the project risk management approach, ensuring that the project risk management is fully integrated with the overall project management

9. _____   The processes that are required to ensure timely and appropriate planning, collection, creation, distribution, storage, retrieval, management, control, and monitoring, as well as the ultimate disposition of information

10. _____ The published standard for risk management

11.	The processes of conducting risk management planning, identification, analysis, response planning, and risk control for a project
12.	The processes necessary to purchase or acquire products, services, or results needed from outside the project team
13.	The processes required to manage the timely completion of the project
14.	The process that further evaluates higher-priority risks in terms of impact on costs and/or schedule
15.	The processes that identify, define, combine, unify, and coordinate the processes within the project management process groups
16.	The processes that define and refine the project objectives and plan the project approach to achieve the objectives and scope of the project
17.	The processes that measure and monitor progress against the project management plan
18.	A standard that defines the aspects of project risk management that are recognized as good practice on most projects
19.	The processes for the organization, management, and leadership of the project team
20.	The process that assesses and evaluates the probability of an individual risk occurring and assesses the impact if the risk occurred
21.	The processes required to ensure that the project includes all the work required and only the work required to complete the project successfully
22.	The processes that formalize acceptance of the product, service, or result
23.	The process that evaluates the prioritized risks for the most appropriate responses
24.	The processes that integrate the project resources to carry out the work of the project management plan
25.	A standard that provides the fundamentals of project management as they apply to a wide range of projects

Answer Key   Chapter 2

Review Question Answers

1. **Answer: B**

   Quantitative analysis evaluates risk in terms of budget and schedule impact. Quantitative analysis is conducted on the highest-priority risks.

2. **Answer: C**

   Answers A, B, and D are all true statements regarding the project management process groups. C is false, as the processes are meant to be applied as necessary for the project requirements and not all processes are needed for all projects.

3. **Answer: A**

   The Project Management Institute (PMI) is a not-for-profit organization with a focus on advancing the practice of project management. Although a U.S.-based organization, PMI has a global reach and includes chapters and credential-holders all over the world.

4. **Answer: C**

   The risk management processes include Plan Risk Management, Identify Risks, Perform Qualitative Risk Analysis, Perform Quantitative Risk Analysis, Plan Risk Responses, and Control Risks.

5. **Answer: D**

   There are five project management process groups/domains, which are groups of related processes, within the project management framework: initiating, planning, executing, monitoring and controlling, and closing.

6. **Answer: B**

   The *PMBOK® Guide* provides an approach to project management, and ISO 31000 is a published standard for risk management.

7. **Answer: C**

   Qualitative analysis evaluates all risks, assessing probability and impact. The objective or reason behind the process is to prioritize the risks, potentially for further analysis or action.

8. **Answer: A**

   The iterative nature of the project management process groups means that they interact based on the Plan-Do-Check-Act cycle, a continuous improvement model.

9. **Answer: D**

   The Plan Risk Management process, also known as "establishing the context" in ISO 31000, determines the scope and objectives of the project risk management approach.

10. **Answer: B**

    The project management framework includes ten knowledge areas and five process groups.

11. **Answer: B**

    Risk identification is ongoing throughout the project from inception to completion. Often, high-level risk identification occurs prior to chartering to ensure that the project is feasible.

12. Answer: C

The initiating processes generally begin the project, and the closing processes generally end the project. However, planning, executing, and monitoring and controlling happen concurrently and repeatedly throughout the project.

13. Answer: C

The false statement is C. Plan Risk Responses is known as "risk treatment" in ISO 31000. The other statements are accurate regarding risk response planning.

14. Answer: B

The *PMBOK® Guide* is a guide to the approach to and best practices for project management. It is not a mandatory methodology.

15. Answer: A

The risk responses and risk management approach are audited during the Control Risks process.

Vocabulary Review Answers

1. Identify Risks
2. Initiating process group
3. Cost knowledge area
4. Stakeholder knowledge area
5. ISO
6. Quality knowledge area
7. Control Risks
8. Plan Risk Management
9. Communication knowledge area
10. ISO 31000
11. Risk knowledge area
12. Procurement knowledge area
13. Time knowledge area
14. Perform Quantitative Risk Analysis
15. Integration knowledge area
16. Planning process group
17. Monitoring/controlling process group
18. *Practice Standard for Project Risk Mgt*
19. HR knowledge area
20. Perform Qualitative Risk Analysis
21. Scope knowledge area
22. Closing process group
23. Plan Risk Responses
24. Executing process group
25. *PMBOK® Guide*

Chapter 3

Stakeholder Engagement

Stakeholder Education

As mentioned previously, one of the key roles and responsibilities of the project manager is educating the project team, stakeholders, and leadership as to the risk management exposure of the project, the desired risk management approach, and the stakeholders' roles in project risk management.

Stakeholder education, awareness, engagement, and support are critical success factors for project risk management. Stakeholders, particularly key stakeholders (those who are in leadership or decision-making roles for the project), need to be educated as to:

- The project risk management approach, tools and techniques, and methodology that will be utilized on the project
- Project risk communication vehicles, information, frequency, and ownership, through the risk register, risk response plan, and other risk reports
- The allocation of contingency and management reserve funding
- The ownership of decisions relating to project risk management
- Project risk management roles and responsibilities

Coaching Team Members

The project team members also need to be educated on the project risk management approach, roles and responsibilities, and expectations. This coaching should occur as early as the project kick-off meeting to ensure that all team members recognize the importance of project risk management, the impact of project risk management on achieving the project objectives, and the expectations of them as team members.

The project manager is responsible for ensuring that this coaching and training occurs and is maintained throughout the project. This responsibility can include looking for opportunities to provide coaching and training on the various risk management techniques, ways to identify risks, the importance of variance and trend analysis, and what is needed to implement and monitor the designated risk responses.

Ideally, risk management is fully integrated with project management, and the team members will not feel that risk management activities are extra work or an additional burden on them as team members.

Group Decision-Making Techniques

Throughout the project, the project manager will be responsible for facilitating decision-making with a number of stakeholders. The project manager should explicitly identify how decisions will be made on the project as it relates to project risk management.

Group decision-making will fall into one of the following categories:

- Unanimity – This decision-making approach implies that all key members must agree in order to finalize a decision. Needless to say, seeking unanimity can be challenging from a time perspective, especially in environments in which there are significant differences in opinions.

- Majority – This decision-making approach accepts a decision as long as more than half of the members agree. Before the members of the group are asked to vote, the project manager should ensure that everyone understands that this will be the approach and seek agreement that the non-majority members will support the decision.

- Plurality – This decision-making approach accepts the decision agreed upon by the largest subset, even if a majority vote is not reached. For example, if four stakeholders agree with option A, two with option B, and three with option C, option A would be pursued, even though it does not have the majority agreement.

- Dictatorship – This decision-making approach implies that one person is making the decision. This is often appropriate for decisions that should rest solely on the sponsor or the customer. Again, it is important to understand and document what specific decisions or areas fall under dictatorship decision-making.

DACI Model

The DACI Model, a popular Six Sigma tool, is helpful in clarifying who has the authority to make decisions. DACI is an acronym representing the roles of Drivers, Approvers, Contributors, and Informed individuals.

Drivers are responsible for coordinating the project overall and making decisions about how to proceed. Approvers may or may not be involved in the detailed work of the project team, but their approval is required for key decisions. Contributors do not have approval authority but can provide information that is needed in order to make decisions. Informed individuals are those who must be given information once a decision is made.

There are a number of other tools and techniques that can be used to guide decision-making for project management and project risk management. These tools and techniques are discussed in more depth later in this book, but can include:

- Decision trees
- Force field analysis
- Failure Mode and Effect Analysis (FMEA)

Group Creativity Techniques

A number of creativity techniques are used for many of the project risk management processes. The project manager is expected to leverage a number of different techniques in order to identify the risks of the project, assess the impact of the risks, and determine the most appropriate response.

Brainstorming

Brainstorming is designed for participants to think and contribute creatively with minimal structure or boundaries. Versus a structured or regimented approach, brainstorming leverages lateral thinking and allows for the development of creative ideas or approaches. All participants are encouraged to participate in brainstorming sessions and be open to hearing all of the ideas shared in the group.

Often, some ideas will spark or feed other ideas, and contributions will be built collectively from the creative energies of the group. When facilitated appropriately, brainstorming can also be a fun and energizing activity that can encourage the project team members to bond and enhance their group dynamics.

Nominal Group Technique

The nominal group technique involves problem identification, solution generation, and decision-making. The nominal group technique is frequently used for groups who want to make a decision quickly, as by a vote, but want everyone's opinion to be taken into consideration before the vote is taken.

Each member of the group provides his or her view of the solution with a short explanation. Duplicate solutions are eliminated from the list, and then members rank the remaining solutions. During this process, members should be encouraged to share the reasons for their choices in order to identify common ground and potentially meld and improve similar ideas.

There are commonly five steps in the nominal group technique process:

1. Introduction and explanation of the purpose and procedure
2. Silent generation of ideas, during which the participants write their ideas
3. Sharing of ideas by all participants
4. Group discussion including questions and answers
5. Voting and ranking of the ideas

Delphi Technique

The Delphi technique is used to generate information from a panel of experts. Participants are asked questions or presented with a scenario for response via an anonymous survey mechanism. The responses are consolidated and redistributed back to the panel for further review, comment, or agreement.

The number of rounds can vary depending on the audience and topic. The Delphi technique is especially valuable in environments where participants may not feel comfortable speaking up in a non-anonymous setting or where very dominant personalities make the risk of "group think" more likely.

Idea/Mind Mapping

Unlike linear note-taking or writing, idea or mind mapping seeks to allow an individual or group to think more creatively. Mind mapping has been used for centuries by thinkers including DaVinci, Darwin, Edison, and Einstein.

The general structure of a mind map includes:

*   A central idea or image
*   One main topic on each branch and sub-topics on "sub-branches"
*   Use of different colors
*   Space for unexpected topics or ideas

Mind mapping can be done using flip charts, white boards, or other manual tools. In addition, there are a number of software applications for mind mapping.

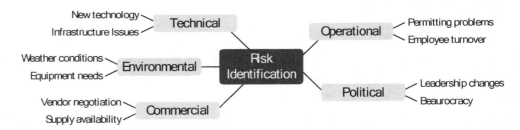

Figure 3-1: Idea/Mind Mapping

Affinity Diagram

Created in the 1960s by Japanese anthropologist Jiro Kawakita, affinity diagram organizes a large number of ideas by their natural or logical relationships. Affinity diagrams are often constructed using sticky notes or cards on a large work surface, so it is also frequently referred to as a "sticky note process."

Ideas captured through brainstorming or other means are listed on individual notes and spread on a large surface for visualization. Using the feedback from the group, the ideas are then grouped by logical relationships or categories.

Affinity diagrams are beneficial when there are a large number of ideas that appear chaotic, when issues seem large or difficult to grasp, and when group consensus is needed.

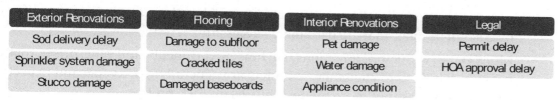

Exterior Renovations	Flooring	Interior Renovations	Legal
Sod delivery delay	Damage to subfloor	Pet damage	Permit delay
Sprinkler system damage	Cracked tiles	Water damage	HOA approval delay
Stucco damage	Damaged baseboards	Appliance condition	

Figure 3-2: Affinity Diagram

PMBOK® Guide, page 246

Risk Attitudes and Tolerances

Organizational and stakeholder risk attitudes and risk tolerances must be explicitly identified and managed before and during the project. While organizational risk attitudes are typically overarching and long-term, stakeholder risk attitudes and tolerances can change and evolve depending on the environment, circumstances, and specific project implications.

Organizational Risk Culture

Each organization possesses and displays an overall risk attitude that exerts influence. However, while a working team's approach to risk is largely a function of the risk attitudes of the constituent individuals, a corporate organization is different.

Each corporate organization can be said to have its own distinct "corporate risk culture" which is more than the sum of its component parts and which influences every action and decision, often covertly.

The drivers of corporate risk culture may include:

- The influence of organizational history and corporate memory
- Recent events which have had a significant effect on the organization
- Reputational issues, past and present
- Stakeholder expectations and influences
- The leadership style adopted at all levels in the organization
- Characteristics of the industry sector
- The current economic environment and conditions
- The national and international context for corporate activities

Organizations perceive risk as the effect of uncertainty on their project and larger organizational objectives. Every organization is different, and the degree to which different organizations are willing to accept risk varies. Organizational risk tolerance is reflected in the organizational policies, such as pre-established prohibitions on pursuing fixed-price contract projects.

Risk responses reflect an organization's perceived balance between risk-taking and risk avoidance. Risks that are threats to a project may be accepted if the risks are within the organization's tolerances and are in balance with the rewards that may be gained by taking the risks.

Organizations in different businesses deal with risk in their own ways.

- Start-ups and speculative endeavors may have a high tolerance for risk: many projects undertaken are expected to fail, but these are compensated for by a small number that are extremely successful.

- More conservative organizations, such as governments and enterprises that provide solutions to customers for a fee, are generally risk-averse and expect consistent success but more modest returns on each project.

The specific organization's risk tolerance must be a primary consideration in the evaluation and selection of projects. A consistent approach to risk should be developed for each project, and communication about risk and its handling should be open and honest.

Risk Tolerances

Individuals and groups adopt attitudes toward risk that influence the way they respond. These risk attitudes are driven by perception, tolerances, and other biases that should be made explicit wherever possible.

The stakeholders of the project may have strong individual opinions on project risk. Although some stakeholders may be risk-tolerant, others may wish to staff and structure the work to minimize extreme outcomes. Technical contributors tend to prefer low risk.

One often-repeated example of stakeholder risk preference is attributed to the NASA astronauts, who observed that they were sitting on the launch pad atop hundreds of systems, each constructed by the lowest bidder. Your risk tolerance frequently depends on your perspective.

Risk Attitudes

In evaluating the organization and the project stakeholders, the project manager may find the following risk attitudes:

- Risk-averse
- Risk-tolerant
- Risk-neutral
- Risk-seeking

Risk-Averse

Risk-averse stakeholders are uncomfortable with uncertainty and have a low tolerance for ambiguity. They seek security and resolution in the face of risk. They prefer facts over theories and are more interested in established methods and procedures than new or untested approaches.

These stakeholders have increased sensitivity and greater reactions to threats. As they are uncomfortable with negative uncertainty, they tend to identify those threats more readily and may feel that risks are more severe than they actually are. I consider these folks the "glass-half-empty" group, a.k.a. pessimists.

From a response perspective, a risk-averse stakeholder will prefer aggressive risk responses to avoid or minimize as many threats as possible.

When considering opportunities, however, the risk-averse stakeholder may not see as many opportunities or may tend to underrate their significance. This can mean that they are not prepared to take the steps necessary to enhance or capture opportunities.

Generally speaking, the risk-averse stakeholder tends to overreact to threats and under react to opportunities. As the project manager, it is important to identify the causes, sources, or reasons for such a stakeholder's risk aversion and factor that into communications with and the management of that stakeholder.

Example: Risk-Averse Attitude
Cathy Shulze joined Meta Corp a few months ago as the new Vice President of Service. Not only is she new to the role, but Cathy has a very limited budget for her service teams. When evaluating projects under consideration for the coming year, Cathy favors projects that are smaller, very well defined, and projected to consume a minimum of the budget. Cathy has requested that the most senior, experienced project manager be assigned to her projects.

Risk-Tolerant

Risk-tolerant stakeholders are reasonably comfortable with most uncertainties, accepting that they exist as a normal feature of everyday life, including projects and business.

Risk-tolerant people tend to take uncertainty in stride, and it exerts no apparent or significant influence on their behavior. For both threats and opportunities, this may lead to a failure to appreciate the importance of a risk's potential effects on the achievement of project objectives.

Whether the impact is positive or negative, the laissez-faire approach often fails to result in proactive action and, as such, may be considered the most dangerous of all the risk attitudes. Acceptance of risk as part of the "normal situation" may mean it is not managed appropriately, leading to more problems from impacted threats. In addition, there may be a loss of potential benefits as a result of missed opportunities.

This attitude may appear balanced, but progress cannot be made from perfect balance. In some ways, this stakeholder may appear to be "checked-out" from the concerns or interests of the project. I find that I encounter this attitude when someone is retiring, leaving the company, or getting ready to leave for vacation or sabbatical. These risk-tolerant stakeholders just do not seem to have a vested interest in the success of the project.

Example: Risk-Tolerant Attitude

Brent Jamison has been the Director of Marketing for a financial services firm for fifteen years. Although Brent is one of the key stakeholders for the new customer management system, he has not been actively engaged in the project. He has remarked that he does not feel it necessary to take time during the meetings to discuss risk management.

"Some things go as planned, and some don't. We'll deal with it when it happens," he recently said to the project manager.

Rumor has it that Brent is planning on retiring before the new system is completed and ready for roll-out.

Risk-Neutral

A risk-neutral attitude sees present risk-taking as a price worth paying for future pay-offs. Risk-neutral stakeholders are neither risk-averse nor risk-seeking but rather seek strategies and tactics that have high future pay-offs.

Typically, risk-neutral stakeholders think abstractly and creatively. They are able to envision possibilities and entertain ideas, and they are not afraid of change or the unknown. Faced with both threats and opportunities, the risk-neutral approach is quite mature. Risk-neutral stakeholders focus on the longer term and take action only when it is likely to lead to significant benefits or avoid the probable effects of threats.

Example: Risk-Neutral Attitude

Jalina Katon is the Chief Strategist for Millbury Associates, a marketing and public relations firm. Jalina is always on the lookout for new opportunities and new markets to expand Millbury Associates' client base.

In part because of Jalina's creativity and market research, Millbury has enjoyed growth in markets that they previously did not consider as potential opportunities. Jalina encourages "out-of-the-box" thinking among her team and will pursue projects that show potential for longer-term gains.

Risk-Seeking

Risk-seeking stakeholders tend to be adaptable and resourceful and are not afraid to take action. Risk-seeking stakeholders are sensitive to possible opportunities and may overestimate their importance and wish to pursue them aggressively.

They welcome the challenge of tackling uncertainty head-on, which can lead to a somewhat casual approach toward threats. The thrill of the chase can outweigh the importance of potential harm, leading to unwise decisions and actions.

Risk-seeking stakeholders are also likely to identify fewer threats, as they see these as part of normal business. Threats that are raised are likely to be underestimated both in probability and possible impact, and acceptance may be the preferred response rather than any type of proactive action. I consider these folks the "glass-half-full" group.

Example: Risk-Seeking Attitude

People who know Kristen Beane often comment that she "lives life to the fullest." Kristen, wealthy from an inheritance, is always searching for and open to the next challenge, in both her personal and professional life.

Kristen's company, Wild Expeditions, coordinates excursions to remote areas around the world. She has been known to close her eyes, spin the globe, and plan an excursion to the location she's pointing to when the globe stops spinning.

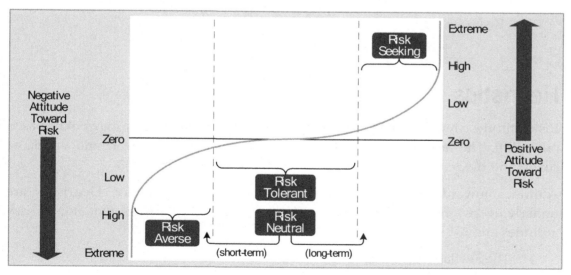

Figure 3-3: Situational Influences on Risk Attitude

Understanding and Managing Risk Attitude, page 47

Depending on their roles on the project, their past experiences, and their work within the organization, individual stakeholders' risk attitudes will vary. It is critical that the project manager understands these different risk attitudes and is able to communicate appropriately with each stakeholder based on his or her attitude.

Exercise: Risk Attitudes

1. What attitude do you believe you exhibit most often?

2. Is your attitude different personally than it is professionally?

3. If so, why?

4. How would your management of stakeholders with these four attitudes differ from a project risk management perspective?

   - Risk-averse

   - Risk-tolerant

   - Risk-neutral

   - Risk-seeking

Heuristics

Risk attitudes are driven by perceptions. Those perceptions may or may not be based on reality. The factors that lead to those perceptions may be overt and visible or covert and hidden.

Attitudes toward risk are significantly influenced by heuristics. Heuristics are underlying psychological influences. The most typical heuristics that impact risk attitudes are:

- The availability heuristic
- The representativeness heuristic
- The anchoring and adjustment heuristic
- The confirmation trap heuristic

The Availability Heuristic

The basic principle of the availability heuristic is that if a particular data item is easier to recall than others, then its relevance is assumed to be higher. The driver is the extent to which the data item is available to memory.

Example: The Availability Heuristic
Two brothers, John and Jason, have a business "flipping" properties, buying houses in poor condition and renovating them for sale for a profit.
The older brother, John, recently sold a house and had a problem with the buyer's financing. This was due to the fact that the recent sales in that neighborhood did not support the high asking price.
Because of this, John is very nervous about the neighborhood comps on recent sales when evaluating how much money to invest in the latest property. However, because his brother Jason has not had this problem with any previous sales, he does not perceive this as a big risk to the project.

The Representativeness Heuristic

The representativeness heuristic selects some data items over others as relevant reference points for assessing situations. While the availability heuristic gives greater weight to items that are more easily remembered, the representativeness heuristic classifies the current situation or item by comparing it with a small range of stereotypes.

The closer the match is between the situation and the stereotype, the stronger the influence the stereotype has on the assessment. The stereotype is viewed as representative of the situation or item under consideration and may cause other characteristics or considerations to be ignored.

Example: The Representativeness Heuristic
The sponsor has provided her final approval for the system renovation project and is ready to assign a project manager. One of the stakeholders has requested that she select a project manager from the Indianapolis project team.
"The Indianapolis project managers always have strong results on their projects and are very good at communicating throughout the initiative," she reasoned.

The Anchoring and Adjustment Heuristic

The anchoring and adjustment heuristic comes into play when an individual is asked to provide an estimate despite not having hard data from which to make that estimate. Instead of making a random guess, he or she will select a starting point and then adjust the estimate from there.

Essentially, regardless of how close the first number is to accuracy, it is given credibility and an associated belief that there must have been a good reason that it came to mind first. This first number is considered the anchor, and potentially more realistic adjustments are made to raise or lower that number.

Example: The Anchoring and Adjustment Heuristic

The project manager is asked to provide an estimate of the overall timeline of a construction project, despite the fact that she has no experience with that type of project. The first estimate that comes to mind is six months, but given that her team is very experienced, she adjusts that timeline down to five months.

The Confirmation Trap Heuristic

A method used as a shortcut in the decision-making process is to assume an answer and then look for evidence that will support or refute that assumption. This is the basis for the scientific method, also known as the hypothetico-deductive method, which begins with an assumption and attempts to prove the assumption false through a series of experiments and deductions.

Unfortunately, there are circumstances in which scientists, politicians, opinionated people only seek evidence that supports their original assumptions and publish that evidence as truth, without seeking evidence that their assumption could be false.

Essentially, with this heuristic, any contrary evidence that does not fit a pre-formed explanation is rejected or forced to fit, while all evidence that confirms it is accepted uncritically and given full weight in the decision-making process.

The confirmation trap heuristic occurs when a person is facing an uncertain situation and subconsciously brings a preexisting judgment to the task of assessing the level of risk. The individual approaches the new, uncertain situation with a feeling of familiarity that clouds his or her judgment going forward. This is also known as the corollary syndrome.

Example: The Confirmation Trap Heuristic

A handyman is hired to build a feature wall in a home that includes an outset of stacked stone with a fireplace flanked by shelves and cabinetry on either side. Despite the fact that the handyman has never completed such a project, specifically with an inset fireplace, he gives a confident estimate of the time and cost to complete the project.

The handyman bases his confidence on the fact that he has done other construction projects of similar sizes and is assuming this project will require the same amount of time and money as these past projects.

Cognitive Biases

A cognitive bias is a pattern of deviation in judgment that occurs in certain situations. These biases affect how stakeholders make decisions, form their beliefs, and behave in various environments and scenarios.

Five common biases are found in project management: optimism bias, loss aversion, framing effect, hindsight bias, and strategic misrepresentation.

1. Optimism bias – This is an optimistic evaluation of the situation that overestimates positive results and shows excessive confidence. The optimism bias can be seen in a number of approaches:

   - Overconfidence – making fast and intuitive decisions when more deliberate decision-making would be appropriate

   - Wishful thinking – believing something is true because an individual wants it to be true

   - Planning fallacy – underestimating the time and/or cost to complete the work or a task

   - Confirmation bias – highlighting information that confirms an individual's assumptions (the confirmation trap heuristic)

2. Loss aversion – This occurs when people prefer to avoid loss rather than acquire gains. This can be seen in a number of preferences:

   - Status quo bias – preferring to keep things the same as they already are and considering changes to be likely to lead to loss

   - Ostrich effect – avoiding risky or difficult situations rather than being willing to learn from them ("putting on blinders" or taking an "out of sight, out of mind" approach)

3. Framing effect – This is when a person sees a situation or problem through his or her own narrow lens based on individual experiences, beliefs, and assumptions.

4. Hindsight bias – This occurs when people misremember their predictions, exaggerating in hindsight what they knew in foresight. This happens when they see past events as having been more predictable than they actually were. They may say they "knew it all along" or "knew it was going to happen like that."

5. Strategic misrepresentation – This is the planned, systematic distortion or misstatement of facts in response to incentives. This can include deliberately underestimating costs and overestimating benefits in order to get project approval.

Stakeholder Identification and Analysis

A key role of the project manager is to not only to identify the project stakeholders but also to analyze and understand their influence over and involvement with the project as it may be affected by factors including but not limited to their levels of risk tolerance. This identification and analysis is conducted within the Identify Stakeholders process.

A stakeholder analysis evaluates the project stakeholders, determining whose interests should be taken into consideration throughout the project. This includes determining their expectations of and influence over to the project and to project risk.

Conducting a stakeholder analysis helps the project manager identify the relationships that can be leveraged to benefit the project through coalitions and partnerships as well as relationships that may need to be managed more closely due to resistance or lack of support.

There are a number of models that can be used to classify and organize stakeholders:

- Power/interest grid – groups stakeholders based on their level of authority (power) and their level of concern (interest)

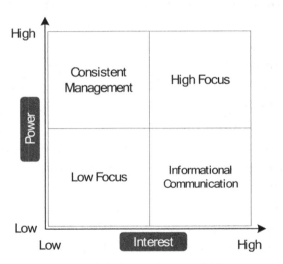

Figure 3-4: Power Interest Grid

- Power/influence grid – groups stakeholders on their level of authority (power) and their active involvement (influence)
- Influence/impact grid – groups stakeholders based on their active involvement (influence) and their ability to effect changes to the project (impact)

- Salience model – classifies stakeholders based on their:
  - Power (ability to impose their will)
  - Urgency (need for immediate attention)
  - Legitimacy (how appropriate their involvement is)

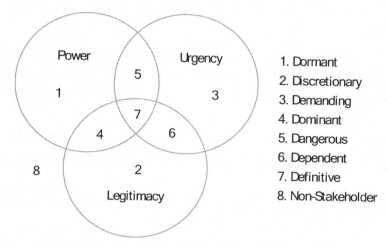

1. Dormant
2. Discretionary
3. Demanding
4. Dominant
5. Dangerous
6. Dependent
7. Definitive
8. Non-Stakeholder

Figure 3-5: Salience Model

The output of the Identify Stakeholders process is the stakeholder register. The stakeholder register contains pertinent information on the stakeholders, such as their identification information, an assessment of their major requirements and main expectations, their potential influence, and some classification, such as internal/external or supporter/neutral/resistor.

Risk Roles and Responsibilities

Effective project risk management requires effort from multiple parties, not just the project manager. It is important to the success of project risk management that these roles and responsibilities are identified, agreed upon, documented, and managed early in the project.

One method of documenting roles and responsibilities for project risk management is publishing a responsibility assignment matrix (RAM). One of the most common RAMs uses the acronym RACI (responsible, accountable, consulted, informed) for each individual and each task.

- Responsible individuals are responsible for performing the activity.
- Accountable individuals are the escalation point and may be responsible for approving the output.
- Consulted individuals may be consulted about the particular task or contribute to the the task in some way.
- Informed individuals simply receive timely information about the task.

Task	Andrew Sponsor	John PM	Angela Risk Champion	Thomas Team Member	Heather Team Member
Risk management plan development	C	A	I	I	I
Risk register development		A			C
Risk process facilitation		A	C	C	C
Risk analysis		R	C	C	C
Risk response development		A	R	R	C
Risk monitoring and reporting	I	A	C	I	I

R = Responsible   A = Accountable   C = Consulted   I = Informed

Figure 3-6: RACI Chart

PMBOK® Guide, page 349

Roles that should be considered or identified include but are not limited to:

- Project manager
- Project sponsor
- Risk champion
- Risk owners
- Action owners
- Project team member

Project Manager

In working with the project sponsor, and based on the project constraints and organization's risk culture, the project manager will determine the acceptable levels of risk for the project. The project manager is instrumental in developing and approving the risk management plan.

The project manager is responsible for team risk management, which involves promoting the appropriate risk management processes with the project team members and ensuring that they are aware of and compliant with the defined project management approach.

Throughout the project, the project manager identifies and most often owns various project risks. Oversight and control responsibilities include the approval of risk response plans and the application of contingency reserves. The project manager is also responsible for risk status reporting, including highlighting risks that are outside of his or her scope and control. These risks are escalated to the project sponsor and/or the the project steering committee.

The project manager monitors the efficiency and effectivess of the risk management processes and risk responses in order to identify gaps and exposure and to capture lessons learned.

From a procurement perspective, the project manager oversees the risk management approaches and reponses by any vendors, contractors, subcontractors, sellers, etc., to ensure that they align with the project risk management approach of the project. Vendor risk reporting may be integrated with the overall project risk reporting.

Project Sponsor

The project sponsor is the individual responsible for approving and funding the project initiative. The sponsor sets the project risk threshholds based upon the identified project constraints, the organizational risk culture, and the documented project benefits. The sponsor's role in project risk management typically includes supporting and encouraging the project risk management approach that is agreed upon, which can require influencing various members of the organization.

The sponsor also reviews the risk outputs, deliverables, and reports to ensure that there is consistency and effectiveness. Decisions on project strategy, including go/no-go decisions, esclations, and evaluations based on risk status come from the sponsor.

Organizationally, the sponsor ensures that there are adequate resources available to respond to identified risks. The sponsor typically "owns" the project's management reserve, which is a financial reserve allocated for unknown risks. Based on escalations from the project manager, the sponsor is responsible for releasing management reserve funds to be applied to those risks.

The sponsor regularly reports on risk status, applied management reserve, and risk response effectiveness to senior management.

Risk Champion

Organizations may have identified risk champions. Often, this role is fulfilled by a member of the PMO. The risk champion's role on the project may be full- or part-time, depending on the requirements, the environment, and the extent of their role.

The risk champion oversees and manages the risk management process on a day-to-day basis. He or she prepares the risk management plan, facilitates risk workshops and risk reviews, and creates and maintains the risk register. He or she ensures the quality of the risk data, analyzing it and producing the appropriate agreed-upon reports.

The risk champion also interviews the risk owners for the most appropriate risk responses to pursue. Periodically, the risk champion reviews the progress of the risk responses in order to advise the project manager on the status of risk management for the project. The risk champion also coaches and mentors team members on the organizationally supported risk management approach.

If there is no identified risk champion, the responsibilities of this role fall onto the project manager. On the exam, this role may also be referred to as that of the "project risk manager."

Risk Owners

Some organizations identify risk owners. A risk owner is the person within a project who is best placed to manage a particular risk. This role is held by individuals, not organizations or teams.

Project teams need to resist the tendancy to nominate the person who identifies a risk as the risk owner. Although this person had enough knowledge to identify the risk, it does not guarantee that he or she would be best at owning that risk. Risk owners must have an appropriate level of authority to appoint the action owners, those individuals who actually implement the necessary actions required to fulfill the response.

The risk owner develops the response or responses to his or her assigned risk in the form of risk actions. These risk actions are then assigned to the appropriate action owners. The risk owner monitors the progress of these responses and reports that progress to the identified risk champion.

Action Owners

Action owners are appointed and assigned by the risk owners. The action owners perform the actions that make up the identified risk responses.

The role of an action owner is temporary, only requiring the implementation of the agreed-upon actions and reports of their progress on their actions to the risk owner.

Project Team Members

Project team members participate actively in the project risk management processes, providing inputs to the risk reports, participating in risk workshops or interviews, and implementing assigned tasks.

Review Questions   Chapter 3

1. The last few times you traveled on business, the counter agents at the airport were very rude. You just learned that your friend accepted a job at that same airline. While you want to be supportive of her opportunity, you do not understand why she would go to work for such an unpleasant company. What heuristic have you applied?

   A. Hindsight
   B. Confirmation
   C. Anchoring
   D. Representativeness

2. In conducting a stakeholder analysis, a number of tools can be used to rank and rate your stakeholders. The salience model of stakeholder classification groups stakeholders based on:

   A. Their power, urgency, and legitimacy
   B. Their level of authority and their level of concern
   C. Their active involvement and their ability to effect changes
   D. Their level of power and influence

3. Which of the following statements is least accurate?

   A. Individuals who are risk-tolerant are reasonably comfortable with most uncertainties.
   B. The risk-neutral approach focuses on the longer term and only supports action when there is likely to be significant benefit.
   C. Individuals who are risk-seeking tend to take a very aggressive approach toward threats.
   D. A risk-averse attitude may underrate the significance of opportunities and may not capture them.

4. Which of the following examples would best represent the availability heuristic?

   A. There are no rooms available at the sponsored hotel, so you will need to drive further to the race.
   B. Your friend has agreed to run the marathon with you, so you are looking forward to the race.
   C. During your last marathon, the weather was very cold, so you are concerned about the weather conditions for your upcoming race.
   D. The race directors are offering race awards for every age division, so you are confident you will place and win an award.

5. All of the following may be drivers of corporate risk culture except:

   A. The leadership style in the organization
   B. The project manager's past successes
   C. The organization's history
   D. The current economic environment

6. A key stakeholder is:

   A. Anyone in a decision-making or managerial role who is impacted by the project outcome
   B. Anyone who is participating actively on the project
   C. The individual who is funding the project
   D. The sponsor and the project manager

7. This technique enhances brainstorming with a voting process to rank the ideas.

    A. Idea/mind mapping
    B. Delphi technique
    C. Affinity diagram
    D. Nominal group technique

8. The PMO has informed you that Brandie Beane will be joining your project in a part-time capacity. Brandie will oversee the risk management process, assist with developing the risk management plan, and facilitating the risk workshops. What role is Brandie playing on the team?

    A. PMO risk liaison
    B. Risk champion
    C. Risk owner
    D. Risk sponsor

9. This type of bias is often seen in risk-seeking individuals.

    A. Hindsight bias
    B. Extreme bias
    C. Optimism bias
    D. Opportunity bias

10. While collecting requirements, you want to solicit feedback from a group of experts in a format in which they are most able to give their individual and honest feedback. What group creativity technique would be best in this situation?

    A. Interviewing
    B. Delphi technique
    C. Affinity diagram
    D. Nominal group technique

11. Also known as the corollary syndrome, this occurs when a person is facing an uncertain situation and subconsciously brings a preexisting judgment to the task of assessing the level of risk.

    A. The confirmation trap heuristic
    B. The anchoring and adjustment heuristic
    C. The availability heuristic
    D. The representativeness heuristic

12. With your team, you have generated a large number of potential requirements. You would like to arrange the ideas into groups for further analysis. What technique should you consider using with your team?

    A. Idea mapping
    B. Affinity diagram
    C. Nominal group technique
    D. JAD session

13. You are mentoring a junior project manager, and you have noticed that he is reluctant to engage with some of the more challenging stakeholders. Whenever he knows they will be at a meeting, he seems to have a scheduling conflict. This ostrich effect is known to occur with individuals with the following type of bias.

    A. Wishful thinking
    B. Framing
    C. Loss aversion
    D. Confirmation

14. The four primary risk attitudes are:

    A. Risk-taker, risk-oppose, risk-neutral, risk-tolerant
    B. Risk-averse, risk-seeking, risk-taker, risk-responsive
    C. Risk-neutral, risk-tolerant, risk-seeking, risk-oppose
    D. Risk-seeking, risk-tolerant, risk-neutral, and risk-averse

15. You and your spouse are considering putting your house on the market. When you ask your spouse for an estimate on what the necessary updates will cost, your spouse states with a shrug, "$30,000, but we may want to do the yard, which could add costs. I would say it would probably be about $35,000." This is an example of:

    A. The anchoring and adjustment heuristic
    B. The confirmation trap heuristic
    C. The availability heuristic
    D. The representativeness heuristic

Vocabulary Review   Chapter 3

Action owner	Dictatorship	Representativeness heuristic
Affinity diagram	Framing effect	Risk-neutral
Anchoring/adjusting heuristic	Hindsight bias	Risk-tolerant
Availability heuristic	Idea/mind mapping	Risk-averse
Brainstorming	Loss aversion	Risk champion
Cognitive bias	Majority	Risk owner
Confirmation trap heuristic	Nominal group technique	Risk-seeking
DACI model	Optimism bias	Strategic misrepresentation
Delphi technique	Plurality	Unanimity

1. _____ An optimistic evaluation of the situation that overestimates positive results and shows excessive confidence

2. _____ A popular Six Sigma tool that is helpful in clarifying who has the authority to make decisions

3. _____ Pursues the decision agreed upon by the largest subset, even if a majority vote is not reached

4. _____ A pattern of deviation in judgment that occurs in certain situations

5. _____ All key members must agree in order to pursue the decision

6. _____ Seeking only evidence that supports an assumption and publishing that evidence as truth without seeking evidence that the assumption could be false

7. _____ Sees present risk-taking as a price worth paying for future pay-offs

8. _____ The person who performs the actions that make up the agreed-upon risk response

9. _____ Captures responses from a panel of experts through an anonymous survey mechanism, with the consolidated responses to be redistributed for further comment and agreement

10. _____ The action of misremembering predictions, exaggerating in hindsight what was known in foresight

11. _____ If a particular data item is easier to recall than others, then its relevance is assumed to be higher

12. _____ Pursues the decision as long as more than half of the members agree

13. _____ When people prefer to avoid losses rather than acquire gains

14. _____ Enhances brainstorming by adding a voting process

15. _____ A stakeholder who is reasonably comfortable with most uncertainty, accepting that it is a normal feature of business

16. _____ Organizes a large number of ideas by their natural or logical relationships

17. _____ A stakeholder who is uncomfortable with uncertainty and has a low tolerance for ambiguity

18. _____ Seeing a situation or problem through a narrow lens based on individual experiences, beliefs, and assumptions

19. _____ The person who oversees and manages the risk management process on a day-to-day basis

20. _____ Providing an estimate by selecting a starting point and adjusting the estimate from there, despite not having hard data from which to determine the starting point

21. _____ Implies that one person is making a decision

22. _____ The person within a project who is best placed to manage a particular risk

23. _____ Creativity technique that allows participants to think and contribute creatively with minimal structure or boundaries

24. _____ A stakeholder with a casual approach toward threats who actively pursues overestimated opportunities

25. _____ Allows the individual or group to think more creatively by mapping out ideas and sub-ideas

26. _____ Selects some data items over others as relevant reference points for assessing situations

27. _____ The planned, systematic distortion or misstatement of facts in response to incentives

Answer Key   Chapter 3

Review Question Answers

1. **Answer: D**

   The bias/prejudice that you apply to an entire organization based on your limited exposure is an example of the representativeness heuristic.

2. **Answer: A**

   The salience model classifies stakeholders based on three factors: power, urgency, and legitimacy. The salience model is typically displayed as a Venn diagram.

3. **Answer: C**

   Individuals who are risk-seeking typically overemphasize opportunities and minimize threats. A risk-averse individual would take an aggressive approach toward threats.

4. **Answer: C**

   The availability heuristic occurs when people use their most immediate frame of reference and apply that incident, knowledge, or experience to the current situation. In this case, because the weather was cold at the last race, that has become a concern for future races.

5. **Answer: B**

   An individual project manager's success, failures, or experiences would not influence corporate risk culture. Corporate risk culture is driven by the sum of experiences, influences, industries, etc., and is not the product of any one individual.

6. **Answer: A**

   A key stakeholder is a stakeholder who is in a decision-making or management role.

7. **Answer: D**

   The nominal group technique, a group creativity technique, enhances brainstorming by adding a voting process to the ideas that are generated.

8. **Answer: B**

   The risk champion is the risk process "apostle" for a project. The role may be full-time or part-time and is often fulfilled by a PMO member. While the role may vary, the risk champion typically provides oversight, develops or assists with the development of the risk management plan, etc.

9. **Answer: C**

   Because risk-seeking individuals tend to focus on opportunities over threats, they often have an optimism bias. An optimism bias focuses on the positive aspects of a situation while minimizing or disregarding the threats.

10. **Answer: B**

    The Delphi technique captures expert feedback using some type of survey mechanism. Participants provide their feedback anonymously. The responses are consolidated and redistributed for further comment and/or consensus.

11. Answer: A

The confirmation trap heuristic is applied when an individual assumes an answer or position and then finds facts or information to support that position.

12. Answer: B

An affinity diagram groups a large number of items by categories.

13. Answer: C

The ostrich effect occurs with people with a loss aversion, a hesitation to take on a situation due to fear of failure or difficulty.

14. Answer: D

The four risk attitudes are risk-seeking, risk-tolerant, risk-neutral, and risk-averse.

15. Answer: A

Taking a guess at a value and then adjusting it based on further information is known as the anchoring and adjustment heuristic.

Vocabulary Review Answers

1. Optimism bias
2. DACI model
3. Plurality
4. Cognitive bias
5. Unanimity
6. Confirmation trap heuristic
7. Risk-neutral
8. Action owner
9. Delphi technique
10. Hindsight bias
11. Availability heuristic
12. Majority
13. Loss aversion
14. Nominal group technique
15. Risk-tolerant
16. Affinity diagram
17. Risk-averse
18. Framing effect
19. Risk champion
20. Anchoring/adjusting heuristic
21. Dictatorship
22. Risk owner
23. Brainstorming
24. Risk-seeking
25. Idea/mind mapping
26. Representativeness heuristic
27. Strategic misrepresentation

Risk Planning

■ ■

In This Chapter
- Risk Management Critical Success Factors
- Risk Definitions
- Risk Contingency and Management Reserve
- Risk Management Planning
- Critical Success Factors
- Plan Risk Management Process

■ ■

Risk Management Critical Success Factors

For project risk management to be successful, the following success factors should exist:

Commitment

Risk management is dependent on both organizational and individual commitment.

Organizationally, the risk management approach should align with the organization's strategic goals, and many risk responses may require upper-management support and approval.

Risk management also involves all members of the project team, from identifying potential risks and analyzing their probable effects to implementation of appropriate risk responses.

Scalability

The level of effort spent on risk management should be scalable and appropriate as it relates to the relative importance of the project to the organization, the organization's risk tolerance, and the project's defined constraints.

Communication

For all aspects of risk management, ongoing dialogue and the ability to communicate honestly is key in not only identifying potential risks but also determining the most appropriate responses for handling those risks.

Integration

Risk management is integrated with project management and is dependent upon the successful implementation of project management processes and practices.

Risk Definitions

As in all of the PMI credentialing exams, there is a high focus on vocabulary and terminology. Keep in mind that you may have used or experienced some of the terms below in a different context that what is described here. On the exam, always stay in the PMI mindset and align with its terminology.

Risk Appetite

Risk appetite is the degree of uncertainty that an organization is willing to take on in anticipation of a reward. An organization's risk appetite is a product of that organization's risk culture, as previously discussed.

For example, a speculative firm will be willing to invest in an initiative of the chance of a large potential payout. Examples abound on *The Discovery Channel*, as depicted in shows such as *Deadliest Catch*, *Bering Sea Gold*, and *Wicked Tuna*.

In contrast, organizations that run more narrow margins, such as healthcare providers, will have lower risk appetites. Taking on risky ventures would not serve to grow their businesses to a degree that the risk would be worth the investment.

Risk Tolerance

Risk tolerance is the degree of risk that an individual stakeholder is willing to withstand. This is highly individualized and can vary and change throughout the project.

A stakeholder's risk tolerance is a product of his or her role, experience, and biases and perspectives. His or her risk tolerance may also vary according to the different project constraints. For example, a stakeholder who is contributing the budget to a project will most likely have lower risk tolerance toward cost risk but may have a higher tolerance toward schedule risk.

It is the responsibility of the project manager to identify the key stakeholders' risk tolerances and revisit/re-evaluate those tolerances throughout the project.

Risk Threshold

A risk threshold is the level of uncertainty or impact at which a stakeholder may have a specific interest. The threshold typically represents the point at which an action may be necessary or be escalated.

The project risk thresholds are typically dictated by the project constraints. The thresholds are agreed upon, documented, and communicated to the appropriate parties to ensure that the full team is aware of them.

For example, an identified project risk that represents a greater-than-$50,000 impact, an agreed-upon threshold, would result in project cancellation.

I observed a fantastic example of a documented and executed risk threshold not too long ago on the show *Dude, You're Screwed* (please excuse the title!). The premise of the show is that a team of highly trained military men selects one individual to drop blindfolded in a remote area with minimal survival gear. He must then make his way to civilization. The stranded "dude" is continually monitored by the other men, who track his core body temperature, heart rate, etc. There is an identified risk threshold set on body temperature, and if the stranded "dude" falls below that threshold, they immediately evacuate him. Everyone on the team knows what the threshold is and also what actions will be taken if that threshold is hit.

Project Risk

A project risk is an uncertain event that, if it occurs, will have an impact on at least one of the project objectives. That impact or effect may be positive or negative. Often, in practice, the focus is on negative risks. From an exam perspective, PMI will expect the candidate to understand both positive and negative risk.

Opportunities

Project risks likely to result in a positive impact are known as opportunities. An opportunity that is realized is known as a benefit. For example, there may be a risk that the project will deliver early, allowing the company to be the first to market.

Threats

Project risks likely to result in a negative impact are known as threats. A threat that is realized is known as an issue or a problem. Generally speaking, an issue is considered a realized negative risk that needs to be escalated for resolution, while a problem is a realized negative risk that the project manager can address without escalation. For example, there may be a risk that the project launch will be delayed, resulting in damage to the company's reputation.

Black Swan Risk

A "black swan" risk is one that is unexpected and unanticipated. It may even have been thought to be impossible. Upon evaluation, a black swan risk would have a probability rating of 0%.

The origin of the name is historical, from Europe, when it was believed that swans could only be white. This belief was dashed when a species of black swans was discovered in Australia.

Emergent Risk

An emergent risk is a risk that arises later in a project and could not have been identified earlier on. For example, if the sponsor of your project has been abruptly fired, a risk arises that your project may not have sponsorship. Because an emergent risk is an unknown risk that occurs, any responses are most likely to be handled using management reserve versus budget contingency reserve.

Secondary Risk

A secondary risk is a risk that arises as a result of implementing a risk response or action. Had that response not been implemented, the risk would not exist. For example, to avoid the risk of falling down the stairwell, you may choose to take the elevator. This choice creates a risk you could get stuck in the elevator.

Cause and Effect

For every risk, there is a cause or causes and an effect or effects. A cause is a given or potential requirement, assumption, constraint, or condition that creates the possibility of negative or positive outcomes. An effect is an impact on one or more of the project objectives.

Risk Statement Construction

The marker of a good risk statement is that it can answer the following questions:

- What could happen?
- Why could it happen?
- Why do we care?

There are a number of risk statement structures using risk metalanguage.

Examples include:

- Because of <one or more causes>, <risk> might occur, which would lead to <one or more effects>
- IF <event>, THEN <consequences>.
- As a result of <definite cause>, <uncertain event> may occur, which would lead to <effect on objective(s)>

Risk Contingency and Management Reserve

A component of project risk management planning is the allocation of a contingency reserve (also known simply as "contingency") and a management reserve. The determination of exact funding dollars is most likely to be validated through a quantitative risk analysis to truly understand the amount of risk exposure and the amount of contingency to be allocated based on the stakeholders' risk tolerances.

Contingency Reserve

A contingency reserve is a risk funding allocation that is established for each activity, work package, or phase based upon the known risk or uncertainty associated with that component.

Contingency is typically managed and controlled by the project manager and is allocated for what are considered "known-unknown" risks. Known-unknown risks are those that have been identified, but it is uncertain whether they will occur.

Contingency allocations are included in the cost baseline and are typically factored into earned value calculations.

Contingency Buffers

Contingency buffers are time allocations at the activity, work package, or phase level based upon the known risk or uncertainty associated with that component. As with contingency reserves, contingency buffers are controlled by the project manager for "known-unknown" risks.

There are a number of methods for determining the contingency buffer allocation. One approach is to use worst-case estimates, which use a second end date for the project further out. The difference in the dates represents the appropriate allocated buffer.

Another approach to buffer allocation is the use of defined contingency plans to dictate needs based on known risks. Using program evaluation and review technique (PERT) or a Monte Carlo simulation can also predict the amount of buffers needed. These are discussed further in the chapter on quantitative risk analysis.

The project manager is responsible for consistently conducting a reserve analysis to evaluate the remaining uncertainty on the project as compared to the amount of contingency budget reserve and time buffers. Theoretically, a project is a risk-declining model, and as such, the need for contingency time and money should decrease as the project progresses.

Any contingency funds that were applied to a risk event that is now obsolete should be reallocated back to the organization, as there is an opportunity cost if the project holds those funds unnecessarily. This may be one of those situations in which real life appears to contradict the PMI way of thinking. Typically, a project manager may actually prefer to hold onto any allocated contingency for future risk events rather than giving it back to the organization. On the exam, be sure to align with the PMI way of thinking!

Management Reserve

A management reserve is a funding allocation established for the overall project, above and beyond contingency reserves. Managed and controlled by the project sponsor, the management reserve is allocated for "unknown-unknown" risks, risks that have not yet been identified, major scope changes that are unexpectedly required, etc. The management reserve is the means for addressing emergent risks.

Unlike contingency reserves, management reserves are not based on known risks. Because of this, there is no way to predict the need for a management reserve based on the current project's information. However, past project experience may yield data and provide guidance on the possible extent of unanticipated risk exposure.

A management reserve is not included in the cost baseline but is considered part of the overall project budget. If the project manager needs to use the management reserve, they would need to seek approval from the sponsor or owner of the project. Not all organizations use management reserves.

Risk Management Planning

The objective of risk management planning is to determine the overall risk management strategy and integrate project risk management with all other project management activities. The risk management plan establishes guidelines for escalating risk-related information, promotes a common understanding of the risk terms and definitions, establishes the type and level of risk detail to be addressed, and determines the appropriate communication protocols both within the team and between the project team and the other stakeholders.

The process of planning risk management should begin as soon as a project is conceived and should be completed early during project planning. However, it is also critical that risk management planning is revisited throughout the project, specifically when there are changes in the environment, realized risks, or other impacts.

Project teams hold planning meetings to develop the risk management plan. Attendees at these meetings may include the project manager, selected project team members and stakeholders, and anyone else in the organization with the responsibility of managing risk planning and execution activities.

In developing the risk management plan, the project manager and attendees consider the budget, resources, and time allocations for risk management activities and determine the success criteria for risk management. Success criteria should include both project-related criteria, such as cost, time, and scope, and process-related criteria, depending on the inherent level of uncertainty in the project.

To be successful, the organization should be committed to addressing risk management proactively and consistently throughout the project. A conscious choice must be made at all levels of the organization to actively identify and pursue effective risk management during the life of the project.

Common Risk Management Errors

Below are some common risk management errors to be aware of, as documented in the *Practice Standard for Project Risk Management*.

1. Risk identification is completed without knowing enough about the project.

2. Project risk is evaluated using only a questionnaire, interview, or Monte Carlo analysis and thus does not provide specific risks.

3. Risk identification ends too soon, resulting in a brief list rather than extensive list of risks.

4. The risks identified are general rather than specific. This makes it extremely difficult to implement effective risk management responses or address root causes.

5. Some things considered to be risks are not uncertain but are facts and are therefore not risks.

6. Whole categories of risks are missed, such as technology, cultural, or marketplace.

7. Only one method is used to identify risks rather than a combination of methods. A combination helps ensure that more risks are identified.

8. The first risk response strategy identified is selected without looking at other options and finding the best option or combination of options.

9. Risk management is not given enough attention during project execution but is rather thought of as a simple planning activity conducted early in the project.

10. Project managers do not explain the risk management process to their team during project planning.

11. Contracts are signed before risks to the project are discussed. This occurs frequently when there is a sales team responsible for closing a deal as quickly as possible. This leaves the project team to deal with the project risks after the fact.

Exercise: Risk Errors

1. Of these common risk errors, how many have you encountered in your project risk management experience?

2. What errors listed above would you consider the most "dangerous" to a project?

3. For one of the errors you identified in #2, explain how you would identify that the error is occurring or has occurred.

4. How would you address the same error you identified above?

Critical Success Factors

Critical success factors for risk management planning include:

Procedural and Policy Compliance

Any rules and guidelines identified for risk management must be compatible with the organization's culture, stakeholder perspectives, and the organization's goals, values, and objectives.

Stakeholder Involvement

Involvement is necessary not only to leverage stakeholders' expertise and experience but also to ensure understanding and commitment to the agreed-upon risk management processes.

Barrier Identification

For risk management to be successful, buy-in and support are necessary from both the stakeholders and the organization. The project manager should proactively identify and address any barriers to risk management.

Organizational Assets

The following organizational assets will increase the chance of risk management success.

- Predefined risk categories
- Established project management methodology
- Standard templates
- Defined roles, responsibilities, and authority levels
- Project documentation

Plan Risk Management Process

The Plan Risk Management process is conducted early in the project with the intention of developing the risk management plan. According to the *PMBOK® Guide*, the Plan Risk Management inputs, tools and techniques, and outputs are:

Plan Risk Management: Inputs, Tools and Techniques, and Outputs

Inputs	Tools and Techniques	Outputs
1. Project management plan	1. Analytical techniques	1. Risk management plan
2. Project charter	2. Expert judgment	
3. Stakeholder register	3. Meetings	
4. Enterprise environmental factors		
5. Organizational process assets		

Figure 4-1: Plan Risk Management ITTOs

PMBOK® Guide, page 313

Plan Risk Management: Inputs

While the *PMBOK® Guide* is not a methodology, there are three documents that PMI states that every project must have: a project management plan, a project charter, and a scope statement.

Project Management Plan

The project management plan provides direction and instruction to the project team regarding how the project will be managed, executed, controlled, and closed. The project management plan may be summary or detailed, depending on the context of the project and the environment.

The project management plan may contain one or more subsidiary plans. Subsidiary plans provide additional information or details regarding a specific area of focus, such as the scope management plan, quality management plan, or communication management plan.

In addition, the project management plan contains the project baselines, which are the scope baseline, schedule baseline, and cost baseline. These baselines are the intended results of the project and can be considered the "frozen" measuring sticks by which the project's progress can be monitored and measured. Variances from the baseline give the project manager and team insight into the health and technical risk exposure of the project.

Because the intention of the project baselines is to measure the progress and health of the project, the only time they should be modified or updated is when there is a significant authorized change to the project scope.

The reason PMI considers the project management plan mandatory ties in to project risk management. Because the project management plan is a "how-to" guide for the project, it provides some level of redundancy for the project and the organization. Should the project manager or a key team member leave, someone else could theoretically step in and take over the project by leveraging the project management plan.

From a risk management perspective, the risk management plan is the subsidiary plan that documents how risk will be managed for the project. Failing to create a risk management plan during the development of the project management plan makes it difficult to conduct future project risk management processes successfully.

Project Charter

Another mandatory document, the project charter formally authorizes the project and details the business needs that the new product, service, or result will satisfy. The charter is signed by the sponsor and provides the project manager with the authority to use organizational resources for project activities. Depending on the organization and the project, the project manager may be assigned before or after the project is chartered.

The charter links the project to the ongoing work and strategic plan of the organization. It is <u>not</u> continually updated throughout the project or iteratively developed as other project documents are.

The project charter may include such information as:

- Project justification, measureable objectives, and success criteria
- High-level requirements, project description, and risks
- Summary milestone schedule and budget
- Project approval requirements, including what constitutes success, who decides whether the project is a success, and who is to sign off on the project once it is completed
- Project manager assignment (if the PM has been assigned), responsibility, and level of authority
- Project sponsor name and level of authority

Stakeholder Register

The stakeholder register contains pertinent information on each of the stakeholders, such as their identification information, major requirements, main expectations, and potential influence, as well as a classification of them as internal/external, supporter/neutral/resistor, etc.

The stakeholder register is used to identify stakeholders who should be involved with risk management planning and should participate in the risk planning meetings. Because this is not risk identification, not all stakeholders will be involved.

Enterprise Environmental Factors

Enterprise environmental factors are internal and external factors that can influence a project's success, including:

- Organizational culture
- Organizational structure
- Internal and external political climate
- Existing human resources
- Available capital resources
- Regulatory environment
- Financial and market conditions

These factors are things that we must consider and assess as to how they will impact the project. For example, when planning project risk management, it is important to consider the organizational culture. Is the culture risk-averse, risk-neutral, risk-tolerant, or risk-seeking? What are the risk characteristics of the industry? What resources are available that can be applied to project risk management?

Organizational Process Assets

Organizational process assets include any of the organization's assets that may be used to enable project success. Leveraging organizational process assets typically increases your efficiency as a project manager. Organizational process assets generally fall into two categories:

- Processes, guidelines, and procedures
  - o Organizational standard processes
  - o Standardized guidelines
  - o Templates
- The corporate knowledge base
  - o Lessons learned
  - o Historical information
  - o Past project files

For example, for planning risk management, organizational process assets that could be used include a project risk management plan template, organizational definitions of risk probability and impact, a risk breakdown structure template, past project files, other historical information that reveals how risk management was implemented on past projects, etc.

Plan Risk Management: Tools and Techniques

Planning meetings and analysis are the primary techniques used for planning risk management, and these techniques encompass the three *PMBOK® Guide* tools and techniques: analytical techniques, expert judgment, and meetings.

Planning Meetings and Analysis

Participants in the planning meetings may include:

- Project manager
- Selected project team members
- Selected stakeholders
- Members of the organization with risk responsibility
- Subject matter experts
- Facilitators

Objectives of the planning meetings are to establish:

- Methodology
- Templates
- Roles and responsibilities
- Terms and definitions
- Schedules and budgets

These planning meetings involve certain key team members in the process, increasing engagement and buy-in. The participants' past experience and knowledge are taken into consideration and evaluated as relative, timely, and comprehensive. If there are gaps in the participants' experience and/or knowledge, it may be necessary to augment the group with outside experts, if available.

Plan Risk Management: Output

Risk Management Plan

The risk management plan, a subsidiary plan to the project management plan, includes information on the stakeholders, planning processes, project tools, and metrics, and it states the standards and objectives for risk management for the project.

The risk management plan may be developed generally for projects in an organization, but each specific project has some unique risk elements that should be reflected.

A risk management plan should include the following components.

- Project description – Documents the project objectives, the external dependencies, and the results of the stakeholder analysis

- Risk management scope and objectives – May include variance thresholds and prioritization of the project objectives

- Methodology – Defines the approaches, tools, and data sources that may be used to perform risk management on the project and includes the key risk deliverables

- Roles and responsibilities – Defines the lead, support, and risk management team members for each type of activity in the risk management plan and clarifies their responsibilities, determines the rules of escalation, and outlines the governance-related rules for reporting and disclosures

- Budgeting – Assigns resources, estimates funds needed for risk management for inclusion in the cost performance baseline, and establishes protocols for the application of the contingency reserve

- Timing – Determines when and how often the risk management process will be performed during the project life cycle, establishes protocols for the application of the schedule contingency reserve, and establishes risk management activities to be included in the project schedule

- Definitions of risk probability and impact – Tailors general definitions of probability levels and impact levels to the individual project and defines different levels of the risks' probabilities and impacts

Defined Conditions for Impact Scales of a Risk on Major Project Objectives (Examples are shown for negative impacts only)					
Project Objective	Relative or numerical scales are shown				
	Very low .05	Low .10	Moderate .20	High .40	Very High .80
Cost	Insignificant cost increase	<10% cost increase	10-20% cost increase	20-40% cost increase	>40% cost increase
Time	Insignificant time increase	<5% time increase	5-10% time increase	10-20% time increase	>20% time increase
Scope	Scope decrease barely noticeable	Minor areas of scope affected	Major areas of scope affected	Scope reduction unacceptable to sponsor	Project end item is effectively useless
Quality	Quality degradation barely noticeable	Only very demanding applications are affected	Quality reduction requires sponsor approval	Quality reduction unacceptable to sponsor	Project end item is effectively useless
This table presents examples of risk impact definitions for four different project objectives. They should be tailored in the Risk Management Planning process to the individual project and to the organization's risk thresholds. Impact definitions can be developed for opportunities in a similar way.					

Figure 4-2: Risk Impact Definitions

PMBOK® Guide, page 318

- Risk categories – Provides a structure that ensures a comprehensive process with a consistent level of detail for systematically identifying risks and contributes to the effectiveness and quality of the risk identification process

  o An organization can use a previously prepared categorization framework. This might take the form of a simple list of categories or might be structured into a risk breakdown structure (RBS). A RBS is a hierarchically organized depiction of identified project risks arranged by risk categories and subcategories that identifies the various areas and causes of potential risks.

- Probability and impact matrix – Prioritizes risks according to their potential effects on the project's objectives

  o A typical approach to prioritizing risks is to use a probability and impact matrix. The specific combinations of probability and impact that lead to a risk being rated as of high, moderate, or low importance are usually established by the organization.

Probability	Threats					Opportunities				
0.90	0.05	0.09	0.18	0.36	0.72	0.72	0.36	0.18	0.09	0.05
0.70	0.04	0.07	0.14	0.28	0.56	0.56	0.28	0.14	0.07	0.04
0.50	0.03	0.05	0.10	0.20	0.40	0.40	0.20	0.10	0.05	0.03
0.30	0.02	0.03	0.06	0.12	0.24	0.24	0.12	0.06	0.03	0.02
0.10	0.01	0.01	0.02	0.04	0.08	0.08	0.04	0.02	0.01	0.01
	0.05	0.10	0.20	0.40	0.80	0.80	0.40	0.20	0.10	0.05

Impact (numerical scale) on an objective (e.g.. cost, time, scope, or quality)

Each risk is rated on its probability of occurring and impact on an objective if it does occur. The organization's thresholds for low, moderate, or high risks are shown in the matrix and will determine whether the risk is scored as low, moderate, or high for that objective.

Figure 4-3: Probability and Impact Matrix

PMBOK® Guide, page 331

- Stakeholders' risk tolerances – Provides documentation regarding the stakeholders' risk tolerances as they pertain to this particular project

- Reporting formats – Defines how the outcomes of the risk management process will be documented, analyzed, and communicated and describes the content and format of the risk register, as well as any other risk reports required

  o A common problem found in standard reporting templates is field size limitations on what is reported. For example, a typical template may ask for the top five risks and top five issues for that period. However, stakeholder communication must be based on what is important to convey that particular period, and for one week, this may include three risks, but the next week it may include twelve. Limiting reporting is not appropriate. This may be a question on the exam!

- Tracking – Notes how risk activities will be recorded for the benefit of the current project, for future needs, and for lessons learned, as well as whether and how risk management processes will be audited

Review Questions   Chapter 4

1. You have assumed the responsibility for a high-risk project that is instrumental to your company's growth. As you begin to evaluate the project, you take into consideration the availability of skilled resources that will be needed for the project. You are considering:

   A. The organizational process assets
   B. The enterprise environmental factors
   C. The project management plan
   D. The organizational methodology

2. Risk tolerances are determined in order to help:

   A. The team rank the project risks
   B. Management know how other managers will act on the project
   C. The team schedule the project
   D. The project manager estimate the project

3. You are new to the project organization within your company. You have been asked to develop a project management plan, and you have sent an inquiry to the PMO asking for any templates or sample plans that may exist. The templates and sample plans:

   A. Are considered enterprise environmental factors
   B. Would constitute the need for a scope change request
   C. Are not the most efficient manner of establishing the project documentation
   D. Are both components of the organization's process assets

4. Risk management planning:

   A. Should begin as soon as a project is conceived
   B. Is optional on most projects
   C. Is the sole responsibility of the project manager
   D. Should be completed prior to the project's authorization

5. The level of risk management is dependent upon:

   A. The amount of funding available for the project
   B. The particular requirements of the project
   C. The timeline available to conduct risk management
   D. The expertise of the project team

6. One of your team members believes that the risk of the CEO stepping down should be evaluated and included. However, your other team members feel very strongly that the CEO would never step down, at least not during the lifespan of your project, and evaluation is therefore unnecessary. The risk of the CEO stepping down is known as a:

   A. Sitting duck risk
   B. Red herring risk
   C. Lame duck risk
   D. Black swan risk

7. **Templates that are preloaded with information common to most projects:**

    A. Make planning faster and decrease the likelihood that necessary work will be overlooked
    B. Are not commonly available in most project environments
    C. Make planning slower, as they need to be customized to fit the project
    D. Increase the probability that past mistakes will be repeated on future projects

8. **Which of the following statements is most accurate regarding the risk management plan?**

    A. A completely customized risk management plan is required for all new projects.
    B. Much of the information in the risk management plan can be developed generally for all projects in the organization, with the inclusion of some unique risk elements for each specific project.
    C. A risk management plan can be developed for the organization and applied to all projects completed within that organization.
    D. The risk management plan is a mandatory document for all projects that will cost more than $50,000 and/or will take more than 90 days to complete.

9. **The risk methodology:**

    A. Defines the project management processes that will be used on the project
    B. Describes the project life cycle and the phase names
    C. Defines the approaches, tools, and data sources that may be used to perform risk management on the project
    D. Defines the individual responsibilities for risk on the project

10. **An outside team-building event is being held at an off-site location. The project team members are traveling in from various regional offices to participate in the one-day activity. This will be the first time many of them meet one another. Select the most accurate risk statement.**

    A. Because of the possibility of rain, an alternate plan should be devised to be put in place in the event of poor weather.
    B. Because this is the first time many of these people will meet, a social gathering is planned that will help facilitate team building.
    C. Because the full team does not usually get to interact in person, an off-site location was reserved to improve team dynamics.
    D. Because the event is outdoors, there is a chance of rain, which could lead to the cancellation of some activities.

11. **The following are components of the risk management plan except:**

    A. A definition of the risk categories
    B. A description of the stakeholders' risk tolerances
    C. The timing of risk activities
    D. The project budget

12. **An emergent risk:**

    A. Is a risk that needs immediate, aggressive attention and needs to be escalated to the project leadership
    B. Is a risk discovered later in the project that could not have been predicted or identified earlier
    C. Is a risk that is not fully formed but may occur
    D. Is a risk that will only impact the project under certain conditions

13. Which of the following statements is not true about positive risks?

    A. A positive risk is also called an opportunity.

    B. Positive risks may not always be appropriately evaluated by the project management team.

    C. Positive risks are always managed externally to the project.

    D. The project manager should consider positive risks as well as negative risks when managing a project.

14. As a subsidiary plan, the risk management plan:

    A. Is separate from the project management plan

    B. Is a component of the project management plan

    C. Will be completed prior to the development of the project management plan

    D. Is mandatory for all projects

15. All of the following should be included in the project risk management plan except:

    A. The timing of risk management activities

    B. The reporting format for risks

    C. How the risk activities will be tracked, communicated, and escalated

    D. The configuration management approach

Vocabulary Review

Chapter 4

Baseline
Black swan risk
Contingency
Emergent risk

Enterprise environmental factors
Management reserve
Organizational process assets
Project charter

Project management plan
Risk management plan
Stakeholder register
Subsidiary plan

1. _____ Detailed or summary document describing the project management approach for the project, including the project baselines and subsidiary plans

2. _____ A component of the project management plan that documents the planned approach to the project constraints of scope, time, and cost that will be measured against during monitoring and controlling

3. _____ A component of the project management plan that provides additional information and details on a particular project area

4. _____ Risk funding allocation for unknown-unknown risks controlled by the project sponsor

5. _____ The document that authorizes the scope and funding of the project, signed by the project sponsor

6. _____ A risk identified later in the project that could not have been identified earlier

7. _____ Internal and external factors that can influence a project's success

8. _____ A subsidiary plan documenting the project's approach to risk management, including roles and responsibilities, definitions, methodology, communication, risk categorization, and risk scales

9. _____ Risk funding allocation for known-unknown risks controlled by the project manager

10. _____ A detailed list of the project stakeholders, including their roles, their functions, their organization, etc.

11. _____ A risk that is considered impossible to occur

12. _____ Any of the organization's assets that may be used to enable project success, including procedures, guidelines, templates, and the corporate knowledge base

Answer Key   Chapter 4

Review Question Answers

1. **Answer: B**

    Enterprise environmental factors are considered as to their effects or impacts on the project. Enterprise environmental factors include internal and external influences. In this question, the enterprise environmental factor that needs to be taken into consideration is the availability of skilled resources.

2. **Answer: A**

    It is important to know what the various stakeholders' tolerances are in order to know the relative priorities of the project constraints and rank the project risks.

3. **Answer: D**

    Templates and sample plans are types of organizational process assets, a phrase that simply refers to things used on the project.

4. **Answer: A**

    Risk management planning needs to begin as soon as a project is conceived in order to determine the approach and structure for risk management, tolerances, constraints, etc.

5. **Answer: B**

    Risk management is not a one-size-fits-all application and must be tailored to the individual needs of the project and the organization.

6. **Answer: D**

    Because this risk is thought to be impossible, it is considered a black swan risk.

7. **Answer: A**

    Project templates, including any used for project risk management, can be pre-filled with common information. These templates make project management more efficient and are considered organizational process assets.

8. **Answer: B**

    Because every project is different, the risk management plan needs to have at least some level of customization. However, it is helpful to have a pre-filled plan that can be easily modified.

9. **Answer: C**

    The risk methodology defines the approaches, tools, and data sources that may be used to perform risk management on the project.

10. **Answer: D**

    The only accurate risk statement that shows cause > risk > effect is answer D. The other options are not risk statements.

11. **Answer: D**

    The project budget would not be included in the risk management plan. It is important, however, as the budget helps determine risk management approaches and risk responses that are included in the plan.

12. Answer: B

An emergent risk is a risk discovered later in the project that could not have been predicted or identified earlier.

13. Answer: C

Positive risks (opportunities) are most often managed internally, not externally.

14. Answer: B

The risk management plan, as a subsidiary plan, is a component of the project management plan.

15. Answer: D

Configuration management is the process by which changes to the technical specifications or scope can be made. The configuration management approach is documented in the project management plan, not the risk management plan.

Vocabulary Review Answers

1. Project management plan
2. Baseline
3. Subsidiary plan
4. Management reserve
5. Project charter
6. Emergent risk
7. Enterprise environmental factors
8. Risk management plan
9. Contingency
10. Stakeholder register
11. Black swan risk
12. Organizational process assets

Risk Identification

In This Chapter

- Risks: Overall and Individual
- Risk Effects
- Critical Success Factors
- Identify Risks Process

Risks: Overall and Individual

Risk is evaluated both at the level of overall project risk and at the level of individual risk.

Overall project risk is the amount of uncertainty about achieving the larger or total project objectives. Generally speaking, the overall project risks are concerned with the project's ability to achieve the desired cost, time, scope, and quality requirements, based on stakeholder needs and their associated tolerance for uncertainty.

A measurement or indication of overall project risk can be used to establish the appropriate amount of contingency resources that should be allocated for the project.

Example: Overall Project Risk

Because the company has produced a similar product in the past, there is a high probability that the scope and quality objectives will be achieved.

However, due to an increase in the manufacturing costs and the lack of availability of the appropriate resources, the budget and schedule objectives will be difficult to achieve.

Individual risks, in contrast, are specific events or conditions that could affect smaller, individual project objectives. These risks may have a positive or negative effect on these project objectives and are the day-to-day focus of the project risk manager as he or she works to allow for the most efficient use of project resources as the project progresses.

Example: Individual Project Risks

Opportunities:

- The product may be first to market
- The client is offering an incentive if the product can be delivered early

Threats

- There may not be sufficient skilled resources
- The production may take longer than anticipated

Risk Effects

For a risk to be considered, it must have an impact on at least one project objective. The most common project objectives are related to the project's triple constraints: scope, time (or schedule), and cost (or resources).

When identifying project risks, these three areas should be evaluated for risks, starting with the project scope.

Project Scope Risk

For risks associated with the elements of the project management triple constraints, scope risks are generally considered first. Identification of scope risks reveals whether or not the project is feasible. Early decisions to shift the scope or abandon the project are essential for projects with significant scope risks. Two common sources of scope risk are scope creep and scope gap.

Scope Creep

Scope creep is any non-mandatory scope change, and it plagues all projects. There are a number of reasons why this is so common, including new opportunities, interesting ideas, undiscovered alternatives, and other information that emerges as the project progresses, providing a temptation to redefine the project and make it "better."

Scope creep represents unanticipated additional investment of time and money, because of both newly required effort and the need to redo work that has already been completed, specifically in plan-driven or waterfall environments. Scope creep is most damaging when entirely new requirements are added once the project is already underway. Scope creep can come from any direction, but one of the most common and dangerous is when it comes from within the project.

Scope Gap

Scope gap is a legitimate scope requirement discovered late in the project. Typically it is the result of committing to a project before the project requirements are complete. When legitimate needs are uncovered late in the project, change is unavoidable, and the work that arises needs to be completed.

Scope gap often occurs from requirements that are overlooked due to customers, managers, team members, or other project stakeholders being unavailable at the start of the project, leading to incomplete or inaccurate requirements.

Although some instances of scope gap are probably unavoidable, in many cases, these gaps are due to incomplete or rushed analysis or gathering of requirements.

Sources of Scope Risk

There are a number of sources of scope risk for a project, including:

- Requirements that seem likely to change
- The mandatory use of new technology
- The requirement to invent or discover new capabilities
- Unfamiliar or untried development tools or methods
- Extreme reliability or quality requirements
- External sourcing for a key subcomponent or tool
- Incomplete or poorly defined acceptance tests or criteria
- Technical complexity
- Conflicting or inconsistent specifications
- Incomplete product definition
- Large work breakdown structure (WBS)

Identifying Scope Risks

To identify scope risks, clearly define all project deliverables and note any challenges with developing any of the deliverables. Evaluate the project objectives and constraints in order to set limits on the project based on the value of the deliverables.

Separate all work on the project into small pieces, as for the creation of the WBS, and identify any work that is not easily understood. Assign all project work to project team members for ownership. If anyone expresses any type of reluctance to accept his or her assignment, that reluctance should be investigated to determine its causes.

Project Schedule Risk

Project schedule risks commonly fall into three categories: delays, estimates, and dependencies.

Delays

Schedule risks in the category of delays may include delays in information, product or component delays, and delays in decision-making.

For example, an information delay may be due to time differences between parts of distributed global teams, poor access to information, or an interruption of the delivery of needed information. Waiting on the production, completion, or arrival of products or components that are required to complete project work are another source of schedule delays. Depending on the organizational structure, the size of the project, and the complexity of stakeholders, slow decisions can also cause project delays. This could result from poor access to the decision makers or their lack of interest in the project.

Estimates

Schedule risks arising from estimates are one of the more common risks affecting the project schedule. These are typically related to learning curves, poor judgment, or imposed deadlines.

Learning curve issues are common with the introduction of new technology or new resources. Poor judgments in estimating timelines are another common problem, because these estimates are often overoptimistic. Asking resources for their worst-case estimates for the length of a project or component can be very helpful. Not only does it reveal information about the likely duration, but it can also serve to uncover new sources of risk.

A very common situation is one in which projects are assigned with aggressive deadlines that have been set in advance with little or no input from the project team. These aggressive deadlines are often difficult if not impossible to achieve within the other constraints of the project. Even when the project schedule and dependencies show that a deadline is unrealistic, organizations often insist that the project objective still needs to be achieved. These projects may be subject to failure from the beginning.

Dependencies

Project schedule risks arising from dependencies can occur from dependencies on other projects, infrastructure factors, and legal issues.

In larger projects or programs, a number of smaller projects may interact and link to each other. In addition to providing each other with information and deliverables that meet well-defined specifications, all projects within a larger program must also synchronize the timing of their schedule dependencies to avoid being slowed down by other projects.

Infrastructure dependencies include technical services, such as computer systems or networks required by the project, that can be interrupted and access to resources such as help desks and system support that may be inadequate. It is very common for projects that are using vendors or contractors to experience schedule delays related to the legal aspects of executing contracts.

Activity Relationship Dependencies

Activity relationship dependencies are another category that should be considered. There are four types of relationship dependencies: mandatory, discretionary, internal, and external.

Mandatory dependencies are inherent to the work being done and typically involve physical limitations. Mandatory dependencies cannot be changed or modified, increasing schedule risk. Mandatory dependencies are also known as "hard logic."

Example: Mandatory Dependency

The books cannot be shipped until they are printed.

Discretionary dependencies are usually established based on the discretion of the project team when they discuss best practices or experience. These dependencies may also come from outside sources or industry experts. Discretionary dependencies are also referred to as "preferred logic," "preferential logic," or "soft logic."

Because they do not involve physical limitations, it is possible to alter or manipulate discretionary dependencies within the project schedule, relative to the amount of risk involved.

Example: Discretionary Dependency

The screen shots of the new system are to be approved prior to beginning the development of the user guides.

External dependencies are those that involve a relationship between project activities and non-project activities. Because external dependencies are outside of the project team's control, there is increased risk.

Example: External Dependency

The city must issue the permits before construction can begin.

Internal dependencies involve a precedence relationship between project activities that are usually inside of the project team's control.

Example: Internal Dependency

The team cannot test a software program until it is designed and built.

Be careful on the exam not to confuse questions on the dependencies with ethical questions. These activity dependencies are not moral judgments but rather physical or non-physical factors on which the project depends. For example, if the exam states that there is a company policy that requires products to be signed off on by a VP prior to shipping to the customer, that question refers to a discretionary dependency. It does not mean that we would violate the policy but that we physically could if necessary.

Identifying Schedule Risks

To identify schedule risks, determine the root causes of all uncertain estimates, identify all estimates not based on historical data, and note dependencies that pose delay risks.

It is often helpful to identify high-risk activities and schedule them early in the project, so that if there is a delay, there is enough time to adjust the remainder of the schedule.

Critical Path

The critical path is the longest path through the schedule network with zero or negative total float. Total float, also known as float or slack, is the amount of time an activity or sequence of activities can be delayed before it delays the overall project duration.

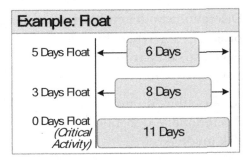

Total float occurs when there are multiple concurrent activities of different durations. The duration difference between the concurrent activities represents the amount of float the shorter path will have.

As illustrated in this graphic, the longest activity concurrently happening is the critical activity and has zero float. This means that if that activity gets delayed, the project will be delayed. The shortest activity has a six-day duration. Because it is happening concurrently with an activity that is 11 days, the activity has five days of total float. The middle activity has an eight-day duration, so it has three days of total float.

If an activity gets delayed beyond any float that is available, the activity now has negative total float. A negative total float indicates that the project is delayed by that many days. For example, if the six-day activity gets delayed by nine days and only had five days of float available, it would then have four days of negative total float. This means that the project would be delayed by four days.

For project schedules that have multiple critical or near-critical paths, risk is increased, due to the fact that if one of those critical activities is delayed, the project will be delayed.

For another example, based on the information in Figure 5-1 below, Activity A and Activity F are on the critical path. They have zero float, as they do not have concurrent activities.

The combined duration of Activities B and C is 7 days. The combined duration of Activities D and E is 11 days. As such, D and E have no float and are on the critical path, but activities B and C can float by as much as four days without affecting the overall project duration.

The four day difference between the two sequences indicates that activities B and C can be delayed, combined, by up to four days before affecting the project duration.

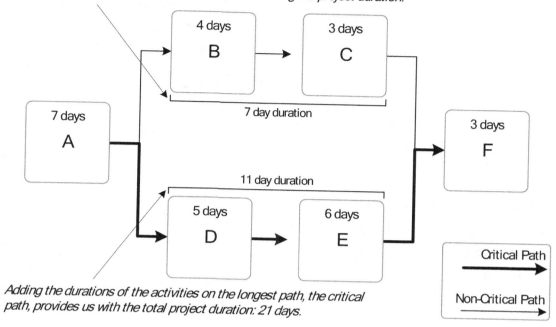

Adding the durations of the activities on the longest path, the critical path, provides us with the total project duration: 21 days.

Figure 5-1: Critical Path Method

PMBOK® Guide, page 177

Exercise: Critical Path Calculation

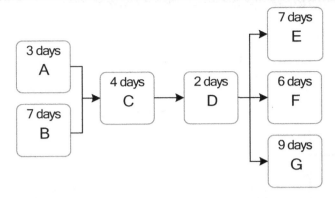

Use the above graphic to answer the following questions.

1. **Which activity has the greatest amount of float?**

   A. Activity E
   B. Activity F
   C. Activity A
   D. Activity D

2. **Which activities are on the critical path?**

   A. A – C – D – G
   B. C – D
   C. B – C – D – E
   D. B – C – D – G

3. **Activity B has __ days of float.**

   A. 0
   B. 6
   C. 4
   D. (4)

4. **Activity A has __ days of float.**

   A. 4
   B. 3
   C. (4)
   D. 0

5. **Activity F has __ days of float.**

   A. 0
   B. 3
   C. (1)
   D. 1

6. **If Activity A is delayed by 9 days, what is the impact on the project?**

   A. There is no impact.
   B. The project is delayed 3 days.
   C. The project is delayed 5 days.
   D. The project is delayed 9 days.

Project Cost/Resource Risk

Project cost and resource risks can be typically categorized as originating from human resources, contracts, and money.

Human Resources

All projects are dependent on human resources, and this can be one of the biggest areas of concern related to risk. Human resource risks include the potential loss of a permanent staff member due to resignation, promotion, reassignment, health, or other reasons or short-term staff loss due to illness or support priorities.

I had one particularly challenging and stressful project that was operating under a very tight delivery timeline. The team really pulled together and worked like rock stars all the way through. As we neared the end of the project and finalized the last of the system tests, I felt the team had earned a celebration dinner before our big install that was scheduled for the following morning. I ordered dinner from the local barbeque restaurant, and everyone enjoyed some well earned downtime, eating and socializing. As we departed for the night, I advised everyone to get some rest in preparation for the big day.

Unfortunately, when I next saw most of my team, it was sooner than I had expected, and it was not in the way I had anticipated. Apparently, something had been "off" with the barbecue, and we all came down with a horrible case of food poisoning. Nothing like a middle-of-the-night rendezvous in the local emergency room with your project team.

Needless to say, I had not identified my entire team being wiped out with food poisoning as a risk. But I can tell you that I have thought of it during every project since. And yes, I now only schedule celebration dinners *after* projects are signed, sealed, and delivered. You could say I am now influenced by an availability heuristic!

Other human resource risks can arise from project team members being unavailable at the start of the project. This frequently occurs when new projects begin while existing projects that were anticipated to have already ended and released their resources are still wrapping up. It can be challenging to find a time when the stars align perfectly so that all of the necessary resources are available right at the start of a new project.

An often-overlooked source of risk is the human motivation of the team members or their lack thereof. This may include a loss of team cohesion or interest, especially for longer-term or generally boring projects.

I had a project that was progressing nicely with a team that was fairly well rounded and delivering as expected. The particular company I was working with was seen as a "forever company" to a lot of the employees, and they planned to stay there until they retired. This is somewhat rare these days, but this company took care of their employees and gave them no reason to feel otherwise.

That was true until the day that they announced that they would have to reduce the workforce due to the decline in the economy. Employees were shocked and seemed to become somewhat paralyzed. The kind-heartedness of the CEO unfortunately led to a very slow, thorough decision-making process to determine which employees were going to be laid off. It was definitely not like "ripping the Band-Aid off." It was a slow, painful, miserable approach.

While the leadership struggled over the decisions that were ahead of them, morale plunged, productivity all but ceased, and my project pretty much crashed and burned. I had identified an emergent risk that I could lose some of my team members to the lay-offs, but I had not even considered the motivational impact.

To leveraging a Maslow assessment of the situation, my team members who were previously and obliviously bouncing around between self-actualization and self-esteem had now plunged desperately to the bottom of the pyramid. Now they were worried about keeping roofs over their heads and food on their tables.

Contracts

Legal contracts also pose another area of resource risk, not only from the procured resources but also from the contracts themselves.

Because projects are temporary, they are typically good candidates for the use of contract resources. Generally speaking, there is always risk associated with using people and services outside the project team for critical project work.

For projects with particularly unusual needs, finding an appropriate supplier may cause significant delays. For example, during Y2K renovations, programmers were in high demand. This caused a delay in staffing a number of time-sensitive projects.

Delayed starts are also fairly common with outsourced work. Before any external work can begin, contracts must be negotiated, approved, and signed. Finally, work done at a distance takes place out of sight, and problems that might easily be detected within a local team inside the organization may not surface as an issue until it is too late.

Contract Types

There are also risks that arise from the contracts themselves. From a procurement perspective on a project, three types of contracts may be used between the project organization and any vendors: fixed-price, cost-reimbursable, and time and material.

Fixed-price contracts involve a fixed total price for the product. The simplest form of a fixed-price contract is a purchase order. Because the buyer is paying one set price, the profit is typically not known by the buyer. In a fixed-price contract, the risk is on the seller, because if there are any changes in conditions or expenses, the seller has to absorb those costs. When we are buyers, we prefer fixed-price contracts, because they present a lower risk for us. However, if the scope of the work is not clearly defined, a cost-reimbursable contract may be the only option.

Cost-reimbursable contracts involve payment to the seller for seller's actual costs, plus a fee that typically represents seller profit. Because the final costs are not known until the work is completed, cost-reimbursable contracts place more risk on the buyer. However, as mentioned above, entering into a cost-reimbursable contract is sometimes unavoidable.

Time and material contracts (T&M) are hybrid contractual agreements that have both cost-reimbursable and fixed-price arrangements and place moderate risk on the buyer. T&M contracts are typically used for staff augmentation, acquisition of experts, and any outside support. A T&M contract can increase in contract value like cost-reimbursable contracts, and because of this, the organization may add a "not-to-exceed" value to prevent unlimited cost growth and limit the risk exposure.

For example, if you take your car into a dealership to be serviced, you expect to pay for parts and labor. However, there is typically a not-to-exceed cost at which the mechanic will call you before fixing the pricy additional problems that they always seem to find.

Money

Insufficient funding can significantly delay the launch of a project. Lack of funding is a contributing root cause to many other risks as well. For example, employee attrition may occur due to lower pay rates, hiring less expensive team members that do not have the appropriate skill levels can damage a project, and shortcutting recommended testing, analysis, and planning to spare the budget can give rise to risks.

Identifying Resource/Money Risks

To identify resource or money risks, identify all required skills you need for which you lack named, committed staffing and determine all situations in the project plan in which people or other resources are overcommitted. Consider the environment and the motivation of the team members.

Evaluate the project schedule to identify all activities with uncertain estimates. For any contracted or outsourced work, identify and document the contract-related risks.

Determine all expected project costs and gain funding approval early for necessary training, equipment purchases, travel, and other expenses that are typically overlooked.

Critical Success Factors

The critical success factors for effective risk identification include:

Early and Ongoing Identification

Risk identification should begin as early in the project as possible, as this enables project decision-making and allows sufficient time for risk response planning. Set intervals of risk identification activities can be established and documented within the risk management plan, but the risk process should also allow for ad-hoc or emergent risk identification and evaluation.

Unbiased Evaluation

There is always the potential for motivational and cognitive biases. Biases, which were presented in Chapter 3, should be explicitly recognized and exposed whenever possible.

Identify Risks Process

The objective of the Identify Risks process is to identify all knowable risks to project objectives, including both threats and opportunities. Risk identification begins early in the project. Rather than a one-time activity, risk identification is an ongoing process that continues throughout the life of the project, as old risks evolve and new risks become known as the project progresses.

The individuals involved in risk identification may vary depending on their areas of expertise and levels of involvement within the project. However, the more eyes there are on risk, the more thorough risk identification and management will be.

Participants can include the following individuals and groups.

- Project manager
- Project team members
- Risk management team (if applicable)
- Customers
- Subject matter experts from outside the project team
- End users
- Other project managers
- Stakeholders
- Risk management experts

I try to invite as many people as possible to the risk party, especially after seeing how detrimental it can be to overlook a particular area.

Typically, I'm the project or program manager, but on one particular project, I was the project manager over only the training aspect of a project. The overall project manager was a sharp, experienced, and thorough project manager, although she kept a lot of information close to the vest, so to speak. She was not a fan of adding extra stakeholders to the project.

The goal of the initiative was to migrate some back-end operational tasks from our operational representatives in the United States to contract resources in India. My team and I landed in India ready to train 60+ representatives on our processes, procedures, and systems in a four-week initiative. Two-thirds of the way through the training program, we suddenly lost connectivity with the infrastructure back in the United States.

In India, we were essentially shut down for over five days, at which point we recognized that there was no way we would be able to complete the training in the time allocated. As a workaround, the project manager had us stay in India an additional week, a very costly solution. Not only was it damaging to the project budget, but it also caused some damage to the project manager's reputation.

After extensive troubleshooting, they determined that the cause of the connection failure was an upgrade in the US infrastructure and back end. Had a member of the IT maintenance team been asked to provide feedback on risks to our project, this potential problem would have been easily identified early on. This was an incredibly valuable lesson for all parties involved and inspired a change in the company's risk identification process for cross-enterprise projects.

Keep your ears, eyes, and options open when identifying risk. There is always someone who knows something that could impact your project!

According to the *PMBOK® Guide*, the Identify Risks process inputs, tools and techniques, and outputs are as follows.

Identify Risks: Inputs, Tools and Techniques, and Outputs

Inputs	Tools and Techniques	Outputs
1. Risk management plan	1. Documentation reviews	1. Risk register
2. Cost management plan	2. Information gathering techniques	
3. Schedule management plan	3. Checklist analysis	
4. Quality management plan	4. Assumptions analysis	
5. HR management plan	5. Diagramming techniques	
6. Scope baseline	6. SWOT analysis	
7. Activity cost estimates	7. Expert judgment	
8. Activity duration estimates		
9. Stakeholder register		
10. Project documents		
11. Procurement documents		
12. Enterprise environmental factors		
13. Organizational process assets		

Figure 5-2: Identify Risks ITTOs
PMBOK® Guide, page 319

Identify Risks: Inputs

Subsidiary Plans

A number of subsidiary plans may be considered and evaluated when identifying project risk. All subsidiary plans describe how a particular aspect of the project is being managed, along with any identified constraints and thresholds. This information can be critical to identifying the risks that relate to that particular area. For example, the quality management plan may describe certain desired quality metrics that may be challenging, given the project staffing and the team's experience.

Subsidiary plans to be evaluated may include the risk, cost, schedule, quality, and human resource management plans.

Scope Baseline

The scope baseline, a component of the project management plan, is the "frozen" version of the project scope. During the monitoring and controlling processes, the progress against the scope baseline is measured to determine any variances that may need to be addressed.

The scope baseline is an output of the Create WBS process and is made up of the project scope statement, the WBS, and the WBS dictionary.

Project Scope Statement

As mentioned previously, PMI states that there are three mandatory documents for a project, and two of them, the project management plan and the project charter, have already been discussed. The third mandatory document is the project scope statement.

The project scope statement describes in detail the project's deliverables and the work required to create those deliverables. The objective of the project scope statement is to provide a common understanding of the project scope among all project stakeholders.

The detailed project scope statement includes the product scope description, the product acceptance criteria, the project deliverables, exclusions, constraints, and assumptions.

Work Breakdown Structure (WBS)

The WBS is a graphical, hierarchical depiction of the work of the project. Essentially, it is a picture of the work described within the project scope statement. The project deliverables are separated into smaller, more manageable pieces known as work packages.

A WBS is an excellent tool to manage against scope risk as it clearly defines the work that is to be done on the project. Nothing is left out of the WBS, and nothing extra is added. If team members are working on tasks that are not a component of a work package, those tasks can easily be identified as scope creep.

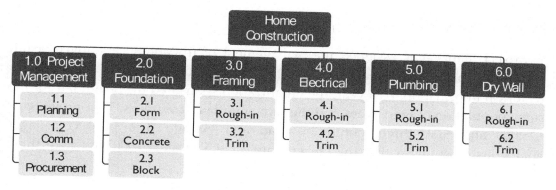

Figure 5-3: Work Breakdown Structure

PMBOK® Guide, page 9

WBS Dictionary

Because the WBS includes limited information, the detailed information for each work package is housed in the WBS dictionary. The WBS dictionary provides information such as resources assigned, dependencies, contract information, and the locations where the work will be conducted.

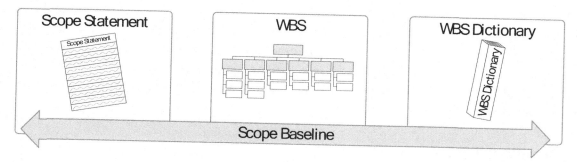

Activity Cost and Duration Estimates

The activity cost and durations estimates are evaluated to determine confidence levels and resulting uncertainties from these estimates. The estimating techniques that are used impact the levels of variability and uncertainty. Estimating techniques include analogous, parametric, three-point (PERT), and bottom-up.

Analogous Estimating

Analogous estimating is a combination of historical information and expert judgment, and it uses a similar past project as the basis of the estimate. Because this is typically done to estimate the overall project duration or cost, it is considered top-down estimating.

While it is quick and easy to do, it is not as accurate as the other techniques. The amount of risk associated with an analogous estimate is much more significant. Analogous estimating is usually used when there is not a lot of detail about the current project. Of the four estimating techniques, the analogous estimate creates the greatest amount of risk or uncertainty.

Example: Analogous Estimate

A project manager is assigned the management of the annual employee health fair. As she has never managed a project of this type or size before, she leverages historical information. Last year, the organization sponsored the health fair for the same population of employees and the same number of vendors. That project cost $25,000 and took three months to plan and execute. The project manager analogously estimates that the current project will cost $25,000 and take three months.

Parametric Estimating

Parametric estimating leverages a statistical relationship between variables to calculate a productivity rate or unit cost. A parametric estimate is based on historical information and is most accurate when the underlying data is representative and scalable.

Example: Parametric Estimate

For the employee health fair this year, all participants will be provided with a custom health and wellness plan. Last year, these packets cost $100 per person, and approximately 30 plans can be developed per hour. The projected attendance of the fair is 300 employees. The project manager estimates it will cost $3,000 for the health and wellness plans and that it will take 10 hours to complete the work of developing the plans.

Three-Point (PERT) Estimating

Three-point estimating, also known as the program evaluation and review technique (PERT) estimate factors in uncertainty by calculating the estimate based on the optimistic, most likely, and pessimistic estimates for cost or duration.

There are two three-point formulas: beta and triangular. The beta three-point is the most commonly used and should be the one used on the exam unless the question is specifically asking about a triangular three-point.

In a beta three-point, the most likely cost or duration is weighted by four. The formula for a beta three-point is:

- (Optimistic + 4(Most Likely) + Pessimistic) / 6

A triangular three-point estimate does not weight the most likely by four and instead simply takes the mean of the three costs. As such, the formula for a triangular three-point estimate is:

- (Optimistic + Most Likely + Pessimistic) / 3

Example: Three-Point (PERT) Estimate

A project manager is evaluating the estimates provided by her team. For the space rental and logistics, she has received the following:

- Optimistic: $1500 and 2 days
- Most likely: $2200 and 5 days
- Pessimistic: $4000 and 9 days

Using a beta three-point, she calculates the following estimates.

- ($1,500 + 4($2,200) + $4,000) / 6 = $2,383
- (2 + 4(5) + 9) / 6 = 5.2 days

Using a triangular three-point, she calculates the following estimates.

- ($1,500 + $2,200 + $4,000) / 3 = $2,567
- (2 + 5 + 9) / 3 = 5.3 days

Bottom-Up Estimating

Bottom-up estimating is the most time-consuming but most accurate estimating technique. In bottom-up estimating, cost estimates are developed for every activity or work package, and those estimates are then added together for an overall project cost estimate. However, bottom-up estimating cannot be used for duration estimating, as it does not account for concurrently running activities.

Of the four estimating techniques, bottom-up estimating has the lowest risk or uncertainty.

Example: Bottom-Up Estimate

The project manager has the following cost estimates.

Room rental: $3,000

Contract resources: $7,000

Brochures: $1,500

Food and beverages: $500

His bottom-up estimate is $12,000.

Exercise: Estimate Activity Durations

You are the project manager for the Chamber of Commerce Annual Banquet and Recognition Event. This is your first time managing a project of this size, and you need to estimate how long the project will take. You must estimate three components of this year's project duration: the event logistics, the venue selection, and the room set-up.

Event Logistics: Last year's event was held on site at the Chamber, and it took approximately three months to complete the project. This included the time it took to develop the guest list and the time it took to choose and order the food. Venue selection and room set-up were not previously included in the project.

Venue Selection: In a review of other past projects that utilized an off-site venue, you see that the time to locate, select, and book a venue has ranged from three weeks in the best case to nine weeks in the worst case. You expect that it will take your team approximately five weeks to identify, select, and book the location.

Room Set-Up: A recent project you completed also involved setting up a room for a banquet. That event hosted 100 guests, and it took approximately four hours to set up the room and prepare the food. You are expecting 300 guests.

1. **What is the best estimate for the venue selection?**
   A. 23 days
   B. 15 days
   C. 6 weeks
   D. 5.3 weeks

2. **What technique is best used to estimate the venue selection?**
   A. Parametric
   B. Analogous
   C. Reserve analysis
   D. Three-point

3. **What is the best estimate for the event logistics?**
   A. 3 months
   B. 6 months
   C. 10 weeks
   D. 12 weeks

4. **What technique is best used to estimate the event logistics?**
   A. Parametric
   B. Analogous
   C. Reserve analysis
   D. Three-point

5. **What is the best estimate for the room set-up?**
   A. 2 days
   B. 12 hours
   C. 1 week
   D. 4 hours

6. **What technique is best used to estimate the room set-up?**
   A. Parametric
   B. Analogous
   C. Reserve analysis
   D. Three-point

Stakeholder Register

The stakeholder register, an output of the Identify Stakeholders process, documents the project stakeholders, their roles in the project, their contact and department information, and other pertinent information related to their risk tolerances, attitudes, and areas of interest. The stakeholder register was described in Chapter 3.

Project Documents

An evaluation of the project documents can identify any gaps, omissions, trends, variances, or other information that may lead to uncertainty. This can include initiating documents such as the business case or ongoing project documentation such as the work performance reports.

Procurement Documents

As mentioned previously, a contributing source of resource and money risks is the area of contracts and procurement activities. A review of any procurement documents, such as contracts, statements of work, and request for proposals (RFPs), can uncover uncertainty or risks. For example, if work with a vendor requires the use of a cost-reimbursable (cost-plus) contract, there will be increased risk for the project organization, as the final costs are not defined.

Enterprise Environmental Factors and Organizational Process Assets

Environmental factors could include an increase in budget restrictions, which would increase the project cost risk. Organizational process assets could include past project files, which can be leveraged to discover for risks identified on similar projects.

Enterprise environmental factors and organizational process assets were discussed in Chapter 4.

Identify Risks: Tools and Techniques

There are a large number of tools and techniques that can be used to identify project risks. In any environment, it is important that a number of different tools and techniques are leveraged in order to facilitate comprehensive risk identification.

The *PMBOK® Guide* includes the following tools and techniques.

- Documentation reviews
- Information-gathering techniques including interviews, brainstorming, Delphi technique, interviews, nominal group technique, post-project reviews, lessons learned, historical information, prompt lists, and questionnaires
- Checklist analysis
- Assumptions and constraints analysis
- Diagramming techniques including FMEA/fault tree analysis, force field analysis, influence diagrams, root cause analysis, and system dynamics
- SWOT analysis

In addition to the *PMBOK® Guide* tools and techniques, the *Practice Standard for Project Risk Management* includes the following:

- Industry knowledge base
- Risk breakdown structure (RBS) review
- Work breakdown structure (WBS) review

These risk identification techniques consider the past (retrospective analysis), the present (current situation analysis), and the future (future analysis). For the benefit of reviewing the various techniques, they are bucketed into past, present, and future. However, it is important to note that the techniques can be applied at different points and are not necessarily limited to the particular bucket under which they are listed below.

Retrospective Analysis	Current Situation Analysis	Future Analysis
1. Industry knowledge base	1. Assumptions and constraints analysis	1. Brainstorming
2. Interviews	2. Checklist analysis	2. Delphi technique
3. Post project reviews and lessons learned	3. Documentation reviews	3. Force field analysis
	4. FMEA/fault tree analysis	4. Nominal group technique
	5. Influence diagrams	5. Questionnaires
	6. Prompt lists	
	7. RBS review	
	8. Root cause analysis	
	9. SWOT analysis	
	10. System dynamics	
	11. WBS review	

Retrospective Analysis

Industry Knowledge Base

Many industries have an established industry knowledge base, such as construction, engineering, and oil or other natural resources. These industry knowledge bases are a rich source of project risk data based on historical project details and experiences.

Leveraging an industry knowledge base provides insight into the risk exposure for the current project while also serving as a benchmark against external organizations. While a knowledge base can provide general industry risk information, it does not contain current project-specific risks.

Interviews

Interviews can be formal or informal, individual or group exercises used to solicit risk information. Expert interviews both inside and outside of your organization can be rich sources of information on risks that a project may encounter. Utilizing the experience and perspectives of others is a potent technique for identifying and managing risks.

When held with stakeholders, the interviews can improve their engagement in the project while also allowing the project manager to address specific risks in more detail. Because the interviewee can bring non-risk-related information into the interview, it is important that the interviewer has prepared an agenda ahead of time, keeps the interview on point, and manages the time of the interview appropriately. The interviewee must feel as though he or she can trust the interviewer with their information and their position on a particular risk or risks, so a level of emotional maturity and trust is also necessary.

Given that interviews can be time-consuming, it is not an optimal technique to use when working with a large number of stakeholders or experts.

Post-Project Reviews and Lessons Learned

The same risks tend to recur in project after project unless the root cause is identified and remedied. Data from earlier work (in the form of project retrospectives, lessons learned, post-mortems, post-project analyses, or close-out reports) can provide extensive risk information.

Everyone is familiar with the idiomatic definition of insanity, which is repeating the same action and expecting a different outcome. Leveraging the past and lessons already learned allows us the ability to break that cycle of insanity in project risk management.

This risk information is not limited to previously identified threats but also previously effective responses, successes in capturing opportunities, and areas of exposure that are organization-specific.

Considering the past will assist in preventing past mistakes while also potentially capturing opportunities similar to those that have arisen in the past. This also contributes to organizational learning that can be applied to future projects.

As is true for many of the techniques addressed here, leveraging the past is not a standalone technique for risk identification. Not all risks have been fully identified, addressed, or documented during past projects. In addition, some organizations struggle to provide an easily accessible source of historic information. That historic information, if available, is considered a component of the organizational process assets.

Current Situation Analysis

Assumptions and Constraints Analysis

Every project and every identified project risk is conceived and developed based on a set of hypotheses, scenarios, or assumptions. Assumptions are ideas that we believe to be true, real, and factual.

An assumptions analysis explores the validity of assumptions as they apply to the project. It identifies risks to the project from any inaccuracies, instabilities, inconsistencies, or incompleteness of assumptions that are made about a project.

The process for conducting an analysis of the project constraints and assumptions is as follows.

1. Document assumptions and constraints
2. Test assumptions and constraints
3. Generate risk

I recently completed a project that was heavily dependent on email, due to the fact that the team was completely virtual. When I developed my duration estimate, it was based on the assumption that the project team would have 24/7 access to email. Did I know without a doubt that they would have uninterrupted access? I did not, but it was the assumption I used when I generated the estimates.

I tested the assumption and the impact of its potential inaccuracy on the project. If the assumption was false and email access was interrupted, how big of an impact would it have? For this particular project, email interruption would have been a significant impact. What was the likelihood of that assumption being false? We had a stable infrastructure with no interruptions in recent history, so I considered it a low likelihood.

Because of its impact, I identified it as a yellow or moderate risk on my risk register, and because it was a moderate risk, we defined a contingent response strategy to implement in the event that email went down. We were certainly glad that we had done so when, right at the most critical juncture of our project, email was down for almost 24 hours. The contingency plan was easily invoked, and we had minimal disruption.

A relatively easy technique requiring no special tools the assumptions and constraints analysis provides exposure to project-specific risks. Assumptions and constraints must be clarified and documented in order to be evaluated, and evaluating assumptions and constraints is good practice for project managers on all projects. Not only does it protect you as the project manager, but it also creates a good record of your decision-making process that can be extremely beneficial for future projects.

Checklist Analysis

Risk identification checklists can be developed based on historical information and knowledge that has been accumulated from previous similar projects and from other sources of information.

The word "checklist" may seem a bit misleading in the context described here. A good way to think of it is as a master list of risks. In other words, if your organization consolidated all of the risk registers from recent projects and removed any redundancies, the result would be this type of risk checklist.

While creating a checklist can be quick and simple, it is impossible to build a complete and exhaustive one. The team should make sure to explore items that do not appear on the checklist. In addition, the checklist should be reviewed during project closure to incorporate new lessons learned and improve it for use on future projects. This can include leveraging some type of unique numbering scheme that is applied to the categories, subcategories, and risks.

Creating a risk identification checklist is considered a professional responsibility of the project manager. Typically, the risk checklist is owned by the project or program management office and aligns with the standard risk breakdown structure.

While it is a powerful starting point for project risk identification, a risk checklist does not include opportunities, as they are project-specific.

Documentation Reviews

A structured review of project documentation, including plans, assumptions, previous project files, contracts, and other information, may be performed to identify any areas or indications of risk or uncertainty. The quality of the plans, as well as the consistency between those plans and the project requirements and assumptions, can be indicators of risk in the project.

Project documentation review can include a review of:

- The assumptions log
- Work performance reports
- Earned value reports
- Network diagrams
- Baselines

Documentation outside of the project that may also be helpful includes:

- Lessons learned
- Published information
- Commercial databases
- Academic studies
- Published checklists
- Benchmarking
- Industry studies

FMEA and Fault Tree Analysis

A failure mode and effect analysis (FMEA) is used for the analysis of potential failures modes within a system. Failure modes are any errors or defects in a process, design, or item.

FMEA is considered a bottom-up technique that examines the failure modes of the components within a system and traces forward the potential effects of that failure mode on system performance.

FMEA is appropriate for analyzing systems that contain little or no redundancy and may also be used if a system contains new technology and the potential effects of failure of the components of the system need to be explored.

FMEA determines:

- Severity (S) – The effect of the failure
- Occurrence (O) – The likelihood the failure will occur
- Criticality (C) – Severity multiplied by occurrence (S x O)
- Detection (D) – The effectiveness of controls to prevent the failure
- Risk priority number (RPN) – S x O x D

Function	Potential Failure Mode	S	O	C	D	RPN
Dispense cash requested by customer	Does not dispense cash	8	5	40	10	400
	Dispenses too much cash	6	3	18	7	126
	Takes too long to dispense cash	3	7	21	8	168

A fault tree is used to analyze a single fault event by identifying the combinations of conditions and component failures that would lead to that fault. Unlike FMEA, a fault tree is a top-down, identifying and analyzing conditions that lead to the occurrence of a defined effect.

The steps involved in a fault tree analysis include:

1. Defining the undesirable event or failure
2. Obtaining a thorough understanding of the relationships
3. Constructing the fault tree
4. Evaluating the fault tree and identifying corrective measures to be taken
5. Implementing these measures in order to protect against the hazards

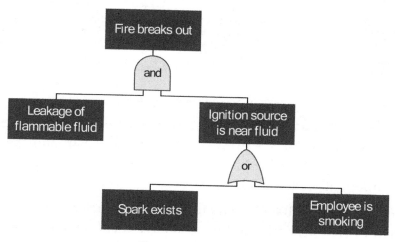

Figure 5-4: Fault Tree

FMEA is more appropriate than a fault tree analysis when a large number of distinct system conditions exist with a range of unacceptable consequences, and a fault tree analysis is more appropriate when there is concern about one or just a few system conditions that pose unacceptable consequences. A fault tree analysis is appropriate for showing how sensitive a system will be to one or more initiating faults.

Fault trees enable the fault/failure logic within a system of a particular effect of interest to be represented in diagrammatic form, whereas FMEA records the system effects of each failure cause in a tabular format.

Influence Diagrams

An influence diagram provides a graphical representation of situations, showing causal influences, the time ordering of events, and other relationships among variables and outcomes.

There are typically four nodes depicted as various shapes in an influence diagram:

- Uncertainty node – An oval
- Decision node – A rectangle
- Value or objective node – An octagon or a diamond
- Function node – A rounded rectangle
- Relevance – Solid arrows
- Information – Dashed arrows

Figure 5-5: Influence Diagram

As seen in Figure 5-4, the decision needs to be made whether to evacuate or stay when there is a potential for a hurricane. The hurricane path and the forecast are both considered uncertainties, with the hurricane path being relevant and the forecast being information to consider.

The decision to evacuate will have two outcomes: the hurricane will hit and we will be safe or the hurricane will miss and we will have spent money unnecessarily. The decision to stay also has two outcomes: the hurricane will hit, and while we did not spend money on evacuating, we are in danger, or the hurricane will miss, and we will be safe and will not have spent any money.

Influence diagrams are used to expose key risk drivers and can generate counter-intuitive insights not available through other techniques. However, it may not always be easy to determine the appropriate structure.

Influence diagrams are also known as relevance diagrams, decision diagrams, and decision networks.

Prompt Lists

A prompt list is a list of common risk categories that can be used as a framework for additional risk identification techniques. Prompt lists stimulate creative thinking and are an excellent tool to use in conjunction with brainstorming. Often, the prompt list serves as the highest level of the risk breakdown structure (RBS).

Common prompt lists include:

PESTLE	TECOP	SPECTRUM
Political Economic Social Technological Legal Environmental	Technical Environmental Commercial Operational Political	Socio-cultural Political Economic Competitive Technology Regulatory/Legal Uncertainty Market

RBS Review

A risk breakdown structure (RBS) is a graphical, hierarchical depiction of risk categories and subcategories for the project. Risk data is organized and structured to provide a standard presentation of project risk categories that facilitates understanding, communication, and management.

As a best practice, a PMO may develop a standard RBS for similar types of projects. This RBS template, a component of the organizational process assets, can then be modified for specific individual projects.

I personally recommend applying some type of standard numbering as well in order to categorize and group risks. That numbering scheme should carry through to the risk register and risk checklist. For example, if the operational category was 4.0, the human resource category would be 4.1, and then HR risks would be 4.1.1, 4.1.2, etc.

The RBS can be used to structure and guide the risk management process.

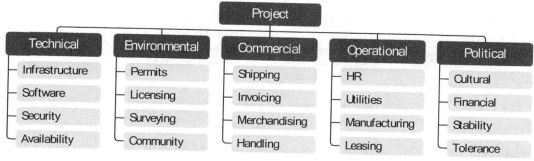

Figure 5-6: Risk Breakdown Structure

PMBOK® Guide, page 317

As mentioned previously, the upper levels of the RBS can be used as a prompt list to ensure complete coverage during the risk identification phase. This is accomplished by using the RBS to structure whichever risk identification method is used.

The major areas can also be used to structure risk identification interviews, providing an agenda for discussion between the facilitator and interviewees. Risks documented on the risk register can be mapped to the lowest levels of the RBS in order to reveal any possible gaps or redundancies in risk identification.

Categorizing risks according to the RBS provides a number of additional insights into the assessment of risk exposure on the project, which would not be available from a simple list of risks even if the list were prioritized. These include:

- Understanding the type of risk exposure on the project
- Exposing the most significant sources of risk to the project
- Revealing root causes of risk
- Indicating areas of dependency or correlation between risks
- Focusing risk response development on high-risk areas
- Allowing generic responses to be developed for root causes or dependent groups of risks

Root Cause Analysis

A root-cause analysis or "cause-and-effect" exercises may be used for risk identification. Effective risk management relies on identifying the root causes of the risks in order to apply more efficient responses. Rather than treating the headache with Tylenol, look for the cause of the headache, such as a sinus infection requiring antibiotics.

There are a number of effective techniques for discovering the sources of problems, including fishbone diagrams (also known as Ishikawa or cause-and-effect diagrams).

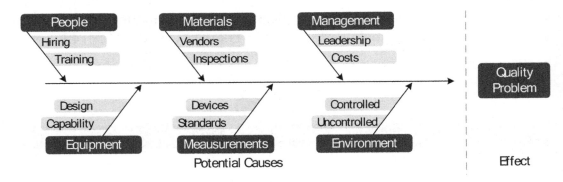

Figure 5-7: Fishbone Diagram
PMBOK® Guide, page 239

A fishbone diagram begins with identifying an undesirable outcome, problem, or quality issue. When it is identified, the project team is then challenged to work backwards to identify all potential causes of the problem.

In addition to uncovering specific risks that might not otherwise be detected, this exercise will often result in a more accurate perception of how probable certain problems are.

One technique used in association with a fishbone diagram is known as the Five Whys. The Five Whys is an iterative, interrogative technique used to explore the cause-and-effect relationships underlying a particular problem. The primary goal of the technique is to determine the root cause of a defect or problem by repeating the question "Why?"

Each question forms the basis of the next question. The number five in the name derives from an anecdotal observation on the number of iterations needed to resolve a problem. The technique was formally developed by Sakichi Toyoda and was used by the Toyota Motor Corporation during the evolution of its manufacturing methodologies.

Not all problems have a single root cause. If there is a need to uncover multiple root causes, the method must be repeated as many times as necessary, with a different sequence of questions each time.

The method provides no hard and fast rules about what lines of questions to explore or how long to continue the search for additional root causes. Thus, even when the method is closely followed, the outcome still depends upon the knowledge and persistence of the people involved.

The following is an example of the Five Whys used to interrogate a problem of team members leaving a company.

1. Why? – They are not happy with their job.
2. Why? – They do not feel challenged.
3. Why? – Their manager is not providing challenging assignments.
4. Why? – The manager is not aware of the level of challenge that would be appropriate for their direct reports.
5. Why? – The manager is not doing quarterly performance reviews with the appropriate assessments of skill level. (ROOT CAUSE)

SWOT Analysis

Evaluating the strengths, weaknesses, opportunities and threats for an organization or project is known as a SWOT analysis. For many projects, particularly those involving delivering solutions, these aspects are examined early in the project, often before the project is chartered.

A SWOT analysis is a good framework to establish during a risk identification brainstorming session. The team would first identify and list the organizational strengths and weaknesses. From there, they can derive opportunities from the strengths, and threats from weaknesses, using risk meta-language.

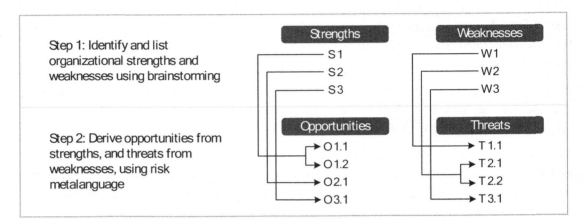

Figure 5-8: SWOT Analysis

Practice Standard for Project Risk Management, page 85

While a SWOT analysis provides a structured approach to evaluate both threats and opportunities, it does not account for external risks. Those risks that are identified are typically high-level and somewhat generic. These risks can then be further evaluated through other techniques.

System Dynamics

System dynamics are a particular application of influence diagrams used to identify risks within a project situation by using feedback and feed-forward loops. System dynamics are utilized when there is a complex, non-linear relationship between entities and information, and they show the impact of risk events on overall project results and a system's sensitivity to specific risks.

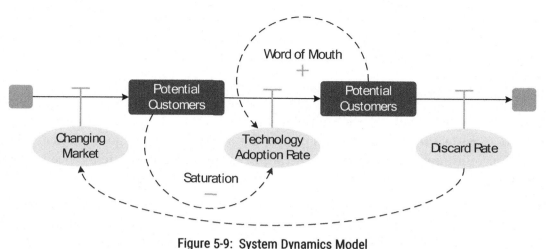

Figure 5-9: System Dynamics Model

Practice Standard for Project Risk Management, page 85

WBS Review

The work breakdown structure (WBS) is a graphical, hierarchical depiction of all of the work of the project. The WBS is an output of the Create WBS process and follows the 100% rule: the lower levels roll up to the higher levels, nothing is left out, and no extra work is included. The lowest level of the WBS is a work package, a group of related activities that are estimated, managed, and controlled by the work package owner.

The WBS can be analyzed and used to structure a number of other risk identification techniques, which help ensures that all elements of the project scope are considered.

Future Analysis

Brainstorming

One powerful risk discovery process is the group creativity technique of brainstorming, as discussed in Chapter 3. Brainstorming sessions are conducted with the project team and can begin with a review of the risk list that was already constructed. The team should work together to brainstorm additional potential project problems and project opportunities.

The brainstorming process occurs as follows.

- The project manager and project team will examine the methods and processes that are being used on the project and consider any aspects that are new or that may be particularly difficult.
- The team should also focus on outside factors that might have an impact on the project, such as natural disasters, weather, government or legal changes, and the actions of competitors.
- The facilitator of the brainstorming session should stimulate the participants to think of new risks and build off one another's ideas.
- The brainstorming session should continue until all of the participants have contributed.

The process can be concluded by restating any risks that are unclear and combining or eliminating risks where there is redundancy. When the brainstorming process is complete, the new risks can be added to the project risk list.

Delphi Technique

Also discussed in Chapter 3, the Delphi technique is a way to reach consensus from a panel of experts. Project risk experts participate in this technique anonymously via a survey or questionnaire mechanism. A Delphi group is a group intelligence process used to tap into anecdotal historical data would otherwise remain hidden.

The facilitator solicits ideas about the important project risks. These responses are summarized and are then recirculated to the experts for further comment and possible revision or reassessment of their previously submitted positions.

Consensus may be reached in a few rounds of this process. The Delphi technique helps reduce biases in the data and keeps any one person from having undue influence on the outcome, such as in environments in which "group think" may be prevalent.

Delphi groups are typically a minimum of four to five experts. This number establishes estimate ranges and stimulates discussion. Delphi groups are collaborative, which leads to group buy-in, ownership, and motivation.

A newer version of the Delphi technique is wideband Delphi, which removes the completely anonymous component from the process. Instead, experts meet and discuss their information, which increases interaction and communication. Their ideas and information are still captured anonymously, but they are then discussed as a group, potentially in multiple rounds, until agreement is reached.

Force Field Analysis

Although typically used in change management, a force field analysis can be used in risk management to identify the driving forces and restraining forces which affect the achievement of the project objectives.

The team starts by identifying the individual project objectives and then brainstorming the forces working to achieve that objective and the forces working against the achievement of that objective.

A scoring model can be used to evaluate the difference in driving versus restraining forces, such as a one (weak) to five (strong) scale.

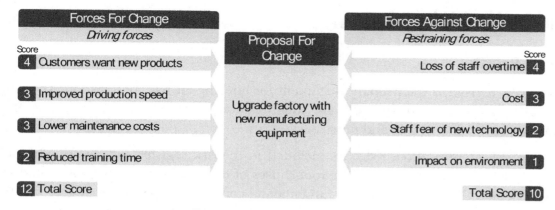

Figure 5-10: Force Field Analysis

Practice Standard for Project Risk Management, page 80

Futures Thinking, Visualization, and Scenario Planning

Futures thinking is another creativity technique that can be used to help a team identify and plan for positive and negative risks that can impact the future. One method is to have the team collaborate to envision a desired end-state. With that vision in mind, the group can then attempt to identify impediments to that future state and work to assess those impediments.

Unlike futures thinking based on a vision, which is a desirable view of the future, scenario planning involves a range of possible views of the future. Scenario planning for risk identification involves evaluating the environment to assess various scenarios that could occur and determine the uncertainties involved.

Nominal Group Technique

As discussed in Chapter 3, nominal group technique is a technique that enhances brainstorming by taking into account all of the participants' opinions through a tallying process.

Each group member gives his or her opinion, and duplicate opinions are removed. The remaining list is ranked by the members. This technique ensures contribution from all participants and can serve as the foundation for other analysis techniques.

Questionnaires

Risk questionniares can be used as a method similar to risk checklists, but where possible risks are phrased as questions rather than as risk statements. For example, on a risk checklist, a risk statement may be "Team members may not be available at the start of the project," but on the risk questionnaire, the same item would be presented as the question "Are the team members available at the start of the project?"

Risk questionnaires are another organizational process asset that may be developed and/or housed by the PMO.

Identify Risks: Output

Risk Register

The risk register is the primary document for housing all risk information. The risk register is developed during risk identification and updated throughout the subsequent risk activities and processes.

Upon risk identification, risks are included in the risk register and described in as much detail as is reasonable. The root causes of these risks are also documented in the register. Root causes are the fundamental conditions or events that give rise to one or more identified risks. They are recorded to be used to support future risk identification for this and other projects.

Upon risk identification, the risk register should contain for each risk:

1. A unique risk identification number – If there is a standard numbering scheme applied to the RBS, the resulting risks under those categories would reflect that numbering.

2. The risk name – The name should be as specific as possible.

3. A description of the risk, including whether it is an opportunity or a threat – The description should be clearly articulated. I call it "passing The MeMe test." My mother is The MeMe. She has been out of the business world for awhile. If she were to read the risk description, would she be able to understand what the risk is about? Be cautious about using acronyms, slang, and technical jargon. If someone were to evaluate your risk register in the future, would they understand the description?

4. Identified risk triggers or precursor events

5. Root causes of the risks

Review Questions

Chapter 5

1. The scope baseline includes all of the following except:

   A. WBS dictionary
   B. Project charter
   C. Scope statement
   D. WBS

2. The PERT estimate is nine hours. The best-case estimate is four hours, and the worst-case estimate is 18 hours. What is the most likely duration estimate?

   A. 11 hours
   B. 9 hours
   C. 8 hours
   D. 5 hours

3. Your team lead has suggested that you evaluate various estimating techniques in order to provide the most comprehensive estimate possible. You decide to use parametric estimating. Parametric cost estimating involves:

   A. Defining the parameters of the project life cycle
   B. Calculating individual cost estimates for each work package
   C. Using a statistical relationship between historical data and other variables to calculate a cost estimate
   D. Using the actual cost of a similar project to estimate total project costs

4. The previous project manager of your newly assigned project leveraged analogous estimating to determine the project costs. The following statement is true about analogous estimating.

   A. It uses bottom-up estimating techniques.
   B. It uses the actual costs of previous, similar projects as the basis for estimating the cost of the current project.
   C. It is used most frequently in the later stages of a project.
   D. It summarizes estimates for individual work items.

5. For a particular component, the work package owner leveraged a triangular three-point estimate to come to a calculation of $111,667. If the optimistic estimate was $98,000 and the most likely estimate was $112,000, what was the pessimistic estimate?

   A. $125,000
   B. $175,000
   C. $223,998
   D. $112,389

6. Which of the following is a true statement about risks?

   A. If a risk is identified in a risk response plan, it means that risk has already happened.
   B. Once a risk has happened, you refer to the risk management plan to determine what action needs to be taken.
   C. A risk that was not planned but has happened is called a trigger.
   D. Risk identification happens in all phases of the project.

7. **Which statement is most accurate regarding risk identification?**
    A. Risk identification is normally the sole responsibility of the project manager.
    B. Risk identification is normally the responsibility of the project sponsor and key stakeholders.
    C. Risk identification only occurs prior to the project being selected.
    D. Risk identification should be done by the entire project team.

8. **Why is it important that scope risks be identified early in the project?**
    A. Scope risks dictate the most likely project costs.
    B. The amount of scope risk determines which project manager would be most appropriate for the project.
    C. Identification of scope risks reveals whether or not the project is feasible.
    D. Scope risks are a component of the cost-benefit analysis.

9. **Scope gap is different than scope creep in that:**
    A. Scope creep refers to legitimate scope requirements that are discovered late, and scope gap refers to non-mandatory scope changes.
    B. Scope gap refers to legitimate scope requirements that are discovered late, and scope creep refers to non-mandatory scope changes.
    C. Scope gap and scope creep are fundamentally the same.
    D. Scope creep is identified by the project manager, and scope gap is identified by the project sponsor.

10. **This is a hierarchical structure of potential risk sources.**
    A. Fishbone diagram
    B. Cause-and-effect diagram
    C. Risk statement
    D. Risk breakdown structure

11. **Which of the following is not a function of an RBS?**
    A. Reveals root causes of risk
    B. Indicates probability of project failure
    C. Exposes the most significant sources of risk to the project
    D. Focuses risk response development on high-risk areas

12. **Which statement is the most accurate regarding the difference in overall project risk compared to individual risk?**
    A. Overall risk is the amount of uncertainty that exists as it relates to achieving project objectives; individual risks are the specific events or conditions that could affect project objectives.
    B. Overall risk is the sum total of all of the risk scores from the project; individual risks are added together to calculate the overall risk.
    C. Individual risks affect only one constraint, and overall risks affect all three constraints.
    D. Overall risks are defined by the stakeholders and upper management, while individual risks are defined and managed by the project team.

13. **You are conducting an FMEA, and your team has provided the following ratings: severity = 5, occurrence = 9, and detection = 4. What is the criticality of this risk?**
    A. High
    B. 45
    C. Moderate
    D. 180

14. As project manager, you are brainstorming with your team to determine implementation risks. The team is struggling to identify any risks, however, because they have not developed this type of product before. What technique may be the most helpful in this kind of situation?
    A. Futures thinking
    B. Nominal group technique
    C. Root cause analysis
    D. Affinity diagramming

15. It is often helpful to consider the Five Whys when doing this type of analysis.
    A. SWOT analysis
    B. System dynamics analysis
    C. Root cause analysis
    D. Futures thinking analysis

Vocabulary Review   Chapter 5

Analogous estimating	Individual risk	Root cause analysis
Assumptions/constraints analysis	Industry knowledge base	Scope baseline
Bottom-up estimating	Influence diagrams	Scope creep
Checklist analysis	Overall risk	Scope gap
Documentation reviews	Parametric estimating	Subsidiary plan
Fault tree analysis	Prompt lists	SWOT analysis
FMEA	RBS review	System dynamics
Force field analysis	Risk questionnaire	Three-point estimating
Futures thinking	Risk register	WBS review

1. _____   An unmanaged change to the project

2. _____   The summing-up of all project costs at the activity or work package level

3. _____   The document that details all indentified risks

4. _____   A graphical representation of situations showing causal influences, time ordering of events, and other relationships among variables and outcomes

5. _____   A framework for identifying risks by evaluating strengths, weaknesses, opportunities, and threats

6. _____   An evaluation of previously identified and documented project risks

7. _____   The analysis of potential errors or defects within a system

8. _____   A list of common risk categories that can be used as a framework for additional risk identification techniques

9. _____   A specific uncertain event or condition which, if it occurs, has a positive or negative effect on at least one project objective

10. _____   A component of the project management plan that includes the project scope statement, the WBS, and the WBS dictionary

11. _____   Using a past similar project as the basis to determine the cost or duration estimate for the current project (also known as top-down estimating)

12. _____   A collection of best practices, lessons learned, and historical information for projects within a particular industry

13. _____   The effect of uncertainty on the project as a whole

14. _____   An evaluation of the defined work of the project

15. _____ A particular application of influence diagrams used to identify risks within a project situation with feedback and feed-forward loops

16. _____ Using a statistical relationship between variables to calculate a unit cost or productivity rate

17. _____ Analysis of a single fault event done by identifying the combinations of conditions and component failures that would lead to that fault

18. _____ An evaluation of the defined risk categories and subcategories done to ensure that all areas of risk are identified

19. _____ A structured review of project documentation, such as project plans, work performance reports, business cases, RFPs, etc.

20. _____ Evaluation of the initiating cause or causes that give rise to a causal chain that may result in risks

21. _____ Used to identify the driving and restraining forces that may affect the achievement of the project objectives

22. _____ A risk identification tool in which possible risks are phrased as questions rather than as risk statements

23. _____ A legitimate requirement identified later in the project

24. _____ An evaluation of those things that are believed to be true or the limitations placed upon the project

25. _____ A component of the project management plan that provides additional details around a specific area of the project

26. _____ A creativity technique that can be used with the team whereby they envision a desired end-state that could occur or exist in the future and identify the uncertainties involved in achieving that end-state

27. _____ Uses optimistic, most likely, and pessimistic duration or cost predictions to develop an estimate

Answer Key   Chapter 5

Chapter Exercise Answers

Exercise: Critical Path Calculation

1. **Answer: C**

   Calculate float for all concurrent activities:

   Activity B (7 days) - Activity A (3 days) = 4 days float for Activity A

   Activity G (9 days) - Activity E (7 days) = 2 days float for Activity E

   Activity G (9 days) - Activity F (6 days) = 3 days float for Activity F

   Activity A has the greatest amount of float

2. **Answer: D**

   The longest path through the network diagram is:

   B (7 days), C (4 days), D (2 days), G (9 days)

3. **Answer: A**

   Activity B is on the critical path therefore it has no float

4. **Answer: A**

   Activity B (7 days) - Activity A (3 days) = 4 days float for Activity A

5. **Answer: B**

   Activity G (9 days) - Activity F (6 days) = 3 days float for Activity F

6. **Answer: C**

   Activity B (7 days) - Activity A (3 days) = 4 days float for Activity A

   A 9 day delay - 4 days of float for Activity A = the project is delayed 5 days

Exercise: Estimate Activity Durations

1. **Answer: D**

   Using a three-point estimate (3 x (4 x 5) x 9) ÷ 6 = 5.3 weeks

2. **Answer: D**

   Three-point

3. **Answer: A**

   3 months

4. **Answer: B**

   Analogous

5. **Answer: B**

   12 hours

6. **Answer: A**

   Parametric

Review Question Answers

1. **Answer: B**

   The scope baseline includes the project scope statement, the work breakdown structure (WBS), and the WBS dictionary.

2. **Answer: C**

   The question provides the PERT estimate and is asking for the most likely estimate. The PERT formula is: PERT Estimate = (optimistic + 4(most likely) + pessimistic) / 6.

   $9 = (4 + 4(ML) + 18)/6$

   $54 = 22 + 4(ML)$

   $32 = 4ML$

   $8 = \text{most likely}$

3. **Answer: C**

   A parametric estimate uses a statistical relationship between variables to calculate an estimate for a unit cost or productivity rate.

4. **Answer: B**

   Analogous estimating uses a similar past project as a basis for developing an estimate.

5. **Answer: A**

   A triangular three-point estimate is calculated as (optimistic + most likely + pessimistic) / 3.

   $\$111,667 = (\$98,000 + \$112,000 + \text{Pessimistic}) / 3$

   $\$335,000 = \$210,000 + \text{Pessimistic}$

   $\$125,000 = \text{Pessimistic}$

6. **Answer: D**

   Risk identification happens throughout the project from conception to completion. Risks are not identified in the response plan. They are in the risk register. The risk management plan does not document the risk responses, as it provides details on how project risk management will be handled for the overall project, not for individual risks. A trigger is a precursor event that indicates that a risk has occurred or is about to occur.

7. **Answer: D**

   The entire team should be involved in project risk identification, as it is not possible for the project manager alone to identify all knowable risks.

8. **Answer: C**

   Scope risk should be identified first, because if it is not possible to deliver the scope of the project, neither the cost nor the schedule matter.

9. **Answer: B**

   Scope gap refers to legitimate scope requirements that are discovered late and must be addressed. Scope creep refers to unmanaged and/or non-mandatory scope changes.

10. **Answer: D**

    The risk breakdown structure (RBS) is a hierarchical, graphical depiction of the risk categories.

11. Answer: B

The RBS cannot predict the probability of project failure, as project success or failure is not dependent on the number of risks or the number of risk categories.

12. Answer: A

Overall risk is the amount of uncertainty that exists as it relates to achieving the project objectives; individual risks are the specific events or conditions that could affect the project objectives.

13. Answer: B

In an FMEA evaluation, criticality is determined by multiplying severity by occurrence.

Severity = 5; occurrence = 9; 5 x 9 = 45.

The risk priority number (RPN) would use all three values: severity x occurrence x detection.

14. Answer: A

Futures thinking allows participants to visualize the future, what the environment will look like with the new product or new scenario, and how it will function.

15. Answer: C

The five whys technique asks the question "Why?" five times in order to drill down to a root cause.

Vocabulary Review Answers

1. Scope creep
2. Bottom-up estimating
3. Risk register
4. Influence diagram
5. SWOT analysis
6. Checklist analysis
7. FMEA
8. Prompt lists
9. Individual risk
10. Scope baseline
11. Analogous estimating
12. Industry knowledge base
13. Overall risk
14. WBS review
15. System dynamics
16. Parametric estimating
17. Fault tree analysis
18. RBS review
19. Documentation review
20. Root cause analysis
21. Force field analysis
22. Risk questionnaire
23. Scope gap
24. Assumptions/constraints analysis
25. Subsidiary plan
26. Futures thinking
27. Three-point estimating

Qualitative Risk Analysis

6

Qualitative Risk Analysis

As risks are identified, they are evaluated in the Perform Qualitative Risk Analysis process. The objective is to prioritize those project risks for potential action based on an evaluation of certain risk characteristics.

Using the risk register developed and updated during risk identification, this process will assess the probability (likelihood) that the risk will occur and the impact (effect) if it does occur.

Once evaluated based on probability and impact, the risks can be prioritized for appropriate action and response. Qualitative risk analysis provides a quick and cost-effective means of establishing priorities and serves as the foundation for potential quantitative risk analysis.

Because a qualitative analysis is a subjective evaluation of the project risks, the assessment will reflect the attitudes, tolerances, and biases of the assessors.

The qualitative analysis of the project risk should be revisited throughout the project to note changes in the project and environment. Trending risk data is a component of controlling risk.

Critical Success Factors

The following factors are necessary for success in qualitative risks analysis.

Agreed-Upon Approach

The organization must have an agreed-upon assessment approach that is applied to all project risks. The assessments generally include an evaluation of risk probability and impact, but they may also include an assessment of urgency (how quickly does the team need to take action on the risk?) and manageability (can the risk even be managed?).

The assessment and evaluation of the risks may result in the decision to establish contingency reserve and move forward with the project despite the level of risk, the decision to stop or re-scope the project, or the decision to inform the customer or sponsor of the risks and escalate to the appropriate parties for a go/no-go decision.

Definitions

Published and agreed-upon definitions of risk probability and impact aid in the accurate assessment of each project risk.

High-Quality Information

High-quality information, which may come from historical information and/or be gathered by workshops and interviews, is a necessary input to ensure accurate assessment of the project risks.

Ongoing analysis

Qualitative risk analysis is an ongoing and iterative process. It must be conducted periodically throughout the project and must not be viewed as a one-time activity.

Perform Qualitative Risk Analysis Process

The Perform Qualitative Risk Analysis process assesses and evaluates the probability of an individual risk occurring and assesses the impact of the risk if it were to occur. This type of evaluation is based on a pre-defined and communicated risk assessment scales, such as $0 - 1$ or $1 - 5$.

Using the probability and impact scores, the risks are then prioritized for additional analysis or response planning as appropriate.

Perform Qualitative Risk Analysis: Inputs, Tools and Techniques, and Outputs

Inputs	Tools and Techniques	Outputs
1. Risk management plan	1. Risk probability and impact assessment	1. Project documents updates
2. Scope baseline	2. Probability and impact matrix	
3. Risk register	3. Risk data quality assessment	
4. Enterprise environmental factors	4. Risk categorization	
5. Organizational process assets	5. Risk urgency assessment	
	6. Expert judgment	

Figure 6-1: Perform Qualitative Risk Analysis ITTOs

PMBOK® Guide, page 328

Perform Qualitative Risk Analysis: Inputs

Risk Management Plan

The risk management plan, a subsidiary plan, will provide details and guidance on the qualitative risk analysis process, including the defined scales or measurements of risk probability and impact.

Scope Baseline

The scope baseline is an output of the Create WBS process and is made up of the project scope statement, the WBS, and the accompanying document to the WBS, the WBS dictionary.

Risk Register

The risk register is started during the Identify Risks process and is elaborated upon during the remaining risk management processes. The risk register lists all of the identified risks with a unique risk identification numbers and description of each risk.

Enterprise Environmental Factors and Organizational Process Assets

Environmental factors may include an increase in budget restrictions, which would increase the project cost risk. Organizational process assets may include past project files, which can be leveraged to identify risks identified on previous, similar projects.

Enterprise environmental factors and organizational process assets were discussed in Chapter 4.

Perform Qualitative Risk Analysis: Tools and Techniques

The *PMBOK® Guide* tools and techniques for the Perform Qualitative Risk Analysis process are:

- Risk probability and impact: assessment and matrix
- Risk data quality assessment
- Risk categorization
- Risk urgency assessment

In addition to the *PMBOK® Guide* tools and techniques, six other tools and techniques may be used to perform a qualitative risk analysis:

- Analytic hierarchy process
- RBS analysis
- Root cause analysis
- Pareto prioritization analysis
- Retrospective analysis
- Estimating techniques

Probability/Impact Evaluation and Matrix

Risk probability assessment investigates the likelihood that a specific risk will occur. Risk impact assessment investigates the potential effect of a risk on project objectives such as schedule, cost, quality, or performance and is attentive to both negative effects of threats and positive effects of opportunities.

Probability and impact are assessed for each identified risk in interviews or meetings with participants selected for their familiarity with the risk categories on the agenda.

The level of probability for each risk and its impact on each objective is evaluated during the interview or meeting and explanatory detail, including assumptions justifying the levels assigned, is recorded.

Risk probabilities and impacts are rated according to the definitions given in the risk management plan, with risks with low ratings of probability and impact included on a watchlist for future monitoring.

Many organizations will define probability on a 0 to 1 scale, with 1 equating to a 100% probability that the event will occur. The impact scale is defined by the organization and, alternatively, may be a 1 to 5 scale or a 1 to 10 scale.

Using this scale, the project team can add probability and impact to assess individual risk scores. In this example, probability is evaluated on a "0 to 1" scale and impact on a "1 to 5" scale.

Risk ID	Risk	Probability	Impact	Risk Score
1	Poor weather conditions	.3	4	1.2
2	Low morale of team members	.4	2	.8
3	Poor cost estimates	.8	3	2.4
4	Lack of technical equipment	.6	5	3
			Total	7.4
			Avg.	1.85

Figure 6-2: Probability and Impact Evaluation

Another common method for qualitative assessment is the use of ranges.

For example:

Probability

- High – 50% or higher (likely)
- Medium –10-50% (unlikely)
- Low – 10% or lower (very unlikely)

Impact

- High – A project objective is at risk, requiring a mandatory change to scope, schedule, and/or cost.
- Medium – Project objectives can be met, but significant replanning is required.
- Low – No major plan changes are required; the risk is an inconvenience or will be handled through overtime or other minor adjustments.

Risks can be prioritized for further quantitative analysis and response based on their risk rating. Usually these risk-rating rules are specified by the organization in advance of the project and included in organizational process assets. Risk-rating rules can be tailored to a specific project during the process of planning the risk management approach.

Evaluation of each risk's importance and hence its priority for attention is typically conducted using a probability and impact matrix. Such a matrix specifies combinations of probability and impact that add up to as low-, moderate-, or high-priority risks.

- The dark gray area (with the largest numbers) represents high risk
- The light gray area (with the smallest numbers) represents low risk
- The medium gray area (in the middle) represents moderate risk

Probability	Threats					Opportunities				
0.90	0.05	0.09	0.18	0.36	0.72	0.72	0.36	0.18	0.09	0.05
0.70	0.04	0.07	0.14	0.28	0.56	0.56	0.28	0.14	0.07	0.04
0.50	0.03	0.05	0.10	0.20	0.40	0.40	0.20	0.10	0.05	0.03
0.30	0.02	0.03	0.06	0.12	0.24	0.24	0.12	0.06	0.03	0.02
0.10	0.01	0.01	0.02	0.04	0.08	0.08	0.04	0.02	0.01	0.01
	0.05	0.10	0.20	0.40	0.80	0.80	0.40	0.20	0.10	0.05

Impact (numerical scale) on an objective (e.g.. cost, time, scope, or quality)

Each risk is rated on its probability of occurring and impact on an objective if it were to occur. The organization's thresholds for low, moderate, or high risks are shown in the matrix and will determine whether the risk is scored as low, moderate, or high for that objective.

Figure 6-3: Probability Impact Matrix

PMBOK® Guide, page 331

An organization can rate a risk separately for each objective. For example, there may be different ratings of a single risk's impact on cost, time, and scope. In addition, it can develop ways to determine one overall rating for each risk. An overall project rating scheme can be developed to reflect the organization's preference for one objective over another, and those preferences can be used to develop a weighting of the risks that are assessed by objective.

Opportunities and threats can be handled in the same matrix and separated by definitions of the different levels of impact that are appropriate for each.

Risk ratings help guide risk responses. Risks that have a negative impact on objectives if they occur and are in the high-risk zone of the matrix may require priority action and aggressive response strategies. Threats in the low-risk zone may not require proactive management action beyond placement on a watchlist or the addition of a contingency reserve.

Opportunities in the high-risk zone that can be obtained most easily and offer the greatest benefit should be targeted first. Opportunities in the low-risk zone should be monitored.

The number of steps in the scale is organizationally determined and organizationally dependent.

Risk Data Quality Assessment

The data used to analyze risks should be evaluated to ensure that it is appropriate, accurate, and timely.

For example, if risks are being analyzed based on real estate data from three years ago, the data may not be truly representative of the current market conditions for real estate.

Risk Categorization

Risks may be categorized by:

- Sources of project risk (for example, using the RBS)
- The area of the project affected by the risk (scope, time, cost, quality, etc.)
- Other useful categories (for example, project phase)

Grouping risks by common root causes can allow for effective response strategies.

Risk Urgency Assessment

A risk urgency assessment evaluates urgency in addressing identified risks and determines which risks need to be addressed the soonest. Urgency may be based on the time needed to implement a risk response, the risk warning signs, or the risk rating.

Analytic Hierarchy Process (AHP)

An analytic hierarchy process (AHP) allows risk scores to be calibrated according to which project objectives are the most important by creating a weighted evaluation of different options.

To conduct an AHP:

1. Using a preference scale, conduct a pair-wise comparison of the objectives.
2. Using the results from the comparison, determine the weighting factor for each objective.
3. Evaluate two identified options against each other as they relates to each of the objectives.
4. Calculate each option's average score and multiply that score by the objective weighting to determine the overall score.
5. Select the option with the highest score.

Example:

Using a preference factor scale, determine pair-wise comparisons.

Preference Factor Scale
1 The two factors are equally important.
2 One factor is slightly more important.
3 One factor is more important.
4 One factor is significantly more important.
5 One factor is absolutely more important.

Step 1

Below is a sample pair-wise comparison comparing scope, time, and cost.

	Scope	Time	Cost
Scope	1	5	3
Time	1/5 (0.2)	1	1/2 (0.5)
Cost	1/3 (0.3)	2	1
TOTAL	1.5	8	4.5

Step 2

Divide each number of the pair-wise comparison by the total and then calculate the average of each. This average is the objective weighting that will be used in step 4.

	Scope	Time	Cost	Average
Scope	.67	.63	.67	.66
Time	.13	.13	.11	.12
Cost	.20	.25	.22	.22

The result of the pair-wise comparison is that 66% of the weighting is on scope, 22% on cost, and 12% on time, meaning that scope is of the most concern, followed by budget and then time.

Step 3

Evaluate the two risks against each other as to the potential impact on the project objectives of scope, time, and cost. Calculate an average score for each risk against each project objective.

In this example, Risk 2 has a significantly larger impact on scope than Risk 1 has. However, Risk 1 has a larger impact on cost and time.

	Scope				Time				Cost			
	Risk 1		Risk 2	Avg.	Risk 1		Risk 2	Avg.	Risk 1		Risk 2	Avg.
Risk 1	1	.20	.25	.20	.20	1	.75	3	.75	.75	1	.83	5	.83	.83
Risk 2	4	.80	1	.80	.80	.33	.25	1	.25	.25	.20	.17	1	1.17	.17
TOTAL	5		1.25			1.33		4			1.2		6		

Average score for each risk against each objective:

	Risk 1	Risk 2
Scope	.20	.80
Time	.75	.25
Cost	.83	.17

Step 4

The risk's average score is then multiplied by the objective weighting to determine the overall score.

	Objective Weighting	Risk 1	Risk 2
Scope	.66	.20	.80
		.20 x .66 = .13	.80 x .66 = .53
Time	.12	.75	.25
		.75 x .12 = .09	.25 x .12 = .03
Cost	.22	.83	.17
		.83 x .22 = .18	.17 x .22 = .04
Overall Score		.40	.60

As a result of this AHP, it is determined that Risk 2 is of the most concern due to its potential scope impact, despite the fact that Risk 1 will have a bigger impact on time and cost.

RBS Analysis

As presented in Chapter 5, the risk breakdown structure (RBS) is a graphical, hierarchical depiction of risk categories and subcategories for the project. Risk data is organized and structured to provide a standard presentation of project risk categories that facilitates understanding, communication, and management.

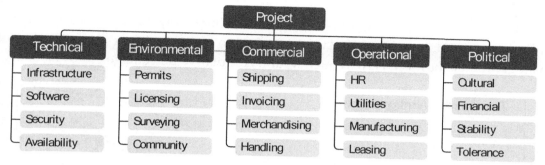

Figure 6-4: Risk Breakdown Structure

PMBOK® Guide, page 331

An RBS analysis can also be used in qualitative analysis to provide the team with insight into the specific categories of risk that may have a higher probability or impact based on the defined project objectives.

Root Cause Analysis

As presented in Chapter 5, a root-cause analysis or cause-and-effect exercises may be used for risk identification. In addition, root cause analysis is helpful in the qualitative risk analysis process. Identifying the root cause of the risks can provide a more accurate assessment of the probability and/or impact of identified risks based on shared or related root causes.

Pareto Prioritization Analysis

The Pareto Principle is also known as the 80/20 Principle, and it can be applied to many things in life. Joseph Juran applied the Pareto Principle to quality issues to say that 80% of quality problems originate from just 20% of causes. It can also be used from a risk management perspective to see how 80% of risks originate from 20% of causes.

Pareto prioritization ranks the causes of poor quality or the causes of risk by overall influence. This data can be displayed in a Pareto chart, which is a special type of histogram that shows causes, frequency, and cumulative percentage.

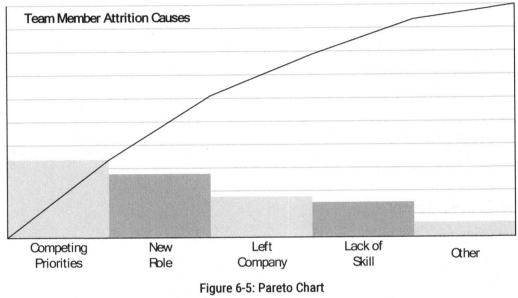

Figure 6-5: Pareto Chart

PMBOK® Guide, page 239

A Pareto prioritization helps project team focus on the causes that will have the biggest impact. From a qualitative risk analysis perspective, a Pareto prioritization provides a visual representation of the impact of the identified root causes.

Retrospective Analysis

A retrospective analysis, as discussed previously, is the analysis of potential risks based upon what occurred in the past on previous projects or the current project. Also used for risk identification, a retrospective analysis is a valuable component of a qualitative risk analysis, as it provides evidence of risk probability and the impact or effect of those risk events if they were to occur.

This allows the team to prevent mistakes that were made on prior projects while also leveraging any possible opportunities similar to those missed or captured in the past. In turn, it contributes to organizational learning that may be applied on future projects.

While retrospective analysis is incredibly valuable for use on any project, it is not a complete approach, as it is not possible that all risks for a project were previously identified earlier in the project or in past projects.

Estimating Techniques

There are multiple approaches to estimating risk impact and risk probability. Simplifying impact and probability scales to project-specific data provides an easier mechanism for team members to use to determine the appropriate score.

Scale	Probability	± Impact on Project Objectives	
		Time	Cost
Very Low	1-10%	< 1 week	<$10k
Low	11-20%	1-2 weeks	$10-20k
Moderate	21-40%	3-5 weeks	$21-40k
High	41-60%	6-9 weeks	$41-70k
Very High	61-99%	> 9 weeks	>$70k

Figure 6-6: Probability and Imapct Scale

Perform Qualitative Risk Analysis: Outputs

The outputs of the Perform Qualitative Analysis process are project document updates. Specifically, the risk register that was established during the risk identification process is updated with all of the information from the qualitative risk analysis.

Updates can include the relative ranking or prioritization of risks, the categorization of risks, and the identification of causes of risk or areas that require particular attention. In addition, it is beneficial to identify which risks require responses in the short term, which need additional analysis, and which are considered low-risk.

Upon performing a qualitative risk analysis, the risk register can be updated with:

- Relative ranking or priority list of project risks – The probability and impact matrix can be used to classify risks according to their individual significance. Using combinations of each risk's probability of occurring and its impact on objectives if it were to occur, risks are prioritized relative to each other by sorting them into groups of high risk, moderate risk, and low risk. Risks may be listed by priority separately for schedule, cost, and performance since organizations may value one objective over another.

  o The project manager can then use the prioritized list of risks to focus attention on items of high significance (high risk) for the most important objectives, where responses can lead to better project outcomes.

- Risks grouped by categories – Risk categorization can reveal common root causes of risk or project areas requiring particular attention. Discovering concentrations of risk may improve the effectiveness of risk responses.

- List of risks requiring response in the short term – Risks that require an urgent response and risks that can be handled at a later date may be put into different groups.

- List of risks for additional analysis and response – Some risks might warrant more analysis, such as a quantitative analysis, as well as response action.
- Watchlists of low-priority risks – Risks that are not assessed as important when assessed qualitatively can be placed on a watchlist for continued monitoring.
- Trends in qualitative risk analysis results – As the analysis is repeated, a trend in particular risks may become apparent and can make risk response or further analysis more or less urgent/important.

As the qualitative risk analysis is repeated throughout the project, the risk register is updated with any trending information.

Review Questions   Chapter 6

1. **A probability impact matrix can be used for:**
   A. Grouping risks to evaluate for further action
   B. Determining the probability and impact of a potential risk
   C. Communicating the level of risk in the project to the sponsor
   D. Separating the opportunities from the threats

2. **In order to be most efficient in targeting risks with the biggest impact, which tool should be used?**
   A. System dynamics chart
   B. Affinity diagram
   C. Pareto chart
   D. Flow chart

3. **The following evaluates identified risks and determines which risks need to be addressed in the short term.**
   A. Analytic hierarchy process (AHP)
   B. Risk urgency assessment
   C. Systems dynamics
   D. Probability impact matrix

4. **In a meeting with your sponsor, you have identified that some of the project constraints are more critical than others. What is the best technique to assess the differences in the importance of the constraints?**
   A. Risk breakdown structure analysis
   B. Futures analysis
   C. Brainstorming
   D. Analytic hierarchy process

5. **The risk management plan has been completed and approved by the key stakeholders. You are working with your team to identify risks to the project and are performing a qualitative risk analysis. The objective of the qualitative risk analysis is to:**
   A. Assess the impact and likelihood of the identified risks
   B. Prioritize the identified risks for further analysis or for response
   C. Determine whether the risk responses have been implemented as planned
   D. Select alternative strategies for dealing with the risks

6. **As the project manager, you need to find out which issue has the maximum impact on a project. Which tool should you use?**
   A. Pareto diagram
   B. Control chart
   C. Trend analysis
   D. Fishbone diagram

7. **What should be done with risks on the watchlist?**

    A. Document them and give them to the customer
    B. Document them for historical use on other projects
    C. Document them and revisit them during project monitoring and controlling
    D. Document them and set them aside because they are already covered in your contingency plans

8. **This can help reduce the influence of bias in a qualitative risk analysis.**

    A. Conducting a Monte Carlo analysis
    B. Interviewing only key stakeholders
    C. Involving the team in the analysis
    D. Establishing definitions of the levels of probability and impact

9. **Which of the following is the most accurate statement regarding conducting a qualitative risk analysis?**

    A. A qualitative risk analysis is more time-consuming than a quantitative risk analysis.
    B. Establishing the definitions of probability and impact can increase the influence of bias.
    C. It is a quick and cost-effective means of establishing priorities for planning risk responses.
    D. The stakeholders' and organization's risk tolerance are not taken into consideration.

10. **A qualitative risk score is:**

    A. Probability multiplied by impact
    B. The percentage of likelihood divided by the impact
    C. Impact divided by probability
    D. The total number of identified risks

11. **A probability and impact matrix:**

    A. Can only be used to show negative risks
    B. Can only be used to show positive risks
    C. Can show both opportunities and threats in the same matrix
    D. Is developed as part of the quantitative risk analysis

12. **Each of the following may be included in the risk register based on the qualitative risk analysis except:**

    A. Risks grouped by category
    B. Probabilistic analysis of the project
    C. List of risks requiring response in the short term
    D. List of risks for additional analysis and response

13. **You have been assigned a bridge demolition and rebuilding project. A risk analysis has already been completed on the project and the resulting risk was 7.9. This project can be considered:**

    A. High-risk
    B. Moderate-risk
    C. Low-risk
    D. Impossible to determine

14. The following is biggest weakness of using a retrospective analysis to evaluate project risk.

    A. All risks may not have been fully identified, addressed, or documented on past projects.
    B. Just because it occurred in the past doesn't mean it will affect the current project.
    C. If the project manager wasn't involved in the previous project, the subjective evaluation will be different.
    D. Every project is different, and therefore the past data would not be of high quality and able to be applied to the current project.

15. You are performing an AHP analysis of various risks. The budget objective has a weighting of .29. For budget implications, risk A has an average score of .56, risk B has an average score of .32, and Risk C has an average score of .12. What is risk B's overall score against the budget objective?

    A. .32
    B. .09
    C. .16
    D. .03

Vocabulary Review   Chapter 6

Analytic hierarchy process   Pareto prioritization analysis   Retrospective analysis
Estimating techniques   Probability   Root cause analysis
Impact   Probability and impact matrix   Watchlist
Pareto chart   RBS analysis

1. _____   The likelihood that a risk event will occur within the project timeline

2. _____   A review of historical project information used to elicit data that can be helpful in assessing the probability and impact of the currently identified project risks

3. _____   The effect of a risk event on one or more of the project objectives

4. _____   A special type of histogram that ranks the causes of poor quality or project risks by overall influence

5. _____   Risks that are deemed low-probability and low-impact that require no action and will only be monitored

6. _____   An evaluation of those causes most likely to generate risks that impact the project

7. _____   An evaluation of the RBS to determine areas or categories of risks that will have an impact on the project

8. _____   An evaluation of the root causes of the project risks done in order to assess the probability and impact of the identified project risks

9. _____   A decision-making tool used for evaluating risks based on their assessed probability and impact

10. _____   A method used to calibrate preferences for achieving the different objectives of a project

11. _____   Techniques that establish parameters around different probability and impact ratings

Answer Key

Chapter 6

Review Question Answers

1. **Answer: A**

   The probability impact matrix is a visual depiction of the various levels of risk prioritization based on probability and impact. The matrix allows the risks to be grouped for further action. Risk scores falling in the highest zone most likely require proactive action. Those in the middle zone may be candidates for contingent responses. Those in the lowest range are most likely placed on the watchlist.

2. **Answer: C**

   A Pareto chart ranks risks based on size of impact to determine shared root causes, following the 80/20 rule.

3. **Answer: B**

   A risk urgency assessment evaluates the immediacy needed in addressing identified risks. Some risks require action in the short term, while others may not need to be addressed until further into the project.

4. **Answer: D**

   An analytic hierarchy process (AHP) will allow for a pair-wise comparison of each of the constraints, creating a weighting factor.

5. **Answer: B**

   The objective of a qualitative risk analysis is to prioritize risks based on their probability of occurring and their impact if they were to occur.

6. **Answer: A**

   A Pareto diagram is a special type of histogram ranked by frequency of occurrence.

7. **Answer: C**

   Risks on the watchlist should be periodically revisited during monitoring and controlling to ensure that nothing has changed from a probability and/or impact perspective.

8. **Answer: D**

   Having set definitions and descriptions that correspond to risk probability and impact ratings gives participants a better understanding of the relative scales.

9. **Answer: C**

   Qualitative analysis is typically a quick and cost-effective process for ranking and prioritizing project risks.

10. **Answer: A**

    A qualitative risk score is probability multiplied by impact.

11. **Answer: C**

    Both opportunities and threats can be shown in the same probability and impact matrix. However, they must be separated onto different sides of the matrix.

12. Answer: B

A probabilistic analysis of the project involves estimating whether the project will be able to achieve the budget and schedule objectives. A quantitative risk analysis provides this, as risks are evaluated in terms of cost and schedule impact.

13. Answer: D

Because no scale is provided as to the evaluation of the probability and impact, it is impossible to assess the level of risk. For example, if the scale were 1- 8, this would be a high risk. However, if the scale were 1-100, this would be an extremely low risk.

14. Answer: A

A retrospective analysis, while valuable, relies on the past, and the past is only as good as the experiences it contained and the documentation of those experiences. Depending on the environment or situation, not all risks experienced in the past may have been fully identified, addressed or documented.

15. Answer: B

Risk B's average score is 0.32. To determine the overall score against the budget objective, multiply risk B's score by the budget objective weighting of 0.29.

0.32 x 0.29 = 0.0928

Vocabulary Review Answers

1. Probability
2. Retrospective analysis
3. Impact
4. Pareto chart
5. Watchlist
6. Pareto prioritization analysis
7. RBS analysis
8. Root cause analysis
9. Probability and impact matrix
10. Analytic hierarchy process
11. Estimating techniques

Quantitative Risk Analysis

In This Chapter

- Quantitative Risk Analysis
- Critical Success Factors
- Perform Quantitative Risk Analysis Process

Quantitative Risk Analysis

Quantitative risk analysis quantifies the possible outcomes for the project and their probabilities and assesses the probability of achieving specific project objectives, such as a budget or schedule objective. Quantitative analysis identifies those risks needing the most attention and may also be used to determine project management decisions when conditions or outcomes are uncertain.

Quantitative risk analysis is performed on risks that have been prioritized through the qualitative risk analysis process as potentially substantially impacting the project. This analysis may be used to assign a numerical rating to those risks individually or to evaluate the aggregate effect of all risks affecting the project.

This analysis provides a numerical analysis of the highest risks on the project to:

- Determine which risk events warrant a response
- Determine overall project risk (risk exposure)
- Determine the quantified probability of meeting project objectives
- Determine cost and schedule reserves
- Create realistic and achievable cost, schedule, or scope targets

Quantitative risk analysis should be repeated after risk responses are planned and as risks are monitored and controlled to determine if the overall project risk has satisfactorily decreased. Trends can indicate the need for more or less risk management action.

Consider the following to compare qualitative risk analysis with quantitative risk analysis:

Qualitative Risk Analysis	Quantitative Risk Analysis
• Risk-level analysis	• Project-level analysis
• Subjective evaluation of probability and impact	• Determines probabilistic estimates of time and costs
• Quick and easy to perform	• Time-consuming
• No special software required	• Requires specialized tools
• Leads to quantitative risk analysis	• Identifies risks with greatest impacts on project

Critical Success Factors

Factors for success in quantitative risk analysis include:

High-Quality Data

If historical data is not available, information for quantitative analysis may be captured through interviews, workshops, etc. Data from unbiased sources is critical to the analysis.

Prioritized List of Risks

Risks must have been identified and then prioritized through qualitative analysis.

Appropriate Project Model

Project models used may include the project schedule, cost estimates, decision tree, and other total project models

Overall Project Risk

This overall project risk is derived from individual risks, based upon an appropriate methodology, such as a Monte Carlo simulation or a decision tree. Individual project risks are incorporated, and then the overall impact on the project is calculated.

Perform Quantitative Risk Analysis Process

The Perform Quantitative Risk Analysis Process further evaluates the effects of risks and assigns a numerical, or quantitative, rating to provide a probabilistic analysis of the project.

Perform Quantitative Risk Analysis: Inputs, Tools and Techniques, and Outputs

Inputs	Tools and Techniques	Outputs
1. Risk management plan	1. Data gathering and representation techniques	1. Project documents updates
2. Cost management plan	2. Quantitative risk analysis and modeling techniques	
3. Schedule management plan	3. Expert judgment	
4. Risk register		
5. Enterprise environmental factors		
6. Organizational process assets		

Figure 7-1: Perform Quantitative Risk Analysis ITTOs

PMBOK® Guide, page 334

Perform Quantitative Risk Analysis: Inputs

Subsidiary Plans

Three subsidiary plans are identified as inputs to the Perform Quantitative Risk Analysis process. The risk management plan defines the approach to conducting any type of quantitative analysis, such as Monte Carlo simulations.

The cost and schedule management plans are also inputs. Because quantitative risk analysis evaluates risk in terms of the cost and schedule impacts, these plans are leveraged to understand the cost and schedule objectives, the level of detail and accuracy of the budget and schedule, and tolerances and the thresholds related to the budget and the schedule.

Risk Register

The risk register, an output of the Identify Risks process, is also an input here. When the Perform Qualitative Risk Analysis process is complete, the risks have been evaluated for probability and impact and have been prioritized. Only those risks prioritized as having a potentially significant impact are evaluated in the Perform Quantitative Risk Analysis process.

Enterprise Environmental Factors and Organizational Process Assets

Environmental factors that may be taken into consideration include the organization's appetite, willingness, or capabilities to perform quantitative risk analyses. Because quantitative analysis typically requires access to high-quality data and sophisticated tools, not every organization is capable of or desires to pursue quantitative analysis.

Organizational process assets that may be leveraged include past project files that can be leveraged to identify risks similar to those of previous projects and their associated quantified impacts.

Enterprise environmental factors and organizational process assets were discussed in Chapter 4.

Perform Quantitative Risk Analysis: Tools and Techniques

The *PMBOK® Guide* simply groups the quantitative analysis tools and techniques into data gathering and representation techniques and quantitative risk analysis modeling techniques. However, there are a number of techniques used to perform quantitative risk analysis, including the following.

- Bowtie analysis
- Decision tree and expected monetary value (EMV) analysis
- Fault tree analysis
- Monte Carlo simulation
- Risk-based critical chain analysis
- Risk-based earned value analysis
- Risk metric analysis
- Sensitivity analysis
- System dynamics

Bowtie Analysis

A bowtie analysis facilitates the discovery of predecessors to project problems by incorporating both sides of a risk scenario, what would come before and what would come after a specific risk event.

Typically, the left side of the diagram is a fault tree depicting the causes of the risk event and the measures that may be taken to prevent those causes. The right side of the diagram depicts the consequences of the risk event and the measures that may be taken to mitigate the consequences.

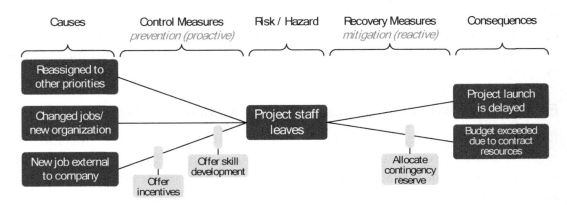

Figure 7-2: Bowtie Diagram

Decision Tree and Expected Monetary Value (EMV) Analysis

When only a small number of options or potential outcomes are possible, decision trees may be useful for quantitative risk assessment. Decision trees are generally used to evaluate alternatives before selecting one of them to execute.

Whenever there are points in the project where several options are possible, each can be planned and assigned a probability (the sum total of which is 100%). An expected estimate for either duration or cost may be derived by weighting the estimates for each option and adding these figures to get a blended result.

For this example, a project plan containing a generic activity, which could be any of the three options, with an estimate of 16 days would result in a more realistic plan than simply using the 12-day estimate of the "most likely" option.

The schedule exposure of the risk situation here may be estimated by noting the maximum adverse variance (an additional four days, if the activity is schedule critical) and associating this with an expected probability of 35%.

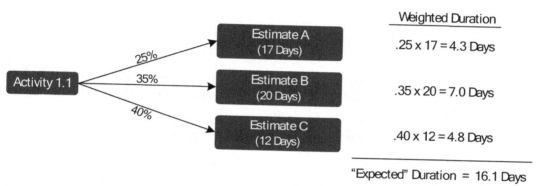

Figure 7-3: Decision Tree Analysis

PMBOK® Guide, page 339

Exercise: Decision Tree

Upon evaluation of the project requirements, the web development team lead provides you with the following duration information:

- If a senior developer is available full time, the estimated duration is four days.
- If a senior developer is available part time, the estimated duration is nine days.
- If a senior developer is not available and the work is completed by a junior developer, the estimated duration is 16 days.
- There is a 50% chance that the senior developer will only be available part time and a 10% chance that they will be available full time.

Considering the risk, what is the expected duration?

Expected Monetary Value

An expected monetary value (EMV) analysis is a statistical concept that calculates the average financial outcome or impact when the future includes scenarios that may or may not happen (i.e. analysis under uncertainty). EMV for a scenario is calculated by multiplying the value of each possible outcome by its probability of occurrence and adding the products together.

EMV requires a risk-neutral assumption, not risk-averse or risk-seeking. In EMV analysis, values may be positive or negative numbers, depending on the situation under analysis. Ascertain how the numbers should be represented requires a careful evaluation of questions about EMV on the exam.

For example, in a scenario in which you are evaluating the risk exposure on a new product that you are introducing to the market, positive values are good, reflecting increased profit, and negative values are bad, reflecting a loss of profit. However, if the scenario is evaluating money that will be spent, positive values are bad and negative numbers are good. Because of this, the first thing you need to do when presented with an EMV question is evaluate it to understand whether you are dealing with money that is being spent or money that is being made.

The second factor you need to take into consideration when faced with an EMV question is the value you need to determine. If the question is asking for the EMV of the risk scenario, the result will be the sum of the "branches" of the scenario under consideration. If it is asking you to determine the total value of the scenario, the EMV will need to be added back to the initial estimate.

As for any math question on the exam, use your calculator, double-check your math, and remember that I personally recommend marking the math questions for review. If the question is lengthy, as these tend to be, skip down to the bottom of the question to be sure of what they are actually asking you before you begin any math.

Example: EMV Analysis

You are evaluating three bids from potential vendors for your project.

- Vendor A provided a bid of $100,000.
- Vendor B provided a bid of $125,000.
- Vendor C provided a bid of $135,000.

Based on historical information and expert judgment, you determine the following.

- Vendor A has a 70% probability of delivering late at an additional cost of $80,000 and a 30% probability of delivering early at a savings of $15,000.
- Vendor B has a 50% probability of delivering late at an additional cost of $35,000 and a 50% probability of delivering early at a savings of $9,000.
- Vendor C has a 20% probability of delivering late at an additional cost of $25,000 and an 80% probability of delivering early at a savings of $7,000.

To determine the <u>expected monetary value</u> (EMV) of the risk of working with each vendor, multiple probability by the financial impact and sum the results.

To determine the <u>total value</u> of each bid, add the EMV to the original bid amount.

- Vendor A EMV = $51,500 + Bid $100,000 = Total Value: $151,500
- Vendor B EMV = $26,000 + Bid $125,000 = Total Value: $151,000
- Vendor C EMV = ($600) + Bid $135,000 = Total Value: $134,400

Based on the analysis, you select Vendor C, as the total value of the risk scenario for Vendor C is $134,400, lower than the other two vendors.

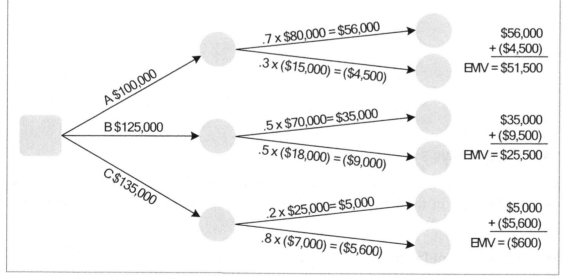

Exercise: Expected Monetary Value

You are evaluating two potential profit scenarios for a new product launch. Product A is estimated to make a base profit of $30,000, and Product B is estimated to make a base profit of $50,000.

There is a 20% chance that Product A will be poorly received by the market at a loss of $10,000, a __% chance that it will be well received by the market at an increased profit of $20,000, and a 30% chance that it will exceed market expectations at an increased profit of $50,000. What are the EMV of the risk scenario and the total value for the product?

There is a 40% chance that Product B will be poorly received by the market for a loss of $20,000, a __% chance that it will be well received by the market at an increased profit of $30,000, and a 30% chance that it will exceed market expectations at an increased profit of $40,000. What are the EMV of the risk scenario and the total value for the product?

Fault Tree Analysis

Fault tree analysis is discussed in Chapter 6 on qualitative risk analysis. A fault tree can also be used in the Perform Quantitative Risk Analysis process to quantify the probabilities and impacts of the various faults.

Monte Carlo Simulation

A project simulation uses the project model to translate the specified detailed uncertainties of the project into their potential impacts on project objectives. One of the most common simulation tools or approaches used is known as the Monte Carlo simulation.

In a Monte Carlo simulation, the project model is computed thousands of times (iterated), with the input values (e.g., cost estimates or activity durations) chosen at random for each iteration from the probability distributions of these variables.

The output of a simulation is a probability distribution (e.g. total cost or completion date) that is calculated from the iterations.

A Monte Carlo simulation iterates the project model thousands of times to compute the probabilities of all of the possible outcomes for the project based on the identified risks. The results are typically presented in a histogram showing a range of possible outcomes and the number of times a particular outcome is achieved. It may also be presented in an S-curve that plots the range of possible outcomes against the cumulative probability of achieving a given value.

For a cost risk analysis, a simulation uses cost estimates. For a schedule risk analysis, the schedule network diagram and duration estimates are used.

The output from a cost risk simulation is shown below. It illustrates the respective likelihood of achieving specific cost targets. Similar distributions can be developed for schedule outcomes.

WBS Element	Low	Most Likely	High
Design	$8,000	$14,000	$20,000
Build	$32,000	$40,000	$70,000
Test	$22,000	$32,000	$46,000
Total Project	$62,000	$86,000	$136,000

Interviewing relevant stakeholders helps determine three-point estimates for each WBS element. These estimates can be input into simulation software for a cost risk analysis as seen below.

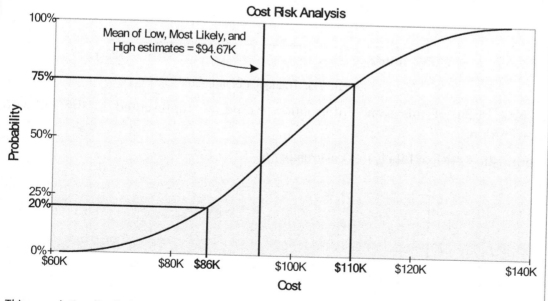

This cumulative distribution shows that the project is only 20% likely to be completed at or below the $86k "most likely" estimate. If a conservative organization wants a 75% likelihood of success, a budget of $110k is required. That is a contingency of nearly 28% (($110k - $86k)/$86k).

Figure 7-4: Continuous Distribution
PMBOK® Guide, page 336, 340

Monte Carlo Simulation Example:

The project team has provided its estimates for each phase of the project, including its best case (optimistic), most likely, and worst case (pessimistic) estimates. Based on this information, the project manager submits a cost estimate of $164,000.

	Best Case	Most Likely	Worst Case
Phase 1	$18,000	$19,000	$31,000
Phase 2	$34,000	$35,000	$47,000
Phase 3	$41,000	$43,000	$54,000
Phase 4	$39,000	$41,000	$53,000
Phase 5	$24,000	$26,000	$42,000
	$156,000	**$164,000**	**$227,000**

From this information, it is known that the lowest possible cost is $156,000 and the highest possible cost is $227,000. Using this information, the mean can be calculated at $182,333 (11% higher than the most likely estimate) and the median at $191,500 (17% higher than the most likely estimate).

This information can be represented by a triangular probability distribution:

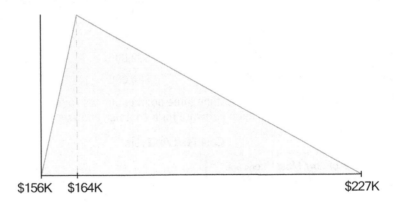

$156K $164K $227K

Figure 7-5: Triangular Distribution

A beta PERT of this same information would be represented in the following distribution:

Optimistic + 4(Most Likely) + Pessimistic / 6 = $173,167

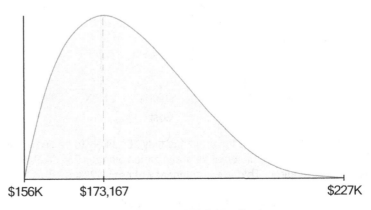

$156K $173,167 $227K

Figure 7-6: Beta PERT Distribution

Using the same project information, the output of a Monte Carlo simulation would provide the probability confidence levels and the amount and percentage of contingency that would need to be allocated based on the submitted cost estimate of $164,000.

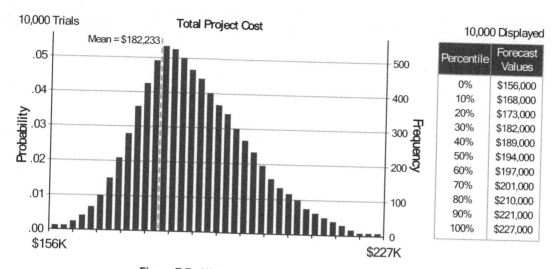

Figure 7-7: Histogram from Monte Carlo Simulation

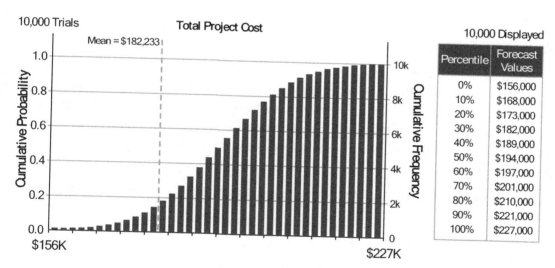

Figure 7-8: S-Curve Graph

For example, if the organization seeks a 50% confidence level (P50), a contingency of $30,000 (18%) would need to be allocated to the project. If the organization were more conservative and sought an 80% confidence level, that contingency amount would increase to $46,000 (28%).

Probability %	Forecast	Contingency	%
P0	$156,000	-$8,000	-5%
P10	$168,000	$4,000	2%
P20	$173,000	$9,000	5%
P30	$182,000	$18,000	11%
P40	$189,000	$25,000	15%
P50	$194,000	$30,000	18%
P60	$197,000	$33,000	20%
P70	$201,000	$37,000	23%
P80	$210,000	$46,000	28%
P90	$221,000	$57,000	35%
P100	$227,000	$63,000	38%

The contingency amount is calculated by subtracting the original estimate of $164,000 from the forecast (Contingency $ = Forecast – Estimate).

To calculate the contingency percentage, divide the forecast by the estimate and subtract one (Contingency % = (Forecast ÷ Estimate) – 1).

Probability Distributions

A number of different probability distributions can be generated from project modeling and simulation. As seen previously, the probability distribution can be a continuous distribution, a triangular distribution, or a beta PERT distribution. Additional distributions that may be developed during a quantitative risk analysis include uniform distributions, normal (Gaussian) distributions, and log-normal distributions.

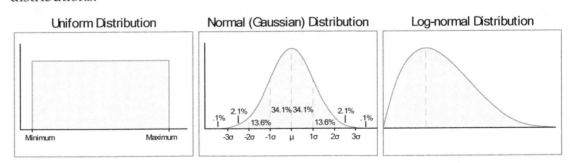

Figure 7-9: Other Probability Distributions

- Uniform distributions – Also known as rectangular distributions, these are distributions with constant probability, where no one outcome is any more likely than another.

- Normal (Gaussian) distributions – Also referred to as bell curves, these are common distributions for representing real-valued random variables whose distributions are not known.

- Log-normal distributions – Also known as Galton distributions, these are distributions with a positive skew that are often used to describe natural phenomena, such as in economics, where evidence shows that the income of 97-99% of the population is distributed log-normally.

Latin Hypercube Sampling

Because performing a Monte Carlo simulation requires running iterations thousands of times, an alternative option is to perform a Latin Hypercube sampling.

Latin Hypercube is a stratified approach, selecting a limited set of values from each strata or segment rather than pulling all random variables. This improves accuracy with a smaller sample size and is typically preferable over Monte Carlo simulations. This is a preference specifically when the speed of the computers running the computations is a concern.

Risk-Based Critical Chain Analysis

Critical chain project management (CCPM) is a method of planning and scheduling that places the emphasis on the resources that are required to complete the activities. In CCPM, the placement and use of time buffers account for limited or constrained resources. The result is a resource-constrained critical path known as the critical chain.

A buffer placed at the end of the critical chain is known as the project buffer and protects the target finish date from slippage along the critical path. Feeding buffers are added at the point of path convergence, where non-critical paths converge into the critical chain.

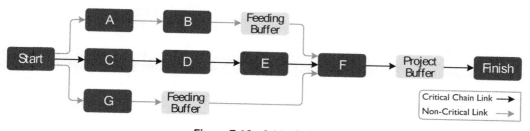

Figure 7-10: Critical Chain

In order to use CCPM, a fully resourced project schedule must be completed. In addition, team members need to be familiar with CCPM and have an agreement as to the sharing of the time buffers.

Risk-Based Earned Value Analysis

Earned value analysis (EVA) compares the value earned in the project to the planned value (to determine schedule status) and to the actual costs (to determine budget status). The earned value analysis can provide insight and quantify uncertainty about the project schedule and budget.

To evaluate the amount of schedule risk for a project that is in progress, the earned value (EV) of the project is compared to the planned value (PV) of the project as of the status date. To evaluate the amount of cost risk, the earned value (EV) is compared to the actual costs (AC) of the project as of the status date.

Earned Value

Earned value is calculated based on what percentage of the budgeted work of the project the team has completed. The completed percentage can be determined in terms of either time or effort.

For example, for an eight-month, $100,000 project, the project may be considered 25% complete after the second month of work or after the project has earned $25,000 in value. However, just because 25% of the time has passed, it does not necessarily mean that 25% of the work has been completed. A more accurate assessment of percentage complete would be based on completed effort.

Considering human behavior, the majority of the work typically occurs just prior to a deadline. It has been demonstrated that Thursday tends to be the most productive day of the week in environments that have status reports due on Friday. Thus, using a time-based percentage complete can be very misleading. However, capturing an effort-based percentage complete can be challenging in most environments, as reporting and progress is not captured at that level.

Schedule Analysis

Planned value is the budgeted spending of the project from the start date through the status date.

For example, the budgeted spend for a project is:

- Period 1: $10,000
- Period 2: $20,000
- Period 3: $30,000
- Period 4: $25,000
- Period 5: $15,000

The planned value (PV) after period 1 would be $10,000. The cumulative PV at the end of period 2 would be $30,000, etc. The total PV at the end of the project would be $100,000.

If the earned value (EV) is $25,000 and the planned value (PV) is $30,000, the project would appear to be behind schedule, as less has been earned than was planned.

- Schedule variance (SV) = earned value (EV) – planned value (PV)
- Schedule variance (SV) = $25,000 - $30,000 = ($5,000)
- Schedule performance index (SPI) = earned value (EV) ÷ planned value (PV)
- Schedule performance index (SPI) = $25,000 ÷ $30,000 = 0.83

Based on the schedule performance index (SPI), the project is 17% behind schedule.

Variable	Acronym	Description
Planned Value	PV	The amount of money budgeted for a component between its start date and the status date. Typically cumulative.
Budget at Completion	BAC	The total amount of money allocated to the component. Equal to the total PV at the end of the component.
Earned Value	EV	Estimated value of the work completed. EV = BAC x percent complete
Schedule Variance	SV	The difference between the earned value and the planned value. SV = EV – PV
Schedule Performance Index	SPI	The ratio of earned value to planned value. SPI = EV ÷ PV

PMBOK® Guide, Glossary

Exercise: Earned Value - Schedule

Your 10-month project has a budget of $20,000. You are evaluating progress of your project after two months. According to your team, the project is 30% complete. Based on your project budget, you planned to spend $8,000 by this date.

Budget at completion (BAC) =

Percentage complete =

Earned value (EV) =

Planned value (PV) =

Schedule variance (SV) =

Schedule performance index (SPI) =

What is the status of the schedule?

Cost Analysis

To evaluate the status of the budget, compare the earned value (EV) to the actual costs (AC).

For example, the actual costs (AC) for the project are:

- Period 1: $7,000
- Period 2: $11,000

The total actual costs (AC) are $18,000. If the earned value (EV) is $25,000 and the actual costs (AC) are $18,000, the project would appear to be under budget, as more has been earned than has been spent. Essentially, it only cost $18,000 to complete $25,000's worth of work.

- Cost variance (CV) = earned value (EV) – actual costs (AC)
- Cost variance (CV) = $25,000 - $18,000 = $7,000
- Cost performance index (CPI) = earned value (EV) ÷ actual costs (AC)
- Cost performance index (CPI) = $25,000 ÷ $18,000 = 1.34

Based on the cost performance index (CPI), the project is 34% under budget.

Variable	Acronym	Description
Actual Cost	AC	The actual cost of the component to date. Typically cumulative.
Cost Variance	CV	The difference between the earned value and the actual cost. CV = EV - AC
Cost Performance Index	CPI	The ratio of earned value to actual cost. CPI = EV ÷ AC

PMBOK® Guide, Glossary

Exercise: Earned Value - Cost

You are the project manager for a six-month, $120,000 project. According to the work performance information, your team is roughly 40% complete with their work.

According to the project budget, estimated costs to date should be $50,000. Costs billed to date are $40,000.

Budget at completion (BAC) =

Percentage complete =

Earned value (EV) =

Actual cost (AC) =

Cost variance (CV) =

Cost performance index (CPI) =

What is the status of the budget?

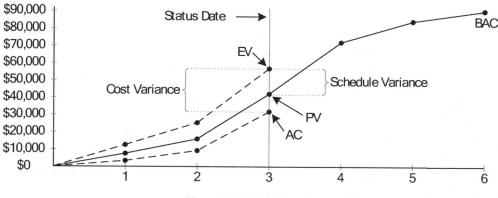

Figure 7-11: EVM Graph

Risk Metric Analysis

An evaluation of risk metrics provides insight into the risk exposure of a project. Three categories of metrics can be leveraged for quantitative risk analysis: predictive, diagnostic, and retrospective.

Predictive Metrics

Predictive metrics use current information to provide insight into future conditions. In other words, they use the current environment to predict the future. Because predictive metrics are based on speculation rather than empirical data, they can be unreliable. However, predictive metrics tend to be commonly employed in many environments as a quantitative risk technique.

Predictive metrics are used in project risk management to determine the project scale, identify situations that may require contingency planning, and justify schedule and budget reserves.

For scope or scale risk, predictive metrics can be used to complete size-based deliverable analyses of such factors as lines of code or component counts, assess project complexity, calculate the volume of expected changes, consider the number of planned activities, etc.

An example would be a project that has one half the possible numbers of lines of code and has experienced a risk-based budget variance of 5%. To assume that the current project, at double the current number of lines of code, may experience a 10% risk-based budget variance would be to leverage predictive metrics.

Schedule risk, project duration, total length, duration estimates, number of critical or near-critical paths, logical project complexity, external predecessor dependencies, project interdependencies, and total float, can all help predict the need for additional project contingency reserves.

Diagnostic Metrics

Diagnostic metrics are designed to provide current information about a system based on the latest available data. Diagnostic metrics may detect anomalies or reveal future problems based on the measurements taken throughout the project.

Diagnostic metrics can be used to detect adverse project variances either in advance or as soon as is practical. This is a common component of monitoring and controlling project risks, where the performance measurement baselines (scope, time, and cost) are established and then used as comparative measurements to the actual progress of the project.

These diagnostic metrics are used in risk management to trigger risk responses, assess the impacts of project changes, provide early warnings for potential problems, determine the need to update or develop contingency plans, and decide when to modify or cancel projects. Using earned value to evaluate risk exposure is an example of leveraging diagnostic metrics.

Retrospective Metrics

Retrospective metrics report after the fact on how the process worked and the process's overall health. Retrospective metrics are particularly useful in tracking trends and can be used to calibrate and improve the accuracy of corresponding predictive metrics for subsequent projects. This can be especially valuable for capturing lessons learned during and about the project risk management process to aide in organizational learning and growth.

Sensitivity Analysis

A sensitivity analysis evaluates the project risks against the project model to determine which risks would have the biggest impact on the project.

Not all risks are equally damaging. Schedule impact that does not affect resources is significant only when the estimated slippage exceeds any available float. For simple projects, a quick inspection of the plan using the risk list will determine what risks are likely to cause the most damage.

For more complex networks of activities, using a copy of the project database that has been entered into a scheduling tool is a fast way to detect the risks and combinations of risks that are most likely to result in project delay. Conducting a schedule "what if" analysis uses worst-case estimates to investigate the potential overall project impact.

Unlike activity slippage, which may or may not affect the overall delivery date (based on activities that have float), all adverse cost variances do have an impact on the budget.

It is important to understand your organization's cost accounting procedures, as not all cost impact is accounted for in the same way. If a risk results in an out-of-pocket expense for the project, then it impacts the budget directly. However, if the cost impact involves a capital purchase, then the project impact may be only a portion of the actual cost, and in some cases the entire expense may be accounted for elsewhere.

Overhead costs, such as conference rooms, copies, postage, etc., are rarely charged back to the project directly. Travel costs may be another expense that does not get allocated to the project. It may be beneficial to segregate potential direct cost variances from any that are indirect.

Sensitivity charts are used to visualize impacts (the best and worst outcome values) of different uncertain variables over their individual ranges. A tornado diagram is a type of sensitivity chart in which the variable with the highest impact is placed at the top of the chart and followed by other variables in descending order of impact.

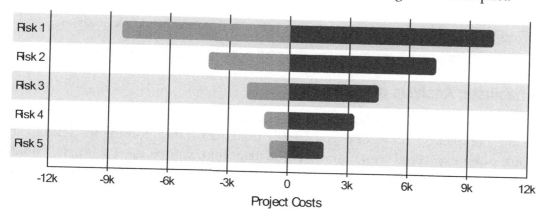

Figure 7-12: Tornado Diagram

PMBOK® Guide, page 338

System Dynamics

System dynamics are a particular application of influence diagrams used to identify risks within a project situation using feedback and feed-forward loops. System dynamics are utilized when there is a complex, non-linear relationship between entities and information and depict the impact of risk events on overall project results or a system's sensitivity to specific risks.

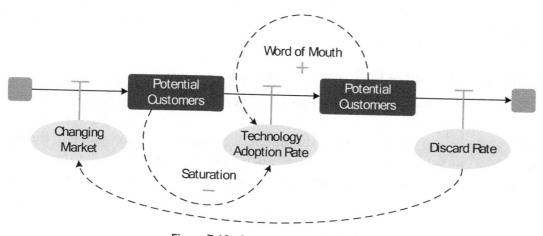

Figure 7-13: System Dynamics Model

Practice Standard for Project Risk Management, page 85

Perform Quantitative Risk Analysis: Outputs

The outputs of the Perform Quantitative Risk Analysis process are project document updates. Specifically, the risk register that was established during the Identify Risks process and updated throughout the Perform Qualitative Risk Analysis process is again updated with all of the information from the quantitative risk analysis.

After a quantitative risk analysis, the risk register can be updated with:

Probabilistic Analysis of the Project

Estimates are made of potential project schedule and cost outcomes listing the possible completion dates and costs with their associated confidence levels. This output, often expressed as a cumulative distribution, can be used with stakeholder risk tolerances to permit quantification of the cost and time contingency reserves. Such contingency reserves are needed to bring the risk of overrunning stated project objectives to a level acceptable to the organization.

Probability of Achieving Cost and Time Objectives

With the risks facing the project, the probability of achieving project objectives under the current plan can be estimated using quantitative risk analysis results.

Prioritized List of Quantified Risks

This list of risks includes those that pose the greatest threat or present the greatest opportunity to the project. These include the risks that may have the greatest effect on cost contingency and those that are most likely to influence the critical path. In some cases, these risks may be identified through a tornado diagram generated as a result of the simulation analyses.

Trends in Quantitative Risk Analysis Results

As the analysis is repeated, a trend that leads to conclusions affecting risk responses may become apparent. Organizational historical information on project schedule, cost, quality, and performance should reflect new insights gained through performing quantitative risk analysis. Such history may take the form of a quantitative risk analysis report. This report may be separate from, or linked to, the risk register.

Review Questions

Chapter 7

1. Based on information from your team, your project is estimated to cost $71,000. Upon completing the Monte Carlo analysis, you have been provided with the following data:

Probability %	Forecast
P0	$59,000
P10	$68,000
P20	$73,000
P30	$82,000
P40	$89,000
P50	$94,000
P60	$97,000
P70	$101,000
P80	$110,000
P90	$121,000
P100	$127,000

Your organization is very risk-averse and is seeking an 80% confidence level. What contingency percentage must be allocated?

A. 55%

B. 15%

C. 42%

D. 70%

2. The last project you managed for this client included 875 planned activities and used an allocated contingency of 10%. The current project is expected to have three times the number of activities, so you suggest a contingency allocation of 30%. This would be predicted using _____ metrics.

A. Diagnostic

B. Pareto

C. Predictive

D. Retrospective

3. Your team lead is concerned about the time and computer speed for running a Monte Carlo simulation. What technique should you suggest to be used in place of the Monte Carlo simulation?

A. Force field analysis

B. Analytic hierarchy process

C. System dynamics

D. Latin Hypercube

4. The organization is very sensitive to any risk impacting the project budget or schedule. You are working with your team and subject matter experts to conduct a quantitative risk analysis on the identified risks. Which statement is least accurate?

A. The outputs of quantitative risk analysis techniques are typically probability distributions.

B. A Monte Carlo simulation takes into consideration both cost and schedule risks.

C. A tornado diagram only represents schedule risk data.

D. Decisions trees are used for both schedule and cost risks.

5. Upon discussion with the work package owner, you learn that based on the vendor that is chosen, there are four potential durations for the work. There is a 20% chance of using a local vendor, which would result in a duration of 12 days; a 30% chance of using a domestic vendor, which would result in a duration of 18 days; and a 10% chance of using an international vendor, which would result in a duration of 27 days. The remaining possibility is to do the work in-house, which would result in a duration of 15 days. What is the best estimate to use?

    A. 16 days
    B. 17 days
    C. 10.5 days
    D. 11 days

6. A project that has a negative cost variance and an SPI less than 1.0 is:

    A. Over budget and ahead of schedule
    B. Under budget and behind schedule
    C. Over budget and behind schedule
    D. Under budget and ahead of schedule

7. Based on the performance measures indicated in the following table, what is the schedule variance (SV) for case 3?

Case	PV	AC	EV
1	$10,000	$8,000	$10,000
2	$12,000	$10,000	$11,000
3	$10,000	$8,000	$9,000
4	$10,000	$8,000	$8,000

    A. -$1,000
    B. $1,000
    C. $2,000
    D. -$2,000

8. As you evaluate a vendor bid of $350,000, you take into consideration the risk associated with potential delays. There is a 65% probability that the vendor will come in behind schedule at a cost of $125,000 and a 35% probability that the vendor will come in early for a savings of $50,000. Based on that information, what is the total value of the bid?

    A. $413,750
    B. $286,250
    C. $63,750
    D. $448,750

9. Which statement below is false regarding quantitative risk analysis?

    A. It is the process of numerically analyzing the effect of identified risks on overall project objectives.
    B. It is performed on risks that have been prioritized through qualitative risk analysis.
    C. It may be used to assign a numerical rating to individual risks or to evaluate the aggregate effect of all risks affecting the project.
    D. It is only conducted at the beginning of the project, before risk responses are made.

10. **Which statement is most accurate regarding Gaussian and beta distributions?**

    A. Gaussian distributions are also known as beta distributions.
    B. The Gaussian distribution has evenly applied distributions from the mean.
    C. The beta distribution is the same as a normal distribution.
    D. They are both known as PERT probability distributions.

11. **If a project has a 60% chance of a $100,000 profit and a 40% chance of a $100,000 loss, the expected monetary value of the project is:**

    A. $40,000 loss
    B. $100,000 profit
    C. $60,000 loss
    D. $20,000 profit

12. **Option A is estimated to take 24 days to complete, option B is estimated to take 16 days to complete, option C is estimated to take 10 days to complete, and option D is estimated to take 14 days to complete. The probability of each option is, respectively, 30%, 12%, 17%, and 41%. What is the best estimate for expected duration?**

    A. 16 days
    B. 15.8 days
    C. 16.6 days
    D. 17.3 days

13. **A Monte Carlo simulation uses a project model and runs multiple iterations with varying input values. The output of a Monte Carlo simulation is a:**

    A. Probability distribution
    B. Sensitivity analysis
    C. Tornado diagram
    D. Fault tree

14. **In a probability distribution:**

    A. The X axis represents likelihood, and the Y axis represents time or cost.
    B. The X axis represents time or cost, and the Y axis represents probability.
    C. The X and Y axes both indicate potential probability.
    D. The X and Y axes differ based on whether it is a beta or a triangular distribution.

15. **Upon evaluation of the project requirements, your product development team lead provides you with the following duration information:**

    If the product can be developed in-house with existing staff, the estimated duration is 14 days. If the product must be developed by a vendor, the estimated duration is 21 days. If a portion is developed in-house and a portion by the vendor, the estimated duration is 19 days. Based on the information you received, there is a 30% probability that the product can be developed fully in-house and a 50% probability that a portion can be developed in-house.

    Considering the risk, what is the best duration estimate?

    A. 18 days
    B. 19 days
    C. 15 days
    D. 16 days

Vocabulary Review   Chapter 7

Actual costs	Earned value	Retrospective metrics
Beta distribution	Expected monetary value analysis	Schedule performance index
Bowtie analysis	Latin Hypercube sampling	Schedule variance
Cost performance index	Lognormal distribution	Sensitivity analysis
Cost variance	Monte Carlo simulation	System dynamics
Critical chain project management	Normal (Gaussian) distribution	Tornado diagram
Decision tree	Planned value	Triangular distribution
Diagnostic metrics	Predictive metrics	Uniform distribution

1. _____ The amount of work budgeted between the start date and the status date

2. _____ Detailed, computer-intensive simulation approach to determining the value and probability of possible outcomes of a project objective such as a project schedule or cost estimate

3. _____ A type of sensitivity chart in which the variable with the highest impact is placed at the top of the chart and followed by other variables in descending order of impact

4. _____ A ratio comparing value earned to actual costs

5. _____ A particular application of influence diagrams used to identify risks within a project situation

6. _____ A method of planning and scheduling that places the emphasis on the resources that are required to complete the activities

7. _____ Analysis technique that evaluates the project risks against the project model to determine which risks will have the biggest impact on the project

8. _____ Metrics that are designed to provide current information about a system based on the latest available data

9. _____ The amount of money spent to complete the work of the project through the status date

10. _____ Value earned in the project based on the percentage of the budgeted work that is complete

11. _____ A ratio comparing value earned to value planned

12. _____ Calculation of a value such as weighted average or expected cost or benefit when the outcomes are uncertain

13. _____ A function that represents the distribution of many random variables as a symmetrical, bell-shaped graph

14. _____ A computerized simulation that applies a stratified approach, selecting a limited set of values from each strata or segment, rather than pulling all random variables

15. _____ The difference between the value earned and the actual costs

16. _____ A continuous probability distribution of a random variable whose logarithm is normally distributed

17. _____ Metrics that report after the fact on how the process worked and the process's overall health

18. _____ A bell-curve probability distribution showing the range and concentration of probabilities of different values

19. _____ Also known as a rectangular distribution, this is a distribution with constant probability

20. _____ Metrics that use current information to provide insight into future conditions

21. _____ The difference between the value earned and the value planned

22. _____ Facilitates the discovery of predecessors to project problems by incorporating both what comes before and what comes after a specific risk event

23. _____ Used to evaluate alternatives before selecting one of them to execute

24. _____ A continuous probability distribution with a probability density function shaped like a triangle and defined by three values: the minimum value a, the maximum value b, and the peak value c

Answer Key   Chapter 7

Chapter Exercise Answers

Exercise: Decision Tree

Part time --- 50% x 9 days = 4.5 days

Full time --- 10% x 4 days = 0.4 days

Junior Developer --- 40% x 16 days = 6.4 days

4.5 days + 0.4 days + 6.4 days = **11.3 days expected duration**

Exercise: Expected Monetary Value

Project A

.20 x ($10,000) = ($2,000)

.50 x $20,000 = $10,000

.30 x $50,000 = $15,000

($2,000) + $10,000 + $15,000 = **$23,000 EMV**

EMV of $23,000 + Initial Estimate of $30,000 = **$53,000 total value**

Project B

.40 x ($20,000) = ($8,000)

.30 x $30,000 = $9,000

.30 x $40,000 = $12,000

($8,000) + $9,000 + $12,000 = **$13,000 EMV**

EMV of $13,000 + Initial Estimate of $50,000 = **$63,000 total value**

Exercise: Earned Value - Schedule

Budget at completion (BAC) = $20,000

Percentage complete = 30%

Earned value (EV) = $6,000

Planned value (PV) = $8,000

Schedule variance (SV) = ($2,000)

Schedule performance index (SPI) = .75

What is the status of the schedule? 25% behind schedule

Exercise: Earned Value - Cost

Budget at completion (BAC) = $120,000

Percentage complete = 40%

Earned value (EV) = $48,000

Actual cost (AC) = $40,000

Cost variance (CV) = $8,000

Cost performance index (CPI) = 1.2

What is the status of the budget? 20% under budget

Review Question Answers

1. **Answer: A**

    An 80% confidence level would correspond to a total estimate of $110,000. This would include $39,000 in contingency above the estimate of $71,000. To calculate the contingency percentage, divide the forecast by the estimate and subtract 1 (Contingency % = (Forecast ÷ Estimate) – 1).

    ($110,000 ÷ $71,000) – 1 = 1.55 – 1 = 0.55 (55%)

2. **Answer: C**

    Predictive metrics use the past to predict the current situation via some type of measurement. If 875 activities needed a 10% contingency, three times that amount of activities would need a 30% contingency.

3. **Answer: D**

    A Latin Hypercube simulation takes values from stratified data, reducing the number of iterations and results. This is helpful when computer processing speed may be an issue.

4. **Answer: C**

    A tornado diagram, the output of a sensitivity analysis, only displays cost risk data, not schedule risk. This is due to the fact that schedule risk impacts would not be accounted for in the same manner, given the occurrence of float for concurrent activities, etc.

5. **Answer: B**

    Using a decision tree, multiply the probability of each scenario by the value of the scenario:

    Local = 0.2 x 12 = 2.4

    Domestic = 0.3 x 18 = 5.4

    International = 0.1 x 27 = 2.7

    In-house = 0.4 x 15 = 6

    SUM: 16.5.

    The closest answer, using the general rules of rounding, is 17 days.

6. **Answer: C**

    A negative cost variance indicates that the project is over budget. A schedule performance index (SPI) less than 1.0 indicates that the project is behind schedule.

7. **Answer: A**

    Schedule variance is calculated as earned value (EV) – planned value (PV).

    $9,000 – $10,000 = -$1,000

8. **Answer: A**

    Using an expected monetary value (EMV) analysis, multiply the probability of the outcome by its value. Sum the results and add that amount back to the original bid to calculate the total value.

    0.65 x $125,000 = $81,250

    0.35 x -$50,000 = -$17,500

    EMV = $63,750

    Total Value = $63,750 + $350,000 = $413,750

9. **Answer: D**

    A quantitative risk analysis may be conducted prior to planning the risk responses. However, it is not conducted only at the beginning of the project, as project data is necessary in order to conduct the analysis. The quantitative analysis should also be repeated throughout the project to evaluate the risk exposure of the project over time.

10. **Answer: B**

    A Gaussian distribution represents values that are evenly spread from the mean, whereas a beta distribution most often has some differences in the spread from the mean.

11. **Answer: D**

    Using an expected monetary value (EMV) analysis, multiply the probability of the outcome by its value and sum the results to determine the EMV.

    0.6 x $100,000 = $60,000

    0.4 x -$100,000 = -$40,000

    EMV = $20,000

12. **Answer: C**

    Using a decision tree, multiply each estimate by the value:

    A = 0.3 x 24 = 7.2

    B = 0.12 x 16 = 1.92

    C = 0.17 x 10 = 1.7

    D = 0.41 x 14 = 5.74

    Expected duration = 16.56

13. **Answer: A**

    The output of a Monte Carlo simulation is a probability distribution.

14. **Answer: B**

    In a probability distribution, the x axis (horizontal) represents the time or cost and the y axis (vertical) represents the probability.

15. **Answer: A**

    Using a decision tree, multiply each estimate by the value:

    In-house = 0.3 x 14 = 4.2

    Vendor = 0.2 x 21 = 4.2

    Split = 0.5 x 19 = 9.5

    Best estimate = 17.9

Vocabulary Review Answers

1. Planned value
2. Monte Carlo simulation
3. Tornado diagram
4. Cost performance index
5. System dynamics
6. Critical chain project management
7. Sensitivity analysis
8. Diagnostic metrics
9. Actual costs
10. Earned value
11. Schedule performance index
12. Expected monetary value analysis
13. Normal (Gaussian) distribution
14. Latin Hypercube sampling
15. Cost variance
16. Lognormal distribution
17. Retrospective metrics
18. Beta distribution
19. Uniform distribution
20. Predictive metrics
21. Schedule variance
22. Bowtie analysis
23. Decision tree
24. Triangular distribution

Risk Response Planning

Risk Response Planning

The objective of the Plan Risk Response process is to determine the set of actions which will most enhance the chances of project success while complying with the applicable organizational and project constraints.

In risk response planning, a response strategy is identified, an owner is assigned, and funding is allocated if necessary for each risk. Risk response planning involves finding ways to make the threat smaller or eliminate it entirely, as well as finding ways to make positive risks more likely or greater in impact.

Risk responses should be appropriate to the level and priority of each risk while remaining cost-effective and realistic within the context of the project. The chosen responses are reviewed over the life of the project for appropriateness as more information about the project becomes known.

Responses may include:

- Doing something to eliminate a threat before it happens
- Doing something to ensure that an opportunity is realized
- Decreasing the probability and/or impact of a threat
- Increasing the probability and/or impact of an opportunity

These risk responses may have effects on the project objectives and can generate additional risks. These additional risks, which arise directly as a result of implementing a risk response, are known as secondary risks. The secondary risks must be analyzed and planned for as well.

It may be impossible to completely eliminate a risk even with the best possible response. The risk that remains after a risk response is implemented is known as a residual risk.

For moderate-level risks, contingency plans may be developed. A contingency plan, or contingent response strategy, is planned in advance but only implemented when the risk event or the risk trigger occurs. Use of a contingency plan is known as active risk acceptance.

Some risks and risk responses may also require the need for a fallback plan. Like a contingency plan, the fallback plan is planned in advance, but it is only implemented when the first planned response is not effective. That original response may have been a proactive strategy (such as avoidance, mitigation, or transference) or a contingency plan. You can think of a fallback plan as a "Plan B."

Critical Success Factors

Critical success factors for risk response planning include:

Communication

Appropriate communication includes openly addressing organizational causes of risk.

Defined Roles and Responsibilities

Risk-related roles and responsibilities must be clearly communicated and agreed upon.

Allocated Resources

Resources including human resources, budget, and time must be available and allocated,

Risk Response Understanding

An understanding of the implications and interactions between risks and risk responses is necessary.

Comprehensive Risk Strategies Employed

Strategies should address both threats and opportunities.

Strategic and Tactical Response Planning

Responses are planned strategically, validated tactically, and integrated into the project management plan.

Response Planning Sequence

1. Identify potential responses.
2. Select the most appropriate response.
3. Tactically plan actions and provide resources.
4. Update the risk register.
5. Consider any residual risks.
   - If residual risk is not acceptable, repeat the process.
6. Update the project management plan and all associated documents.

Risk Responses

Whether responding to threats or opportunities, the strategies must be timely and the selected effort must be appropriate to the severity of the risk. Avoid spending more money preventing the risk than the impact of the risk would cost if it were to occur.

Often, multiple responses can each partially address the same risk, and one response can be used to address more than one risk, especially if it addresses a root cause of multiple risks.

Regardless of the risk response strategy pursued, it is critical that the team, stakeholders, and/or other experts are involved in selecting the most appropriate strategy.

Proactive	Reactive
BEFORE the risk has occurred:	**AFTER the risk has occurred:**

Determine the most appropriate response strategy
 	
 • Mitigate   • Enhance
 • Avoid   • Exploit
 • Transfer   • Share
	• Implement contingency plan
	 • Implement a fallback plan
	    (if original response is not adequate)
	 • Implement a workaround
	    (if there is no contingency plan)

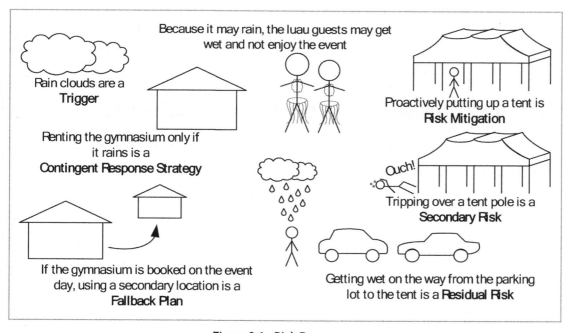

Figure 8-1: Risk Responses

Plan Risk Responses Process

After the risks are analyzed qualitatively and perhaps quantitatively, the responses to those risks are assessed.

Plan Risk Responses: Inputs, Tools and Techniques, and Outputs

Inputs	Tools and Techniques	Outputs
1. Risk management plan	1. Strategies for negative risks or threats	1. Project management plan updates
2. Risk register	2. Strategies for positive risks or opportunities	2. Project documents updates
	3. Contingent response strategies	
	4. Expert judgment	

Figure 8-2: Plan Risk Responses ITTOs

PMBOK® Guide, page 342

Plan Risk Responses: Inputs

Risk Management Plan

The risk management plan, a subsidiary plan, provides details and guidance on planning risk responses, including information on the contingency budget allocation and stakeholder and organizational risk tolerances.

Risk Register

The risk register, an output of the Identify Risks process, is the basis from which the responses will be planned. This process includes using the qualitative and potentially the quantitative evaluations to determine which responses will be most appropriate given the priority of the risk.

Plan Risk Responses: Tools and Techniques

PMBOK® Guide tools and techniques for risk response planning include:

- Strategies for negative risk or threats
- Strategies for positive risks or opportunities
- Contingent response strategies

Additional tools and techniques that may be used for risk response planning, as described in the *Practice Standard for Project Risk Management*, include:

- Creativity techniques
- Scenario analysis
- Multi-criterion selection techniques
- Critical chain project management (CCPM)
- Other techniques

Strategies for Negative Risks or Threats

For project threats, there are four potential responses: avoid, transfer, mitigate, and accept.

Avoid

Risk avoidance involves changing the project management plan to eliminate the threat entirely. Some risks that arise early in the project can be avoided by clarifying requirements, obtaining information, improving communication, or acquiring expertise.

The project manager may also isolate the project objectives from the risk's impact or change the objective that is in jeopardy. For example, if the risk identified exceeds the project's budget, the budget may be increased to accommodate for that risk. That would be considered risk avoidance.

Examples of risk avoidance include extending the schedule, changing the strategy, or reducing scope. Shutting down the project entirely is the most radical avoidance strategy.

Transfer

Risk transference requires shifting some or all of the negative impact of a threat, along with ownership of the response, to a third party. Transferring the risk simply gives another party responsibility for its management. It does not eliminate the risk.

Transferring liability for risks is most effective when dealing with financial risk exposure. Risk transference nearly always involves payment of a risk premium to the party taking on the risk.

Transference tools can be quite diverse and include the use of insurance, performance bonds, warranties, guarantees, etc. Contracts may be used to transfer liability for specified risks to another party.

From an exam perspective, keep in mind that the act of transferring the risk may also serve to mitigate the risk. If a scenario involves some type of contractual relationship, assume first that the response strategy is transfer.

Mitigate

Risk mitigation is a reduction in the probability and/or impact of an adverse risk event to a range within acceptable threshold limits. Taking early action to reduce the probability and/or impact of a risk occurring on the project is often more effective than trying to repair the damage after the risk has occurred.

Adopting a less complex process, conducting more tests, or choosing a more stable supplier are examples of mitigation actions. Mitigation may require prototype development to reduce the risk of scaling up from a bench-scale model of a process or product. When it is not possible to reduce the probability of a risk, a mitigation response might address the risk impact by targeting linkages that determine the severity. For example, designing redundancy into a system may reduce the impact from a failure of an original component.

Accept

This strategy exists because it is seldom possible to eliminate all threats from a project. Risk acceptance indicates that the project team has decided not to change the project management plan to deal with a risk or is unable to identify a suitable response strategy.

This strategy can be either passive or active. Passive acceptance requires no action except documentation of the strategy and leaves the project team to deal with risks as they occur.

Active acceptance involves establishing a contingency reserve, including amounts of time, money, or resources to handle the risks, and defining contingency plans and/or contingent response strategies.

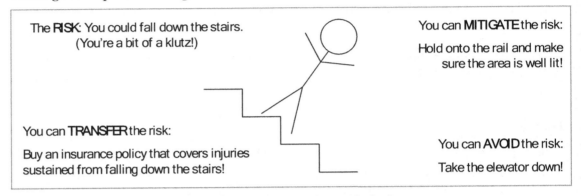

The **RISK**: You could fall down the stairs. (You're a bit of a klutz!)

You can **MITIGATE** the risk:
Hold onto the rail and make sure the area is well lit!

You can **TRANSFER** the risk:
Buy an insurance policy that covers injuries sustained from falling down the stairs!

You can **AVOID** the risk:
Take the elevator down!

Figure 8-3: Responses to a Negative Risk/Threat

Strategies for Positive Risks or Opportunities

For project opportunities, there are four potential responses: exploit, share, enhance, and accept.

Exploit

This strategy may be selected for risks with positive impacts where the organization wishes to ensure that the opportunity is realized. This strategy seeks to eliminate the uncertainty associated with a particular upside risk by ensuring that the opportunity is definitely capitalized upon.

Examples of directly exploiting responses include assigning an organization's most talented resources to the project to reduce the time to completion or providing a lower cost than originally planned.

Share

Sharing a positive risk involves allocating some or all of the ownership of the opportunity to a third party who is best able to capture the opportunity for the benefit of the project.

Sharing can include forming risk-sharing partnerships, teams, special-purpose companies, or joint ventures, all of which can be established with the express purpose of taking advantage of the opportunity so that all parties gain from their actions.

Enhance

This strategy is used to increase the probability and/or positive impacts of an opportunity. Identifying and maximizing key drivers of positive-impact risks may increase the probability of their occurrence.

Examples of enhancing opportunities include adding more resources to an activity to finish it early.

Accept

Accepting an opportunity is being ready and willing to take advantage of it if it comes along but not actively pursuing it.

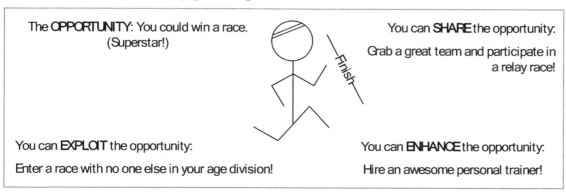

The **OPPORTUNITY**: You could win a race. (Superstar!)

You can **SHARE** the opportunity:
Grab a great team and participate in a relay race!

You can **EXPLOIT** the opportunity:
Enter a race with no one else in your age division!

You can **ENHANCE** the opportunity:
Hire an awesome personal trainer!

Figure 8-4: Responses to a Positive Risk/Opportunity

Exam Hint:

The risk responses for threats mirror the responses for opportunities:

- Avoidance is to threats as exploitation is to opportunities: both involve modifying the plan to eliminate the uncertainty.

- Transference is to threats as sharing is to opportunities: both involve entering into a contractual relationship with an external party.

- Mitigation is to threats as enhancement is to opportunities: both involve modifying the plan to minimize the uncertainty.

- Acceptance is used for both. However, remember that acceptance may be passive or active for threats.

Contingent Response Strategies

Some responses are designed for use only if certain events occur. For some risks, it is appropriate for the project team to make a response plan that will only be executed under certain predefined conditions if it is believed that there will be sufficient warning to implement the plan.

Events that might trigger a contingency response, such as missing intermediate milestones or gaining higher priority with a supplier, should be defined and tracked.

A contingency plan (or contingent response strategy) is an alternative plan that will be used if a possible foreseen risk event becomes a reality. A contingency plan serves to reduce or mitigate the negative impact of a risk event and answer the questions of what action will take place and how, where, when it will take place.

While contingency plans can significantly increase the chances for project success, it is critical that activation guidelines are decided and clearly documented. This includes documenting a cost estimate and identifying the source of funding. Team members must be aware of the contingency plan to minimize surprise and resistance.

If a contingency plan is not developed, the project team may implement a workaround. A workaround is a response to a negative risk that has occurred. A workaround is not planned in advance of the occurrence of the risk event.

Reserve Estimation

Contingency funds are established to cover both identified and unknown project risks. How much money will be spent and when and where it will be spent are not known until the risk event occurs.

The size and amount of a contingency reserve depends on the uncertainty of the particular project. In practice, contingencies run about 10% in projects similar to past projects and in the 20-60% range for new or poorly defined projects.

A contingency reserve is typically divided into budget and management reserve funds for control purposes.

Budget Contingency Reserves

Budget contingency reserves (typically known as "contingency") are reserves that are identified for specific work packages or segments of a project found in the baseline budget or WBS. The reserve amount is determined by costing out the accepted contingency or recovery plan.

Distributing budget reserves is the responsibility of both the project manager and the team members responsible for implementing the specific segment of the project. If the risk does not materialize, the funds are removed from the budget reserve.

Management Reserves

Management reserve funds are needed to cover major unforeseen risks and are applied to the total project. These risks include any major scope changes that develop while the project is in progress. Management reserves are independent of budget reserves and are controlled by the owner of the project, usually the sponsor.

Activity	Estimate	Contingency	Baseline
Analysis	$600	$60	$660
Design	$400	$40	$440
Development	$100	$10	$110
Subtotal	$1,100	$110	$1,210
Management reserve	--	--	$40
Total Project Budget			$1,250

In this example, you can see that contingency was allocated at 10% for each of the major activities. The estimate plus the contingency adds up to the baseline. Notice how there is an additional allocation for management reserve. The baseline plus the management reserve equals the total project budget.

Time Buffers

Managers use time buffers to cushion against potential delays in the project. Like contingency funds, the amount of time kept as a buffer is dependent upon the relative uncertainty of the project. The strategy is to assign extra time at critical moments in the project.

Creativity Techniques

Creativity techniques may be used to determine potential responses. There are a number of creativity techniques used to identify risk responses that were discussed in earlier chapters of this book, including:

- Force field analysis – Evaluating the forces for and against the project
- Delphi technique – Capturing information anonymously from experts, consolidating that information, and redistributing it for further comment and/or agreement
- Root–cause analysis – Identifying the root causes of the risks
- Brainstorming – Free-form thinking to create a variety of response possibilities
- Nominal group technique – Enhancing brainstorming by adding a voting process
- Decision tree analysis – Applying probability and impact to various options to guide decision-making
- Interviews – Conducting one-on-one or group sessions to elicit information

Scenario Analysis

Scenario analysis defines several alternative scenarios and evaluates them for appropriate and cost-effective responses. If the organization has control of the scenarios, the alternatives and responses can be evaluated. If it does not, the analysis can determine effective and necessary contingency planning.

Multi-Criterion Selection Techniques

As in qualitative risk analysis, various available options are evaluated against defined, weighted criteria in order to score them.

Criterion	Weight	Response A		Response B	
		Rating	Points	Rating	Points
Accessibility	3	4	12	7	21
Price	7	8	56	5	35
Implementation	4	10	40	6	24
Ease	6	5	30	10	60
Score			138		140

Critical Chain Project Management (CCPM)

As discussed in Chapter 7, CCPM is a method of planning and managing projects that focuses on the resources that are required to complete project activities. Resources are levelly loaded, but there is flexibility in the start times and resources so they can be switched between activities as needed in order to meet the project schedule objectives.

Buffers are used to monitor and manage schedule performance. Buffers in CCPM, particularly the project buffer at the end, are equivalent to schedule reserves.

CCPM is often seen as a way to compress the schedule because of the underlying assumption that all estimates are padded and can be reduced. The assumption is that most durations are overestimated, when in reality, most duration estimates are underestimated.

Other Techniques

Many of the techniques discussed in earlier chapters can also be used to plan risk responses, including:

- Checklists – Risk checklists developed by the organization may provide insight into the types of responses that were applied on previous projects.
- Decision trees and expected monetary value analyses – The evaluation of the most appropriate response can include an evaluation of the probability of success and/or the probability of various costs, allowing for more effective risk response decision-making.

- Force field analysis – An evaluation of the forces for and the forces against the project and/or the risk responses can be used to evaluate the appropriateness of those responses.

- Industry knowledge base – This is utilized as a basis of industry-specific information pertaining to risk responses.

- Interviews – Working with key stakeholders, team members, risk experts, and organizational subject matter experts can provide insight helpful for selecting the appropriate responses.

- Post-project reviews, lessons learned, and historical information – Responses implemented on previous projects and the efficacy of those responses are captured in various organizational process assets.

- Prompt lists – Prompt lists allow for the categorization of risks and can stimulate creativity surrounding response identification.

- Quantitative risk analysis – Data gleaned from the quantitative analysis allows for responses to be evaluated based on cost and/or schedule impact.

- Root-cause analysis – Identifying root causes of risks enables more efficient targeting of risk responses.

Plan Risk Responses: Outputs

The outputs of the Plan Risk Responses process include project document updates and project management plan updates.

Project Document Updates

Once the appropriate responses are chosen and agreed upon, they are included in the risk register. The risk register should be written to a level of detail that corresponds with the priority ranking and the planned response. The high and moderate risks are often addressed in detail. Risks judged to be low priority are included in a watchlist for periodic monitoring.

The risk register is updated to include:

Residual Risks

Residual risks are risks that remain after risk response planning and risks that have been accepted, for which contingency plans and fallback plans can be created. Residual risks should be properly documented and reviewed throughout the project to see if their ranking changes.

Contingency Plans

These plans describe the specific actions that will be taken if a threat occurs. Contingency plans are documented in advanced and are considered a form of active risk acceptance.

Risk Response Owners

A key concept in risk response planning is that the project manager does not have to do everything and neither does the team. Each risk must be assigned to an owner who may help develop the risk response and who will carry out the risk response. The risk response owner can be a stakeholder or a team member.

Secondary Risks

An analysis of the new risks created by the implementation of the selected risk response strategies should be included in risk response planning. Frequently, what is done to respond to one risk will cause other risks to occur.

For example, a risk of fire can be allocated to an insurance company, potentially causing the risk of cash flow problems. Cash flow should then be analyzed and added to the risk management process if appropriate.

Project Management Plan Updates

On the PMI-RMP exam, it is common for the questions ask, "What do you do next?" or "What is the first thing you do?" If you get a question that states something to the effect of "You have planned your risk responses, so what is the next thing you do?" the correct answer is to update your project management plan, baselines, and/or subsidiary plans. The act of getting approval on the project risk responses is assumed to be part of this process. If you have finished the process of planning your risk responses, this implies that they are approved.

A good way to remember the need to update your plans is that a response is work, work is scope, and if I am adding scope to my project, I need to be sure that my project management plan and baselines reflect that work.

A number of subsidiary plans are also updated with the information from the Plan Risk Responses process. The following items may be updated to reflect changes in process and practice driven by the risk responses.

- Schedule management plan - May include changes in tolerance related to resource loading and leveling
- Cost management plan - May include changes in tolerance related to cost accounting, tracking, reports, and consumption of contingency reserves
- Quality management plan - May include changes related to requirements, quality assurance, or quality control
- Procurement management plan - May be updated to include changes in strategy, such as alterations in the make-or-buy decision or contract type(s)
- Human resource management plan – May be updated to reflect changes in project organizational structure and resource applications and may include changes in tolerance or behavior related to staff allocation and resource loading
- Scope, schedule, and cost performance baselines – May be updated to reflect omitted work or new work that has been approved and generated by the risk responses.

Review Questions   Chapter 8

1. The difference between the cost baseline and the total project budget can be best described as:

   A. They are synonymous.
   B. The total project budget includes management reserve, and the cost baseline does not.
   C. The cost baseline includes management reserve, and the total project budget does not.
   D. The total project budget is managed by the project manager, and the cost baseline is managed by the team.

2. Your client requires a major scope change due to a change in the market conditions. The scope change will add costs to the project. You currently have funding in your budget contingency reserve. What should you do?

   A. Escalate to the sponsor to inquire about the application of management reserve funds
   B. Utilize the contingency reserve until it is exhausted and then escalate if necessary
   C. Deny the change
   D. Ask the client for additional funding to cover the scope change

3. There was a software risk associated with the infrastructure project. To mitigate the risk, you leveraged a software provider that has been known to be compatible with your organization's systems. However, upon install, you realize that the new software is causing a major problem. What is the next thing you do?

   A. Implement the contingent response strategy
   B. Implement the residual risk plan
   C. Implement the risk mitigation strategy
   D. Implement the fallback plan

4. You are the project manager of ABC project. The project is being executed in an earthquake-prone area. To take care of this you buy insurance for earthquakes. This is an example of:

   A. Risk mitigation
   B. Transfer of risk
   C. Risk contingency planning
   D. Accepting the consequences passively

5. One of the risks that have been identified for your current project is the attrition of team members. Midway through the project, you notice that the morale and motivation of the team members is going down. You think that this is a precursor to people leaving the organization. For this risk, low motivation is an example of:

   A. A work-around
   B. A trigger
   C. Risk monitoring
   D. Risk planning

6. You are managing the project of planning a party for your company employees. There is a risk that the employees will not come to the party. You decide to not take any action against this, as the likelihood of this is low. Which risk response strategy are you following?

   A. Acceptance
   B. Avoidance
   C. Mitigation
   D. Transference

7. There is a meeting in Europe for the organization's senior leadership team. To reduce the risk associated with having the executives all on one plane, you send no more than two executives on the same flight. What risk strategy are you using?

   A. Risk avoidance
   B. Risk transference
   C. Active risk acceptance
   D. Risk mitigation

8. There is a potential opportunity if your product is first to market. You decide to team up with another business in order to increase the chances that you will make it to market first. What risk strategy are you using?

   A. Enhancement
   B. Sharing
   C. Exploitation
   D. Teaming agreement

9. Upon evaluation of a complex construction project, your sponsor has asked that you transfer some of the risk. Which of the following should you consider?

   A. Entering into a contract with a vendor who has specialized knowledge of the geographic issues and concerns of the region
   B. Assigning a portion of the work to another team within the organization
   C. Having your team members conduct a geological study of the work area
   D. Identifying a vendor that can ensure that the project will deliver early

10. There is a risk that pedestrians could walk on the new sidewalks before the concrete has cured. As such, your team places caution signs near the sidewalks. This is an example of what risk response strategy?

    A. Share
    B. Exploit
    C. Avoid
    D. Mitigate

11. There is an opportunity to provide a service for one of the largest companies in the region. To improve your chances of getting the job, you decide to partner with another firm to demonstrate that you have the manpower required to complete the job. This is an example of what risk response strategy?

    A. Exploit
    B. Mitigate
    C. Share
    D. Enhance

12. The implementation of selected risk response strategies may create:
    A. Secondary risks
    B. Emergent risks
    C. Contingent risks
    D. Residual risks

13. An output of risk response planning is:
    A. Identified risks
    B. Prioritized list of risks
    C. Identified impacts
    D. Residual risks

14. You were in the middle of a three-year project to deploy new technology to 15 field offices across the country. A tornado caused power outages just when the upgrade was nearing completion. When the power was restored, all of the project reports and historical data were lost with no way of retrieving them. What should have been done to mitigate this risk?
    A. You should have purchased insurance.
    B. You should have scheduled the installation outside of the tornado season.
    C. You should have monitored the weather and had a contingency plan.
    D. You should have planned for a reserve fund.

15. Because there was a risk of rain during an outdoor event, the team decided to put a tent over the main banquet area. A risk has now been identified that the tent may become unsecured with high wind. The possibility of the tent becoming unsecured is an example of:
    A. An emergent risk
    B. A residual risk
    C. A contingent risk
    D. A secondary risk

Vocabulary Review   Chapter 8

Accept   Exploit   Scenario analysis

Active acceptance   Fallback plan   Secondary risk

Avoid   Management reserve   Share

Budget contingency reserve   Mitigate   Transfer

Contingent response strategy   Multi-criteria selection technique   Trigger

Enhance   Residual risk

1. _____   A risk that arises as an outcome of implementing a risk response

2. _____   Changing the plan to ensure that a risk will be realized

3. _____   Actions planned in advance but only implemented when the primary response is not effective

4. _____   Defining a contingent response strategy or allocating contingency time or money to a risk

5. _____   Changing the plan to reduce the probability and/or impact of a risk

6. _____   Defines several alternative scenarios, which are then evaluated for appropriate and cost-effective responses

7. _____   A financial allocation for known-unknown risks managed by the project manager

8. _____   Shifting the negative impact of the risk to a third party in exchange for a premium

9. _____   Changing the plan to increase the probability and/or impact of the risk

10. _____   A financial allocation for unknown-unknown risks managed by the project sponsor or owner

11. _____   Changing the plan to eliminate the threat

12. _____   Planned in advance but only intended for use if the risk event occurs

13. _____   Various options available are evaluated against defined, weighted criteria in order to score the options

14. _____   Risk that remains after actions have been taken

15. _____   Shifting a portion of the ownership of the project to a third party that could best leverage the opportunity

16. _____   Acknowledging the risk without changing the plan

17. _____   A precursor event that indicates that a risk event has or is about to occur

Answer Key   **Chapter 8**

Review Question Answers

1. **Answer: B**

   The cost baseline includes the estimate and the contingency but not the management reserve. The total project budget includes the cost baseline plus the management reserve.

2. **Answer: A**

   Contingency reserve is allocated for "known-unknown" risks. These risks are known, but it is impossible to determine whether they will occur. Because the change in market conditions was not identified as a risk, contingency should not be used. Instead, the situation should be escalated to the sponsor for approval to use management reserve funds.

3. **Answer: D**

   Because the risk was already mitigated (unsuccessfully), an initial response was already applied. The next step is to implement the fallback plan ("Plan B").

4. **Answer: B**

   Purchasing insurance is risk transference. Risk transfer shifts some or all of the impact to a third party in exchange for a premium.

5. **Answer: B**

   A trigger is precursor event that indicates that a risk is about to happen or has happened. In this case, low motivation is a precursor to people leaving the organization.

6. **Answer: A**

   Taking no action is considered passive acceptance.

7. **Answer: D**

   The act of sending two executives reduced the risk. Therefore, this is a mitigation response. A risk avoidance method would be to put no executives on any flights.

8. **Answer: B**

   Partnering up with another company is risk sharing.

9. **Answer: A**

   Transference shifts the ownership of a negative risk to a third party. Because transference involves a contractual relationship, it cannot be handled within the organization. Transference is for negative risks, not opportunities.

10. **Answer: D**

    Because the caution signs will not eliminate the chance of someone walking on the concrete, they are considered a form of mitigation.

11. **Answer: C**

    Partnering up with another company is risk sharing.

12. Answer: A

A risk that arises as an outcome of implementing a risk response is known as a secondary risk. Emergent risks are risks that could not have been identified earlier in the project. Residual risks are risks that remain after actions (mitigations) have been taken. There is no such thing as a contingent risk.

13. Answer: D

Residual risks are an output of risk response planning. For risks that are going to be mitigated, there may be residual risks. Residual risks cannot be identified until after mitigation responses are planned.

14. Answer: B

To mitigate the risk (reduce the probability), the installation should have been scheduled outside of the tornado season. Purchasing insurance is an example of transference. Monitoring the weather and having a contingency plan is practicing active risk acceptance, as is planning for reserve.

15. Answer: D

A secondary risk is a risk that arises as an outcome of implementing a risk response. Putting up the tent was a risk response. Therefore, the tent becoming unsecured is a secondary risk.

Vocabulary Review Answers

1. Secondary risk
2. Exploit
3. Fallback plan
4. Active acceptance
5. Mitigate
6. Scenario analysis
7. Budget contingency reserve
8. Transfer
9. Enhance
10. Management reserve
11. Avoid
12. Contingent response strategy
13. Multi-criteria selection technique
14. Residual risk
15. Share
16. Accept
17. Trigger

Risk Monitoring and Controlling

9

Risk Monitoring and Controlling

Risk monitoring and controlling is an ongoing, iterative process conducted from project initiation to project completion. Multiple project participants are involved with risk monitoring and controlling, including the project manager, project sponsor, various stakeholders, subject matter experts, risk champion, risk response owners, and action owners. It is not feasible for the project manager to effectively control risks alone.

The project environment and progress is monitored for the occurrence of risk triggers. The watchlist is revisited to see if additional risk responses are needed, and the need to recommend corrective actions and change requests is considered. Corrective actions may need to be adjusted to align with the severity of the actual risk events.

Communication regarding risk status is a key component of risk control. This can include collecting and sharing risk status with team members, communicating with stakeholders about specific risks, and creating a database of risk data that may be used throughout the organization on other projects.

Risk processes are evaluated and audited. This includes monitoring residual risks, ensuring that the risk management plan is being executed and that it is effective, evaluating assumptions to ensure that they are still valid, and performing variance and trend analysis on the project performance data. The watchlist, the risk management and response plans, and the project management plan are updated to reflect the current and changed status of the project as necessary.

Contingency reserves are evaluated and monitored for application and changes based on the project progress. This reserve analysis technique has been mentioned previously.

As new risks are identified throughout project monitoring and controlling, the risk management planning processes is conducted iteratively, including qualitative and quantitative risk analysis and risk response planning.

This is also the process during which the need for workarounds is determined. A workaround is a response to a realized negative risk. Workarounds are completely reactive and are not planned in advance. While implementing workarounds is considered the least optimal situation, it is not possible to identify all possible project risks, and workarounds are often necessary.

Project Risk Reports

Monitoring and controlling risks for the project must include timely, efficient, and effective communication about the project risk management. The format, details, and frequency of risk reporting are documented within the project risk management plan, but if that communication appears to be ineffective at any time, it should be revisited.

Information to be communicated on a regular basis includes but is not limited to:

- Top risk list – A list of the highest-priority risks currently open
- Risks that have transitioned to issues – Threats that have occurred and are now classified as issues
- Risk outcomes – The results of risks that occurred, their impacts, the effect of any risk strategies or responses, etc.
- Risk response metrics – An analysis of responses that have been implemented, their cost and schedule impacts, and their effectiveness
- Risk reserve status – Reports of remaining contingency reserve and reserve that has been utilized

Quality Tools

There are seven basic quality tools that can also be applied to project risk management.

1. Cause and effect diagram
2. Flowchart
3. Checksheet
4. Pareto chart
5. Histogram
6. Control chart
7. Scatter diagram

Tool	Description	Example
Cause and Effect Diagram	The cause and effect diagram is a tool that provides a visualization of how various factors are linked to potential problems or effects. This tool is used to identify root causes of project risks in order to be more efficient in planning appropriate responses. A cause and effect diagram is also known as a fishbone or Ishikawa diagram.	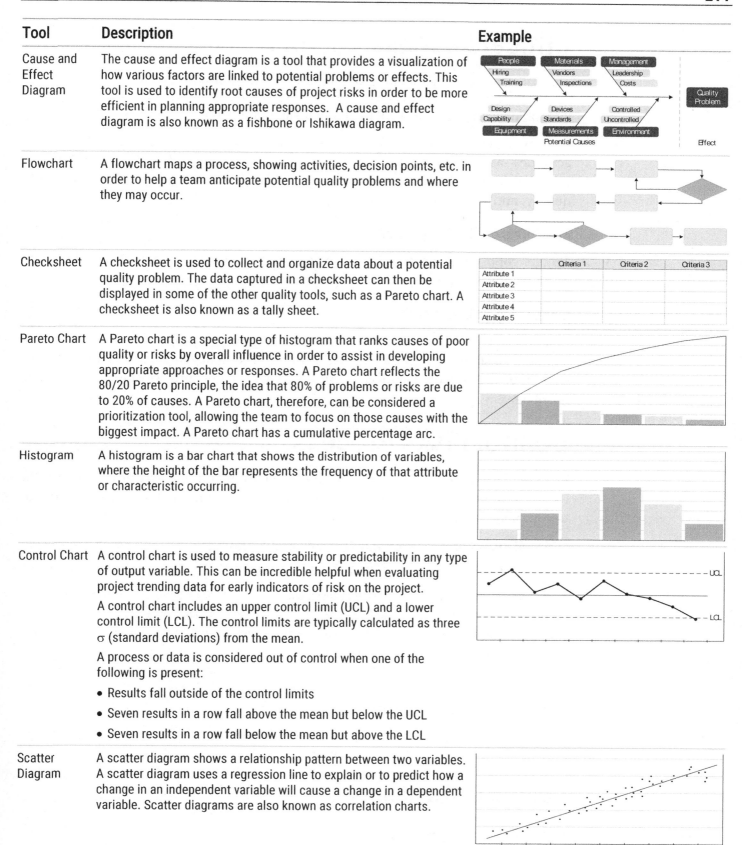
Flowchart	A flowchart maps a process, showing activities, decision points, etc. in order to help a team anticipate potential quality problems and where they may occur.	
Checksheet	A checksheet is used to collect and organize data about a potential quality problem. The data captured in a checksheet can then be displayed in some of the other quality tools, such as a Pareto chart. A checksheet is also known as a tally sheet.	
Pareto Chart	A Pareto chart is a special type of histogram that ranks causes of poor quality or risks by overall influence in order to assist in developing appropriate approaches or responses. A Pareto chart reflects the 80/20 Pareto principle, the idea that 80% of problems or risks are due to 20% of causes. A Pareto chart, therefore, can be considered a prioritization tool, allowing the team to focus on those causes with the biggest impact. A Pareto chart has a cumulative percentage arc.	
Histogram	A histogram is a bar chart that shows the distribution of variables, where the height of the bar represents the frequency of that attribute or characteristic occurring.	
Control Chart	A control chart is used to measure stability or predictability in any type of output variable. This can be incredible helpful when evaluating project trending data for early indicators of risk on the project. A control chart includes an upper control limit (UCL) and a lower control limit (LCL). The control limits are typically calculated as three σ (standard deviations) from the mean. A process or data is considered out of control when one of the following is present: • Results fall outside of the control limits • Seven results in a row fall above the mean but below the UCL • Seven results in a row fall below the mean but above the LCL	
Scatter Diagram	A scatter diagram shows a relationship pattern between two variables. A scatter diagram uses a regression line to explain or to predict how a change in an independent variable will cause a change in a dependent variable. Scatter diagrams are also known as correlation charts.	

Figure 9-1: Seven Basic Quality Tools

PMBOK® Guide, page 239

Critical Success Factors

The critical success factors for risk monitoring and controlling include:

Integration with Overall Project Monitoring and Controlling

Risk management activities must be fully integrated with the project management activities associated with project monitoring and controlling, as the two are inextricably linked. This specifically includes integration between the cost, schedule, quality, and scope requirements and plans.

Monitoring of Risk Trigger Conditions

Trigger conditions dictate the need to enact the project risk responses and thus must be monitored in a consistent and ongoing manner.

Maintaining Risk Awareness

Risk management activities are considered a key part of project status meetings and should be a standing agenda item. In addition, risk management status and activities should be documented and communicated within the project status reports and dashboards.

Control Risks Process

The Control Risks process is an ongoing evaluation and analysis of the project and its risk status. It is considered an iterative process and occurs from project initiation to completion.

Control Risks: Inputs, Tools and Techniques, and Outputs		
Inputs	Tools and Techniques	Outputs
1. Project management plan	1. Risk reassessment	1. Work performance information
2. Risk register	2. Risk audits	2. Change requests
3. Work performance data	3. Variance and trend analysis	3. Project management plan updates
4. Work performance reports	4. Technical performance measurement	4. Project documents updates
	5. Reserve analysis	5. Organizational Process Assets updates
	6. Meetings	

Figure 9-2: Control Risks ITTOs

PMBOK® Guide, page 349

Control Risks: Inputs

Project Management Plan

The project management plan provides details and instruction for the overall management of the project, including the project performance measurement baselines (scope, schedule, and cost) and the subsidiary plans.

As risk management cannot be separated from project management, the project management plan is a critical input. Baselines are used to evaluate any type of variance, indicating possible risks to the project. Subsidiary plans are used to ensure appropriate handling of the various aspects of the project from a risk perspective.

Risk Register

The risk register contains all of the individual risks, their triggers, analyses, selected responses, etc., which are used to control the risks.

Work Performance Data

Work performance data, an output of the Direct and Manage Project Work process, comprises the raw data and details of the project progress. This can include percentage of work complete, work progress, actual money spent, quality measurements, etc.

Work Performance Reports

Work performance reports, an output of the Monitor and Control Project Work process, are the status reports for the project. The work performance reports are used to evaluate the progress of the project and identify any variances and trends that may indicate uncertainty.

Control Risks: Tools and Techniques

The *PMBOK® Guide* techniques that the project manager and project team may use while monitoring and controlling the project risks include:

- Risk reassessment
- Risk audits
- Variance and trend analysis
- Technical performance measurement
- Reserve analysis
- Status meetings

In addition, the *Practice Standard for Project Risk Management* offers two additional techniques:

- Critical chain project management (CCPM)
- Workarounds

Risk Reassessment

Monitoring project risks often results in the identification of new risks, the reassessment of current risks, and the closing of risks that are outdated. Project risk reassessments should be regularly scheduled. The amount of repetition and level of detail that is appropriate depends on how the project progresses relative to its objectives. Typically, the risk owner is responsible for ensuring that these risk reassessments occur on an appropriate basis.

Risk Audits

Risk audits examine and document the effectiveness of risk responses in dealing with identified risks and their root causes, as well as the effectiveness of the overall risk management process. The project manager is responsible for ensuring that risk audits are performed at an appropriate frequency as defined in the project's risk management plan.

Risk audits may be included during routine project review meetings, or separate risk audit meetings may be held. The format and objectives of each audit should be clearly defined before the audit is conducted. The risk audit results in the identification of lessons learned for the project and for future projects in the organization.

As the project manager, it is important to be sensitive to team members' perceptions of the risk audits. Some team members may feel that a risk audit is judgmental and/or a waste of time. Setting expectations proactively on the project regarding risk audits can help alleviate any anxiety surrounding the audits.

Variance and Trend Analysis

Trends in the project's execution are reviewed using the work performance data, earned value analysis, and other statistical information and reports. Deviations from the baselines may indicate the potential impact of threats or opportunities and can help forecast the degree of success in achieving the project's scope. Variance and trend analysis may expose the degree of technical risk faced by the project.

An earned value analysis, as presented in Chapter 7, is used to track project performance over time, capturing variance and trend information. Data such as the schedule performance index (SPI) or cost performance index (CPI) can be published in a control chart to determine stability or predictability.

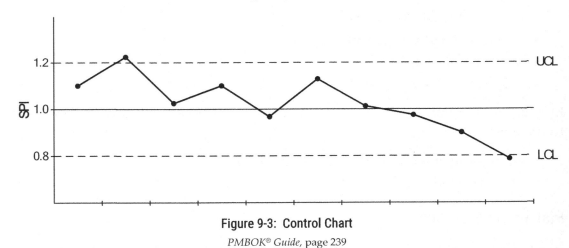

Figure 9-3: Control Chart

PMBOK® Guide, page 239

As described earlier in this chapter, a control chart plots results over time with defined control limits, typically three standard deviations from the mean. Results are considered to be unstable if there are results that fall outside the control limits or if there are seven results in a row below or above the mean.

When there is an assessment of schedule risk, such as the potential for further delays or slippage or in a situation in which the schedule has been previously delayed due to a realized risk, there are two techniques often used to compress the project schedule while maintaining the scope: fast-tracking and crashing.

For schedule compression, fast-tracking is employed first, as it comes with no additional cost. Activities that were planned to occur sequentially are shifted to be completed in full or partial parallel. The same concept as a lead, acceleration of a successor activity, fast-tracking can only be used in activities with finish-to-start discretionary relationships. While the costs will not increase, there may be some additional risk from performing the activities simultaneously versus sequentially.

If fast-tracking does not yield the necessary compression, another option that is considered is crashing. In crashing, the scope remains the same, but money is spent to get the work done more quickly. This could be done by adding more resources, paying overtime, outsourcing the work, paying extra fees, etc.

For both fast-tracking and crashing, activities on the critical path are the primary targets. Compressing non-critical activities only results in more float, which does not affect the overall timeline for delivery.

Technical Performance Measurement

Technical performance measurement compares technical accomplishments during project execution to the project management plan's schedule of technical achievement.

Reserve Analysis

It is the project manager's role to manage the contingency reserve and ensure that it is used only for the identified risks. A reserve analysis evaluates the amount of reserves allocated and remaining compared to the amount of uncertainty remaining on the project.

Typically, a project is considered a risk-declining model, meaning that as the project progresses, the uncertainty or risk should decrease and the understanding of the project should increase. Because of this, the amount of contingency allocated at the beginning of the project may become unnecessary as the project becomes more defined.

It is the project manager's professional responsibility to evaluate the reserve versus the risk. If there is an excess amount of contingency, that excess should be reallocated back to the organization. There is an opportunity cost associated with holding that funding for no purpose, as the organization could benefit from reinvesting it into other needs.

From an opposite perspective, the environment may become more complex and risky over the course of the project. The original allocation of contingency may not be sufficient, and the project manager may need to request additional reserve.

Status Meetings

The most effective setting for monitoring and controlling risks is the project status or team meeting. Risk should be a major topic at all status meetings so the team remains attentive to existing risks, continues to identify new risks, and makes sure plans remain appropriate.

Agenda items should include:

- A review of the highest-priority risks
- Risk or trigger conditions that have occurred
- Risk responses taken during the last period
- An evaluation of effectiveness and additional requirements
- Risks closed during the last period and the associated impacts
- Lessons learned

Critical Chain Project Management (CCPM)

As discussed in Chapter 7, critical chain project management focuses on resource constraints and critical path buffers. In controlling risk, CCPM evaluates the use of buffer penetration to trigger actions adjusted to the relative priority of the activities.

Workarounds

Workarounds are originally unplanned responses developed to deal with the occurrence of unanticipated risk events. Workarounds, unlike contingency responses, are not developed in advance. The use of workarounds may cause distrust of the project manager or the project, as they are very reactive in nature. Often, costly workarounds may be taken due to a lack in planning.

Control Risks: Outputs

Work Performance Information

Work performance information, an output of most of the monitoring and controlling processes, is analyzed work performance data. Whereas work performance data (the input) is raw, work performance information is that same data analyzed and applied to the current status of the project.

Change Requests

As the project progresses and project risks are monitored and controlled, there may be a need to submit various types of change requests. There are four types of change requests: scope changes, corrective actions, preventive actions, and defect repairs. Any of these may result from risk exposure, realized risks, the implementation of risk responses, etc.

Scope Changes

Scope changes are requests to add, remove, or modify the scope or work of the project. For example, if a risk of rain is identified during an outdoor celebration, a scope change may be generated to add a tent to the work of setting up the function.

Corrective Actions

Corrective actions are reactive requests typically related to the budget or schedule. For example, if there is a need to purchase insurance as a risk response and the purchase will exceed the budget, a change request could be generated to downscale the cabinetry to a less expensive model to capture cost savings that can be applied to the insurance purchase.

Preventive Actions

Preventive actions are proactive requests typically related to the budget or schedule and based on trending information. For example, if a project is not yet behind schedule but it is trending in a negative direction, with the latest work activities taking longer to accomplish than originally projected, a preventive action may be submitted to outsource a segment or portion of the work.

Defect Repairs

Defect repairs are change requests related to identified quality issues. For example, if a team that is inexperienced with producing a new type of product were to make a development error that would need to be corrected, a defect repair change request would be generated.

Project Management Plan Updates

As after the Plan Risk Responses process, the project management plan, the baselines, and the subsidiary plans are updated to reflect any changes related to project risk management.

Project Document Updates

As after the other risk processes, the risk register is updated based on the information gathered from risk monitoring and controlling.

Updates can include outcomes of the risk reassessments and risk audits, updates to previous risk management processes, notes on the closing of risks that are no longer applicable, details of what happened when risks occurred, and records of any lessons learned.

Organizational Process Assets Updates

Organizational process assets include any procedures, guidelines, and templates, as well as the project historical data, including lessons learned, post-project reviews, etc. As the risk is monitored and controlled on the project, those organizational process assets may need to be changed or updated.

The final action of risk control is to record the actual, concrete data for the organization's future use. The objective is to ensure that the risk data documented and archived is significant and robust enough to lend to future project risk management.

For all identified risks, it should be documented whether, when, and how often the risk occurred, along with its impact, the effectiveness of the response, and any other effects of the risk. A response analysis should be included, documenting the effectiveness of the risk strategies used (avoidance, mitigation, transference, exploitation, sharing, and enhancement). In addition, any unexpected or undocumented risks should be recorded, along with their associated impacts.

Upon closing the project, the risk checklist should also be groomed and updated, and any redundancies should be removed.

| Review Questions | Chapter 9 |

1. **The difference between work performance data and work performance information can best be described as:**

   A. Information is raw, and data is analyzed.
   B. The two terms are synonymous.
   C. Data is an output, and information is an input.
   D. Data is raw, and information is analyzed.

2. **As you enter the last phase of your project, you identify a number of risks that are now obsolete. What should you do next?**

   A. Submit a lessons-learned report that you did not use all of your contingency
   B. Reallocate the contingency that had been allocated to those risks back to the organization
   C. Delete the obsolete risks from your risk register
   D. Apply remaining contingency to a necessary scope change

3. **A control chart has all of the following characteristics except:**

   A. It illustrates how a process behaves over time.
   B. It is used to determine whether or not a process is stable or has predictable performance.
   C. It illustrates how various factors might be linked to potential problems or effects.
   D. It can be used to monitor any type of output variable.

4. **Which of the following is true about risk audits?**

   A. They must be conducted in house in order to be effective.
   B. They should not be included in routine project review meetings, as they require key stakeholders that may not attend review meetings.
   C. Ideally, they should only be conducted at the completion of a project or a phase.
   D. The project manager is responsible for ensuring that risk audits are performed at an appropriate frequency.

5. **Risk monitoring and controlling can best be accomplished through:**

   A. A monthly risk monitoring meeting
   B. Assigning specialized risk responsibilities to a team member
   C. Including risk management as an agenda item during periodic status meetings
   D. An evaluation of risks at the beginning of each phase

6. **Used in controlling risks, the technical performance measurement:**

   A. Compares technical accomplishments to the project management plan's schedule of technical achievement
   B. Evaluates the team's progress against the cost and scope baseline
   C. Considers the work that is being done, the team members, the effectiveness of the team members' work, and how well the team members are working together
   D. Evaluates the earned value performance of the project to the organization's standard for performance

7. **Which statement is most accurate regarding the monitoring and controlling of project risks?**

    A. It is optional on most projects.
    B. It is conducted throughout the project.
    C. It is the sole responsibility of the project manager.
    D. It is performed at the end of the project.

8. **This technique focuses on resource allocations within the schedule and can be used to monitor the amount of risk reserve time available, which may trigger actions to be taken.**

    A. Critical path method
    B. Critical chain method
    C. Workflow analysis
    D. Resource leveling

9. **All of the following are techniques used to monitor and control project risks except:**

    A. Risk reassessments
    B. Reserve analysis
    C. Delphi technique
    D. Risk audits

10. **This technique examines and documents the effectiveness of risk responses in dealing with identified risks and their root causes.**

    A. Risk reassessment
    B. Risk monitoring
    C. Reserve analysis
    D. Risk audit

11. **These are unplanned responses developed to deal with the occurrence of unanticipated risk events.**

    A. Workarounds
    B. Contingency plans
    C. Risk audits
    D. Risk reassessments

12. **As a result of monitoring and controlling risk, the risk register updates will include all of the following except:**

    A. Closed risks that are no longer applicable
    B. Outcomes of risk reassessments
    C. Identification of risk owners
    D. Outcomes of risk audits

13. **Why are effective status reports important to risk monitoring and controlling?**

    A. They ensure that risks are detected and managed in a timely manner.
    B. They are required as per the risk management plan.
    C. They list all of the risks, risk owners, and response strategies.
    D. They become part of the project archive.

14. **All of the following should be included in the project status report except:**
    A. Significant risks, issues, and problems with your planned responses
    B. The known risks in the near project future and the status of any ongoing risk recovery efforts
    C. Activities planned during the next status period
    D. The risk register

15. **During project executing, a major problem occurs that was not included in the risk register. What should you do first?**
    A. Tell management
    B. Reevaluate the risk identification process
    C. Create a workaround
    D. Look for any unexpected effects of the problem

Vocabulary Review   Chapter 9

Corrective action   Risk reassessment   Work performance data

Defect repair   Scope change   Work performance information

Preventive action   Technical performance measurement   Work performance reports

Reserve analysis   Variance and trend analysis   Workarounds

Risk audits

1. _____ Analyzing work performance data and evaluating that data relative to the project baselines

2. _____ Evaluation of the amount of risk of the project and the corresponding amount of contingency reserve for increase or reduction

3. _____ Detailed review of the project risk management approach and the risk responses taken to evaluate impact and effectiveness

4. _____ A change request to add to, remove from, or modify the work of the project

5. _____ Raw data being generated from the executing processes

6. _____ A change request intended to reverse a negative trend, typically related to the cost or the schedule

7. _____ Comparison of actual technical accomplishments during project execution to the project management plan's schedule of technical achievement

8. _____ Analysis of the work performance information of the project, including variances from the project baselines and performance data over time, done to determine risk exposure

9. _____ A change request intended to bring the project's performance back into alignment with the project baselines

10. _____ A change request to fix a quality issue

11. _____ Status reports detailing current project information

12. _____ Ongoing evaluation of identified risks conducted to confirm earlier analyses and responses

13. _____ A response to a negative risk that has occurred but was not planned in advance

Answer Key   Chapter 9

Review Question Answers

1. **Answer: D**

   Work performance data, an output of the Direct and Manage Project Work process, is the raw data being generated by the project activities. The work performance data is an input to the monitor and control processes, where it is analyzed against the project management plan and the project baselines. The output is work performance information. Work performance data is raw, and work performance information is analyzed.

2. **Answer: B**

   If there are identified risks that are now considered obsolete, any contingency originally allocated for those risks should be reallocated back to the organization. This is the process of a reserve analysis.

3. **Answer: C**

   A control chart does not illustrate how factors are linked to problems or effects. The type of diagram that shows that is a cause and effect diagram.

4. **Answer: D**

   The project manager is responsible for ensuring that risk audits are performed at an appropriate frequency. Those audits may be performed in-house or externally and may be included as a part of project review meetings. Risk audits occur regularly throughout the project, not just at the completion of a project or a phase.

5. **Answer: C**

   Risk should be a standing agenda during the project's periodic status meetings. This leverages insight and feedback from the team and the risk owners and keeps risk as a key topic.

6. **Answer: A**

   The technical performance measurement compares actual technical accomplishments to the project management plan's schedule of technical achievement. This evaluation ensures that the project is delivering appropriately on the technical aspects of the project.

7. **Answer: B**

   Risks are monitored and controlled throughout the project.

8. **Answer: B**

   The critical chain method focuses on resource allocations within the schedule.

9. **Answer: C**

   While the Delphi technique is used for many of the other risk processes, it is not one of the tools and techniques used to monitor and control risks.

10. **Answer: D**

    A risk audit evaluates the effectiveness of risk responses in dealing with the identified risks and their root causes.

11. Answer: A

A workaround is a response to a negative risk event that has occurred. Workarounds are not planned in advance.

12. Answer: C

Risk owners are identified during the Plan Risk Responses process.

13. Answer: A

Status reports include key information on risk management within the project. Providing this information to the stakeholders ensures that risks are managed appropriately.

14. Answer: D

The risk register is not included in the project status reports.

15. Answer: C

The first thing that happens when a major problem occurs is some type of workaround. For example, if you walk in your office and you realize your trashcan is on fire, you put out the fire. You do not call management, re-evaluate the risk identification process, or look for any unexpected effects first.

Vocabulary Review Answers

1. Work performance information
2. Reserve analysis
3. Risk audits
4. Scope change
5. Work performance data
6. Preventive action
7. Technical performance measurement

8. Variance and trend analysis
9. Corrective action
10. Defect repair
11. Work performance reports
12. Risk reassessment
13. Workarounds

Appendix A

Practice Exam

1. As project manager, you have just completed the risk response plan for a multi-million dollar renovation project. What should you do next?
   A. Conduct a risk reassessment during the next risk meeting
   B. Update the WBS with the additional work packages
   C. Calculate the overall project risk rating
   D. Conduct a quantitative risk analysis

2. Alexander is new to the organization and has been assigned a complex, multi-year project to deliver a new technology offering to the field offices. As Alexander begins to evaluate the project for risks, what area would be most appropriate for him to consider first?
   A. The scope of the project
   B. The cost of the project
   C. The schedule for the project
   D. The quality implications of the deliverables

3. Jennifer is a publisher. In order to make sure that her writer delivers on time, she inserts a penalty clause for late delivery into her writer's contract. Jennifer is using which risk response?
   A. Risk avoidance
   B. Risk transference
   C. Risk mitigation
   D. Risk acceptance

4. David is a senior project manager for the Valentine Manufacturing Company. He is currently assigned a high-priority project constrained by a limited budget. What is the most accurate statement regarding the monitoring and controlling of risks on David's project?
   A. It should be done throughout the project.
   B. It would only be necessary if there were a significant change to the project objectives.
   C. It is solely David's responsibility.
   D. It will not be performed until the last phase of the project.

5. Your team has identified project risks, performed a qualitative risk analysis, and determined the most appropriate responses for the prioritized risks. Which statement is least accurate regarding the updates to and communication of the risk register?

   A. The risk register should be written to a level of detail that corresponds with the priority ranking and the planned response.
   B. Risks evaluated to low priority should be included on a watchlist.
   C. The top 20 highest-priority risks should be addressed in detail.
   D. The risk register should include residual risks and the contingency plans.

6. This is the person responsible for ensuring that an appropriate response strategy is selected and implemented and for determining suitable risk actions to implement the chosen strategy.

   A. Project manager
   B. Risk sponsor
   C. Project sponsor
   D. Risk owner

7. This risk response creates changes to the project management plan that are meant either to eliminate a risk or to protect the project objectives from its impact.

   A. Risk transference
   B. Risk avoidance
   C. Risk mitigation
   D. Risk strategy

8. You are assigned a project that is underway. Activity B is a difficult activity and has a projected early start of day 10 and a late start of day 15. The SPI on your project is .72 and the CPI is 1.2. You have 15 stakeholders involved in the project. What are you most concerned about?

   A. Budget
   B. Resources
   C. Float
   D. Schedule

9. You are nearing the completion of your project. Upon evaluation of the previously identified risks, you realize that 18 of the 35 risks can be closed. What is the appropriate handling of closed risks?

   A. Deleting the risks from the risk register
   B. Indicating that the risks are closed on the risk register
   C. Reassigning the risk owners to other risks
   D. Performing quantitative analyses to ensure that the risks can be closed

10. You have taken over a project that has been rumored to be behind schedule and over budget. Many of the team members are disengaged and resentful of the project. The previous project manager left the company abruptly and provided no turnover documentation. During your first week on the project, your primary vendor shuts down. This was not identified as a risk on the risk register. What is the first step you should take?

    A. Invoke the contingency plan
    B. Mitigate the risk
    C. Implement a workaround
    D. Evaluate the project management plan for additional change control procedures

11. This is a set of actions defined in anticipation of the occurrence of a risk, to be executed only if specific, predetermined trigger conditions or the risk itself arises.
   A. Fallback plan
   B. Penalty clause
   C. Contingency plan
   D. Workaround

12. Which risk management technique would be most useful for providing an early warning threshold for sponsor communication and for tracking the spending and release of contingency on a project?
   A. Nominal group technique
   B. Reserve analysis
   C. Interviews
   D. Qualitative risk analysis

13. This risk response changes the project management plan to modify the size of the opportunity by increasing its probability and/or positive impacts.
   A. Risk enhancement
   B. Risk exploitation
   C. Risk strategy
   D. Risk transference

14. Your sponsor wants to discuss with you the most appropriate estimating technique to use on the project. You know that it's important to use a form of expert judgment, but your sponsor feels strongly that analogous estimating should be used. What would be the best option?
   A. Compromising by suggesting parametric estimating, which is a combination of both
   B. Discussing the situation further with the sponsor to understand why he or she wants to use the more time-consuming method of estimation
   C. Utilizing a three-point estimate, as it would be more accurate
   D. Agreeing to use analogous estimating, as it uses expert judgment

15. Your project has a dependency requiring that the design be completed prior to the beginning of manufacturing. What type of dependency is this?
   A. Discretionary
   B. Mandatory
   C. External
   D. Preferential

16. You are developing contingency plans for the risks that are not currently being addressed with proactive responses. The benefits of a documented and published contingency plan include all of the following except:
   A. It allows for fast action and response to risk events.
   B. It provides a justification for reserves.
   C. It determines the need for workarounds and fallback plans.
   D. It ensures that actions are documented to address significant events prior to their occurrence.

17. This risk response changes the project management plan to reduce the probability of occurrence or impact of a risk to below an acceptable threshold.

    A. Risk avoidance
    B. Risk management
    C. Risk mitigation
    D. Risk enhancement

18. There is a 30% probability that a risk event will happen in a given month. The project is a 12-month project. As such, what is the probability of that risk event occurring during the sixth month of the project?

    A. 15%
    B. 30%
    C. 5%
    D. 80%

19. With your key stakeholders and team members, you are determining the various roles and responsibilities for risk management within your project. What is the primary reason for documenting the risk roles and responsibilities?

    A. To ensure alignment with the WBS and the scope baseline
    B. To develop the information required to perform a stakeholder analysis
    C. To ensure that team members are aware of the expectations prior to the risk events occurring
    D. To provide feedback to the human resources department regarding project alignment

20. The project is underway and progressing according to plan. However, when you arrived at the office this morning, a malfunctioning sprinkler head led to the destruction of many hard-copy documents as well as the server. This was not identified as a risk during your risk identification for the project. You now have to take action. A _____ is a response to an unidentified negative risk that has occurred.

    A. Mitigation strategy
    B. Contingent response strategy
    C. Corrective action
    D. Workaround

21. You have evaluated the stakeholder communication needs generally for the project, and now you are specifically evaluating the communication needs as they relate to project risk. When determining the project risk communication needs, you should consider all of the following except:

    A. Gathering input from the stakeholders to ensure that nothing significant is overlooked and that risks are realistically assessed
    B. Identifying only the analyzed risks through the qualitative analysis process
    C. Identifying targeted communications to meet the specific needs of each stakeholder
    D. Ensuring credibility of the process by gaining commitment from the stakeholders regarding the risk responsibilities

22. Exploitation is to opportunities as _____ is to threats.

    A. Acceptance
    B. Mitigation
    C. Avoidance
    D. Transference

23. Your sponsor advises you that there is enough money in the budget to complete the IT project. However, the project is 40% complete, and the cost performance index (CPI) is 0.65. Upon reviewing the original cost estimates, you learn that the project was analogously estimated. The analogous estimate was then used to determine the activity estimates. What should have been done to reach a more accurate estimate?

A. SPI should have been used instead of CPI.
B. Past history should have been taken into consideration.
C. A bottom-up estimate should have been conduct to ensure that the activity estimates were accurate.
D. Estimated costs should have been used to calculate CPI.

24. You are determining the appropriate amount of time to dedicate to risk management activities for your new project. The frequency and depth of reviews and updates to the project risk information will depend upon:

A. Stakeholder availability for interviews
B. The nature of the project and the volatility of the environment
C. Team member commitment and risk roles
D. Previous strategic projects that have been completed

25. As you developed your project schedule, you identified resource constraints as a potential risk cause. Because of this, you decided to utilize the method of planning that leverages time buffers to monitor and manage schedule performance and account for limited resources. This technique is known as:

A. Critical path method
B. Critical chain method
C. Critical scheduling method
D. Resource risk mitigation method

26. You have completed all of your risk planning processes, and now the project is underway. You are continuing to monitor and control the risk environment of the project. During risk response control, when is additional response development needed?

A. When the organization is restructuring
B. When the original risk response is not working as expected
C. When the project objectives change
D. When the contingency reserves are used up

27. You have taken over the management of a strategy-critical project that is exceptionally time-sensitive. The team members represent the different divisions that will be most impacted by the implementation of the project and have been known to have very strong opinions about the project requirements and the development of the project deliverables. The previous project manager had difficulty managing conflict within the team, which caused the project to be delayed. You decide to train the team on conflict resolution strategies. This is an example of:

A. Risk avoidance
B. Risk exploitation
C. Risk acceptance
D. Risk mitigation

28. Your project is high-risk and has significant implications for the growth of the company. In order to monitor and control the project risks, you are adding formal risk items to the status meeting agenda. Which would you be least likely to include on the agenda?

   A. Risk or trigger conditions
   B. Risk responses taken during the last period
   C. Lessons learned
   D. Project management plan changes

29. Your project involves the implementation of sophisticated infrastructure technology. Upon evaluation of the project requirements, you realize that one of the components will require expertise that you do not currently have in-house. Leveraging a vendor that specializes in producing that component will allow you to deliver the project requirements. You enter into a contractual agreement with a vendor with the expertise you require. This is an example of:

   A. Sharing the risk
   B. Transferring the risk
   C. Avoiding the risk
   D. Mitigating the risk

30. You are assuming the management of a project that is already in progress. Upon conducting a stakeholder analysis, you identify a stakeholder that you classify as risk-neutral. What is the best approach for risk communication with that stakeholder?

   A. As they will be sensitive to possible opportunities, offer them detailed information on the opportunities available to the project team.
   B. As they will see present risk-taking as a price worth paying for future pay-offs, offer them information on the current project risk assessment and the actions being taken to minimize threats and maximize opportunities.
   C. As they are highly reactive to threats, offer them detailed information regarding the risk avoidance strategies in place.
   D. As they do not want to be actively engaged in risk management, only give them information on general project status.

31. Your project is dependent upon purchasing a piece of equipment from a vendor. The project is operating with an extremely limited budget. To exploit the probability of delivering under budget, you:

   A. Eliminate that requirement from the project objectives
   B. Enter into a cost-reimbursable contract with the vendor
   C. Begin negotiation for the equipment earlier than planned so as to secure a lower price
   D. Implement an extensive training program to train the team on how to develop the piece of equipment in-house

32. You are providing guidance to a peer project manager who has recently joined your project organization regarding risk monitoring and controlling. You advise her that the most effective setting for monitoring and controlling project risks is:

   A. Change control meetings
   B. Earned value analysis meetings
   C. Team status meetings
   D. Steering committee meetings

33. For your park development project, you have hired a vendor to install all of the concrete walkways. In the past, your organization has had some quality issues with this particular vendor. You need to mitigate the risks associated with poor quality. What would be the most appropriate response?

A. Insisting on the use of a cost-reimbursable contract
B. Assigning a team member to visit the job site to monitor the vendor's results on a pre-determined schedule
C. Developing a workaround to be used in the event of quality issues
D. Escalating the issue to the sponsor for resolution

34. This is the process of numerically analyzing the effect of identified risks on overall project objectives, assigning a numerical rating to those risks individually, and evaluating the aggregate effect of all risks affecting the project schedule and budget, and it presents an approach to making decisions in the presence of uncertainty.

A. Perform Qualitative Risk Analysis
B. Perform Quantitative Risk Analysis
C. Perform Quality Control
D. Perform Quality Management

35. You are working with your sponsor on a stakeholder analysis for your new project. You have identified a stakeholder who appears to be risk-seeking. What is the best approach for risk communication with this stakeholder?

A. As she will be sensitive to possible opportunities, include information on the opportunities available to the project team, but also alert her to the threats facing the project and the actions being taken for those threats.
B. As she will see present risk-taking as a price worth paying for future pay-offs, include information on the current project risk assessment and the actions being taken to minimize threats and maximize opportunities.
C. As she is highly reactive to threats, provided detailed information regarding the risk avoidance strategies in place.
D. As she is focused solely on opportunities, provide detailed information about all opportunity responses planned and completed.

36. The engineering department is developing multiple components for the new manufacturing facility. One particular component is very complex, and the development of that component is new to the department. You decide to prototype that particular component. Prototyping a risky piece of equipment:

A. Mitigates the risk associated with unsatisfactory results
B. Avoids the risk of non-acceptance
C. Exploits the risk of early delivery
D. Transfers the liability to the end-user

37. On your corporate infrastructure project, risk management is a key priority, given the company's sensitivity to market fluctuations. In addition, this is the first project for which formal project and risk management practices are being implemented. You have scheduled quarterly risk audits per the risk management plan. Which statement is least accurate regarding risk audits?

A. Risk audits are the responsibility of the project risk sponsor.
B. Risk audits examine and document the effectiveness of risk responses.
C. Risk audits may be perceived as too judgmental or time-consuming by the project team.
D. Risk audits require a communicated and agreed-upon risk management plan.

38. Your team members have escalated issues with the QA analyst to you and despite your feedback and requests for improvement, the issues are continuing to be a problem for the project team and are disrupting the work that needs to be done. To avoid the risk associated with the QA analyst, you:

A. Refer the QA analyst to the HR department
B. Document the disruption as a risk on the risk register
C. Conduct an off-cycle team meeting to set expectations regarding team behavior
D. Remove the QA analyst from the project

39. You are the project manager for the new marketing campaign. You need to find out which customer complaints occur most frequently about the product that will be replaced with the new marketing campaign. Which tool should you use to illustrate and rank the most frequently occurring complaints?

A. Pareto diagram
B. Control chart
C. Trend analysis
D. Fishbone diagram

40. Which of the following is not a critical success factor for project risk management?

A. Risk management must be fully integrated with project management and is dependent upon the implementation of project management practices.
B. Risk management requires commitment from both the organization and the project manager.
C. The level of effort and implementation for risk management is scalable and adaptable based upon the particular needs of the project.
D. Risk management is defined through organizational policies and procedures and can be applied uniformly on all projects.

41. You are the project manager of a multi-year, international project. The project will have significant implications for the organization's customer base. Because of the impact and reach of the project, you have identified a number of stakeholders. One of the stakeholders is known to be risk-averse. What is the best approach for risk communication with that stakeholder?

A. As they are sensitive to possible opportunities, include detailed information on the opportunities available to the project team.
B. As they feel uncomfortable with ambiguity, provide clear, detailed information regarding the overall risk status of the project and the planned responses.
C. As they will not want to be actively engaged in risk management, only provide information on general project status.
D. As they see present risk-taking as a price worth paying for future pay-offs, include information on the current project risk assessment and how you are capturing opportunities.

42. The construction project for the new high-rise building is running behind schedule and over budget. Upon evaluation of the project performance to date, you identify that one key reason for the delays is the inexperienced project foreman. You make a recommendation to the change control board to partner this foreman with a more experienced one in order to mitigate the risk associated with his inexperience. Once the change is approved, what is the next thing you should do?

A. Archive the change control report
B. Update the schedule to reflect the additional time and effort needed for the mentoring
C. Update the project baselines
D. Consult with the experienced project foreman and provide him with the background information

43. You are conducting a quantitative risk analysis on your project in relation to potential profits earned from a new product. The estimated profit is $350,000. There is a 20% chance that it will exceed expectations at a value of $180,000, a 50% chance it will meet expectations at a value of $40,000, and a 30% chance it will not meet expectations at a value of ($140,000). What is the expected monetary value of the risk?

A. $364,000
B. ($364,000)
C. $14,000
D. ($14,000)

44. You are working with your team leads to develop the cost estimates for the new website project. Your team members are questioning you regarding the difference between the cost baseline and the project budget. How can you best describe the difference between the project budget and the cost baseline?

A. The difference is the cost account.
B. The difference is the management reserve.
C. The difference is the contingency reserve.
D. The difference is the project cost estimate.

45. You just completed the initial analysis phase of your project and reported your findings to the sponsor. The project has significant uncontrollable risks, so your sponsor decides to cancel the project. Cancelling a troubled project is an example of:

A. Mitigating risk
B. Transferring risk
C. Exploiting the project
D. Avoiding risk

46. With your team, you have identified 35 risks. Of the 35 risks, you realize that five of them will have the greatest impact to the project. You would like to display the risks in a format that illustrates this effect. Which of the following is a chart that is useful in prioritizing risk management efforts, as it displays the risk causes ranked by their overall influence?

A. A control chart
B. A fishbone diagram
C. A Pareto diagram
D. A trend analysis

47. A peer project manager has approached you and asked for your advice regarding stakeholder communication on his project. One of the key stakeholders who is involved in the project is considered risk-tolerant. How would you advise the project manager to communicate with that stakeholder regarding project risk management?

   A. As the stakeholder is sensitive to possible opportunities, include detailed information on the opportunities available to the project team.
   B. As the stakeholder will see present risk-taking as a price worth paying for future pay-offs, include information on the current project risk assessment and the actions being taken to minimize threats and maximize opportunities.
   C. As the stakeholder is highly reactive to risk, provided detailed information regarding the risk avoidance and risk exploitation strategies in place.
   D. As the stakeholder has a casual approach to or opinion about risks, set realistic expectations of both the threats and opportunities identified for the project.

48. You have identified risks with the project team and key stakeholders, analyzed those risks, and implemented the designated risk responses. What is the next thing you should do?

   A. Identify and analyze any residual and secondary risks
   B. Update the project management plan and baselines
   C. Provide a written update to the sponsor regarding the risk actions completed
   D. Perform a quantitative risk analysis

49. You are three months into a one-year project and are evaluating the project schedule. It appears as though there are only few activities coming up within the next reporting period that have float. The float of an activity is determined by:

   A. The amount of lag
   B. The amount of time the activity can be delayed before it impacts the critical path
   C. Performing a Monte Carlo analysis
   D. The slack time between activities

50. A construction project is being completed in an area that is at high risk for fires. The organization has purchased an insurance policy that will cover damages from a fire. The premium for the insurance has cost implications and may cause the project to have cash flow problems. Which statement is most accurate regarding this situation?

   A. Purchasing the insurance policy is not considered transferring the risk because it was purchased at the organizational level.
   B. Cash flow problems are a residual risk.
   C. Cash flow problems are a secondary risk.
   D. A workaround plan should be defined in case a fire breaks out.

51. Midway through your project, you are evaluating your project schedule. There have been a number of changes that have affected the project cost and duration. As you analyze the schedule, you realize that there are three critical paths in your project. How will this affect your project?

   A. It will make the project more expensive
   B. It will make the project easier to manage
   C. It will increase the project risk
   D. It will increase the need for additional resources

52. Your customer has requested a significant scope change to the project. You are evaluating your project management reserve and contingency reserve. Management reserve is different from contingency reserve in that contingency reserve:

    A. Can be used at the discretion of the project manager
    B. Can only be allocated by the sponsor
    C. Is not part of the baseline
    D. Is intended to be used for "unknown-unknowns"

53. You are the project manager for a new customer service system implementation. In association with the launch of the new system, you are also responsible for implementing a training program. To develop your duration estimate for the development of the training program, you meet with the training team lead who will be in house for the development work, and based on her feedback, you decide to use a three-point duration estimate. What is the most commonly used formula for a three-point estimate?

    A. (Optimistic time + most likely time + pessimistic time) / 6
    B. (Optimistic time + most likely time + pessimistic time) / 3
    C. (Optimistic time – pessimistic time) / 2
    D. (Optimistic time + 4(most likely time) + pessimistic time) / 6

54. Which of the following would not be a tool or technique used in the monitor and control risks process?

    A. Risk audits
    B. Expected monetary value analysis
    C. Risk reassessment
    D. Status meetings

55. Your PMO offers guidelines on project cost estimation and the evaluation of projects using earned value. For the purposes of earned value analysis, you are instructed to use the cost performance baseline. The difference between the cost estimate and the cost performance baseline can be described as:

    A. Management reserve
    B. Contingency reserve
    C. Residual reserve
    D. Secondary reserve

56. You received notification from the sponsor that the new construction project has been approved and the project charter has been signed. As you begin the planning process for the project, you set aside time to develop the risk management plan with the key stakeholders and the sponsor. The risk management plan should be completed and communicated early in the project for all of the following reasons except:

    A. It sets expectations for risk management activities for the project, increasing the probability of engagement and project success.
    B. It provides the agreed-upon risk definitions so that all team members and stakeholders have a consistent understanding of risk ratings.
    C. It requests the human resources for the team and assigns the risk owners.
    D. It defines the risk budget and the format for risk tracking and communication.

57. The estimated costs for your project are $795,000. Upon evaluation of the project and the associated project risks, you decide to allocate an additional 10% to account for the uncertainty on the project. The sponsor has allocated 15% above the baseline to account for any major scope changes that may be requested by the customer. What is the project budget?

    A. $874,500

    B. $795,000

    C. $1,005,675

    D. $914,250

58. In an effort to minimize risk on the project, your sponsor has instructed you to use a fixed-price contract with any vendors whenever possible. In a fixed-price (FP) contract, the fee or profit is:

    A. Calculated as a percentage of the estimated costs

    B. Not known by the buyer

    C. Determined by the buyer upon project completion

    D. Included as a separate cost during the invoicing process

59. Which statement is most accurate regarding project risk management?

    A. Risk management plays a role in providing realistic expectations for the completion dates and cost of the project, even if there are few options for changing the future.

    B. Risk management should be considered separate from project management and communicated only with the project team.

    C. Risk management is not applicable throughout a project's life cycle.

    D. Risk management decreases in value contribution as the project progresses and more information becomes available to the project team.

60. The customer for your IT renovation project has notified you that they want to add another server and five more software packages to your project. What is the most appropriate way of handling this?

    A. Once the addition is approved through the change control process, utilize contingency reserve to cover the costs.

    B. Once the addition is approved through the change control process, utilize management reserve to cover the costs.

    C. Document the request and update the project management plan.

    D. Submit a corrective action request to the change control board.

61. You are performing a quantitative risk analysis on your project, specifically evaluating the use of an off-the-shelf software versus the development of the software in house. There is a 30% probability that the in-house product would require additional maintenance, and that would cost the organization $9,000. If a risk event has a 30% chance of occurring and the impact of the risk would be $9,000, what does $2,700 represent?

    A. The risk value

    B. The expected monetary value of the risk

    C. The amount of contingency to allocate

    D. The present value

62. You are kicking off the large company infrastructure project as the project manager. The six-month project will involve resources in all of the regional offices, including offices in eight different countries. Upon reviewing the resources and key stakeholders involved in the project, you identify 62 team members other than you. Based upon this information, you note that you have ____ communication channels.

    A. 1953
    B. 1890
    C. 124
    D. 496

63. The project team is evaluating the project risks and determining the most appropriate risk responses. What two risk responses will most likely generate risk-related contract decisions?

    A. Mitigate and transfer
    B. Transfer and avoid
    C. Enhance and share
    D. Transfer and share

64. You are mentoring a project manager who is struggling with his project. The project has been running behind schedule and over budget. You suggest that he conduct an ongoing trend analysis in order to:

    A. Improve variance reporting
    B. Create change requests
    C. Mitigate the harmful effects of scope creep
    D. Forecast future project performance

65. Critical chain project management (CCPM) adds time buffers to absorb variations of the durations of activities that are not on the critical path, reducing schedule risk. What is a weakness of using CCPM?

    A. It conflicts with the critical path method.
    B. It can only be used when resources have not been fully identified.
    C. It may be inadequate to deal with special causes of variance.
    D. It is only done once on the project.

66. This process determines which risks might affect the project and documents their characteristics:

    A. Identify risks
    B. Perform qualitative risk analysis
    C. Perform quantitative risk analysis
    D. Plan risk responses

67. You and your project management team have identified 73 risks on your project, identified and documented the triggers, plotted the risks on a probability/impact matrix, and evaluated the quality of the data that was used. What did you forget?

    A. To conduct simulation and modeling
    B. Risk mitigation activities
    C. To involve the other stakeholders
    D. An overall risk rating for the project

68. A scenario analysis defines alternative scenarios, and those scenarios are then evaluated for appropriate and cost-effective responses. If the organization has control of the scenarios, the alternatives and responses can be evaluated. If not, the analysis can determine effective and necessary contingency planning. Which statement is least accurate regarding a scenario analysis?

   A. Because it is based on project assumptions, it will be very accurate.
   B. It can be used to evaluate the effect of the risk and the response strategy.
   C. It can be time-consuming.
   D. The individuals conducting the scenario analysis should have an understanding of the project and the project objectives.

69. You are the project manager over a project to upgrade all existing patient systems to comply with electronic record requirements as determined by the US government. What would be the most appropriate technique to establish a reserve for the schedule duration, budget, estimated cost, or funds for a project based upon the remaining level of project uncertainty?

   A. Risk reassessment
   B. Reserve analysis
   C. Baseline establishment
   D. Risk audit

70. You are evaluating your current project to determine the need for contingency plans. You have 15 team members at three different locations within the US. This is your first project of this type, and you are operating with a very limited budget. What statement is least accurate regarding contingency plans?

   A. A contingency plan answers the questions of what action will take place, when and where it will take place, and how much will take place.
   B. The contingency plan should be communicated to team members to minimize surprise and resistance.
   C. The contingency plan is an alternative plan that is used if a possible unforeseen risk event becomes a reality.
   D. The contingency plan can significantly increase the chances for project success.

71. You have been assigned the management of a project to implement a new customer satisfaction survey mechanism for a large call center. Customers will be surveyed upon completion of a call with one of the company's 2,000 service representatives. The leadership of the company will use the results of the customer satisfaction surveys to determine the quarterly bonuses for the team managers. Unfortunately, because of the survey calibration associated with the new mechanism, the team managers feel that they may actually receive smaller bonuses than they did in the past.

   In this scenario, what is the negative risk?

   A. The team managers may receive smaller bonuses.
   B. The team managers will not be fully engaged in the project.
   C. The calibration is different.
   D. There are a large number of impacted parties.

72. You have been assigned the management of a project to implement a new customer satisfaction survey mechanism for a large call center. Customers will be surveyed upon completion of a call with one of the company's 2,000 service representatives. The leadership of the company will use the results of the customer satisfaction surveys to determine the quarterly bonuses of the team managers. Unfortunately, because of the survey calibration associated with the new mechanism, the team managers feel that they will actually receive smaller bonuses than they did in the past.

In this scenario, what is the cause of the threat?

A. The large number of team members
B. The implementation of a customer satisfaction survey
C. The differences in the calibration mechanism
D. The team managers being resistant to the change

73. Upon conducting a stakeholder analysis for the organizational reward and recognition project, you realize that your stakeholders have very different risk attitudes. Of the risk attitudes, which one is potentially the most dangerous?

A. Risk-seeking, as they have an aggressive approach to threats
B. Risk-tolerant, as they accept risks as part of the "normal situation" and may not manage risks appropriately
C. Risk-averse, as they feel discomfort about the presence of a threat
D. Risk-neutral, as they seek strategies and tactics that have high future pay-offs

74. You are taking over a project that is nearing completion. You realize that there was no documented risk management approach or documented risk register. Despite resistance from the team and the sponsor, you conduct a brainstorming session to identify risks that may impact the project. You and the team analyze the risks, prioritize the risks, determine the best responses, and update the project documents to reflect the responses. What else needs to happen?

A. Notification of the change control board
B. Submission of the status report to the sponsor
C. Creation of a new performance report
D. Assignment of a risk owner to prioritized risks

75. As the project manager over a web development project, you have identified over 80 risks. Using your past experience and available historical data from other projects, you have prioritized the risks based upon their probability of occurring and the impact on the project objectives should the risks occur.

What did you do wrong?

A. You performed a qualitative risk analysis when the risks should first have been prioritized through a quantitative analysis process.
B. You did not engage the project team in the risk identification process.
C. You did not thoroughly evaluate opportunities.
D. You did not identify enough risks.

76. You and your team have completed the following analysis:

Risk	Probability	Impact	Risk Score
A	.3	4	1.2
B	.8	5	4.0
C	.9	2	1.8
D	.6	3	1.8

Based on this information, what would be the most appropriate information for you to convey in the project performance report?

A. The project is low-risk.
B. The overall project risk score is 8.8.
C. The project is high-risk.
D. The overall project risk score is 2.2.

77. In order to comply with the PMO requirements, high-priority risks must have a documented risk response. Which statement is most accurate regarding risk response planning?

A. It is the responsibility of the project sponsor.
B. It must be completed prior to performing a qualitative risk analysis.
C. It will most likely lead to modifications of the project budget and schedule.
D. It is only necessary for those risks that have undergone quantitative analysis.

78. Which statement is most accurate regarding overall project risks and individual risks?

A. Overall project risks are the day-to-day focus of the project manager, whereas individual risks are the day-to-day focus of the project team.
B. Individual risks are associated with each team member, whereas overall project risks are associated with the project sponsor.
C. Individual risks are identified first, and they then serve as the foundation for the identification of overall project risks.
D. Specific events or conditions that could affect project objectives are individual risks, whereas overall project risks are based upon the project's ability to achieve the desired cost, time, scope, and quality requirements.

79. Your project is approximately 50% complete. Due to a restructuring within the organization, a new stakeholder has been identified that will be significantly impacted by your project. In a discussion of the project risks with the stakeholder, he tells you that he is comfortable with the identified risks, believes that there are risks involved with any project, and does not feel there is a need to do any further risk assessments or evaluation.

How would you describe the stakeholder's risk attitude?

A. He is risk-averse.
B. He is risk-tolerant.
C. He is risk-neutral.
D. He is risk-seeking.

80. You are the project manager for a local zoo enlargement project. A number of risks have been identified and analyzed. One of the identified risks is that the noise from the construction may lead to increased anxiety in the monkeys that are housed closest to the construction site. Your team develops a contingency plan to move the monkeys to a temporary housing location should they exhibit signs of increased anxiety. This is an example of:

   A. Active acceptance
   B. Trigger mitigation
   C. Risk avoidance
   D. Scenario enhancement

81. Based on past experience, when production is doubled, the unit costs decrease by 15%. Using this information, the company determines that production of 800 units will cost $150,000. This illustrates:

   A. The 80/20 rule
   B. The law of diminishing returns
   C. An evolution learning cycle
   D. Parametric cost estimating

82. You have completed the analysis of the risks facing the project. You would like to include a graphical representation of the risks in your status report. What diagram would best represent the risks depicted in order by their overall influence?

   A. Histogram
   B. Ishikawa diagram
   C. Control chart
   D. Pareto chart

83. The new project is highly visible and key to delivering on the organization's strategic goals for the year. The company assigns the most talented resources in order to ensure that the project is delivered as intended. Which of the following statements is most accurate?

   A. Because you are partnering up with the skilled resources, this is an example of risk sharing.
   B. Because the organization provided you with the resources, this is an example of risk transferring.
   C. Because the talented resources will ensure that the project is delivered as intended, this is an example of risk exploitation.
   D. Because the project is visible and tied to the strategic direction, this is an example of risk acceptance.

84. You are estimating the costs for your project and will be using a couple of different techniques, including analogous and parametric estimating. Analogous estimating:

   A. Uses bottom-up estimating techniques
   B. Uses the actual cost of previous, similar projects as the basis for estimating the cost of the current project
   C. Is used most frequently in the later stages of a project
   D. Summarizes estimates for individual work items

85. This is your first project for your new employer. You are in the process of identifying risks, but there are no existing risk register templates available for your use. Given your past project experience, you create a risk register template. What would you not include in the risk register?

   A. Identification number
   B. Schedule
   C. Description
   D. Owner

86. Upon evaluation of the project risks, you determine that 30 of the risks will be accepted without a proactive risk response. Passive risk acceptance requires:

    A. Minimal action
    B. No action other than documenting the strategy
    C. Setting aside contingency funding
    D. A risk response owner

87. This technique computes or iterates the project cost or project schedule many times using input values, selected at random, to calculate a distribution of possible total project costs or completion dates.

    A. Expected monetary value analysis
    B. Monte Carlo simulation
    C. Tornado simulation
    D. Sensitivity analysis

88. Which of the following is a decision-making technique that uses a diagram to compare available alternatives and the implications of those alternatives?

    A. Decision tree analysis
    B. Earned value analysis
    C. Sensitivity analysis
    D. Probability distribution

89. For the process re-design project, you have identified a risk of failed adoption by the organization's employees. In order to determine the most appropriate response, you send a questionnaire to the subject matter experts. Their responses are kept anonymous and upon submission are consolidated with the other responses. The consolidated information is then sent back out to the SMEs for further comment. This is an example of:

    A. Active risk acceptance
    B. The nominal group technique
    C. The Delphi technique
    D. A force field analysis

90. Which of the following is a type of sensitivity chart where the risk with the highest impact is placed at the top of the chart followed by other risks in descending impact order?

    A. Probability distribution
    B. Pareto chart
    C. Ishikawa diagram
    D. Tornado diagram

91. You have recently assumed the management of a project that has been underway for six months. Upon review of the risk register, you believe that many project risks have not been identified, so you decide to interview the key stakeholders and team members to get their input. Which of the following is a weakness of using interviews for risk identification?

   A. When used with stakeholders, interviews can decrease engagement, as stakeholders may feel the time is better spent on project activities.
   B. Specific risks cannot be addressed in detail, only in summary.
   C. Additional information, such as concerns and alternate perspectives that are non-risk-related, could surface and distract from the topic of the interview
   D. The experience and perspectives of others could lead to the identification of opportunities that had not been previously documented.

92. You are working with your project team and key stakeholders on three potential options for addressing an identified project risk. The options will be evaluated against the weighting of four key criteria: accessibility, price, ease, and implementation. Price is the most important criterion, so it has a weighting of 7. Ease has a weighting of 6, implementation has a weighting of 4, and accessibility has a weighting of 3.

   Option A has the following ratings: accessibility 4, price 8, implementation 10, ease 5.

   Option B has the following ratings: accessibility 7, price 5, implementation 6, ease 10.

   Option C has the following ratings: accessibility 6, price 7, implementation 9, ease 6.

   What option is the most appropriate to choose?

   A. Unable to determine based on information provided
   B. Option B
   C. Option A
   D. Option C

93. Which of the following is a quantitative risk analysis and modeling technique used to help determine which risks have the greatest potential impact on the project by examining the extent to which the uncertainty of each project element affects the objective?

   A. Monte Carlo simulation
   B. Earned value analysis
   C. Qualitative risk analysis
   D. Sensitivity analysis

94. Upon developing your schedule, you realize that your project has multiple critical paths. Because of this:

   A. You should consider adding in time buffers on the critical paths.
   B. You should consider additional management reserve.
   C. You should escalate the situation to your project sponsor.
   D. You should take a risk mitigation approach.

95. You are conducting an FMEA on your project. The XYZ function is being analyzed, and four potential failure modes have been identified. Failure mode A has a severity score of 8, an occurrence score of 5, and a detection score of 10. Failure mode B has a severity score of 6, an occurrence score of 3, and a detection score of 7. Failure mode C has a severity score of 3, an occurrence score of 7, and a detection score of 8. Failure mode D has a severity score of 7, an occurrence score of 4, and a detection score of 9.

    What is the risk priority number (RPN) for failure mode C?

    A. 18
    B. 168
    C. 21
    D. 42

96. You are meeting with your project management team and your key stakeholders to evaluate risks and determine the appropriate risk responses. To increase your success in risk response planning, you need all of the following except:

    A. An understanding of the implications of and interactions between risks and risk responses
    B. Responses that are planned strategically and then validated tactically
    C. Defined, communicated, and agreed-upon risk-related roles and responsibilities
    D. Responses that are planned tactically and then validated strategically

97. You are conducting an FMEA on your project. The XYZ function is being analyzed, and four potential failure modes have been identified. Failure mode A has a severity score of 8, an occurrence score of 5, and a detection score of 10. Failure mode B has a severity score of 6, an occurrence score of 3, and a detection score of 7. Failure mode C has a severity score of 3, an occurrence score of 7, and a detection score of 8. Failure mode D has a severity score of 7, an occurrence score of 4, and a detection score of 9.

    What is the criticality score for failure mode B?

    A. 4
    B. 16
    C. 126
    D. 18

98. Workarounds are determined during which risk management process?

    A. Control risk
    B. Plan risk responses
    C. Risk identification
    D. Perform qualitative risk analysis

99. You are conducting a FMEA on your project. The XYZ function is being analyzed, and four potential failure modes have been identified. Failure mode A has a severity score of 4, an occurrence score of 6, and a detection score of 10. Failure mode B has a severity score of 6, an occurrence score of 3, and a detection score of 7. Failure mode C has a severity score of 3, an occurrence score of 7, and a detection score of 8. Failure mode D has a severity score of 7, an occurrence score of 4, and a detection score of 9.

    What failure mode has the highest criticality score?

    A. Failure mode B
    B. Failure mode D
    C. Failure mode A
    D. Failure mode C

100. This technique allows for all participants to provide their opinions through a tallying process. Each group member gives his or her opinion, and duplicate opinions are removed. The remaining list is ranked by the group members.
   A. Nominal group technique
   B. Brainstorming
   C. Delphi technique
   D. Group decision-making techniques

101. Consider the following estimate information:

Phase	Low	Most Likely	High
Design	$6,000	$12,000	$17,000
Development	$5,000	$8,000	$12,000
Testing	$7,000	$10,000	$11,000
TOTAL	$18,000	$30,000	$40,000

If the project sponsor wanted to allocate funding based on the mean of the estimates versus the most likely estimate, how much additional funding would need to be allocated above the most likely estimate?
   A. $2,000
   B. $700
   C. ($670)
   D. $58,000

102. Your project team member is a very high performer and is very committed to the project being successful. However, upon review of the project performance report, she realizes that the project is currently running behind schedule. She notices that the delay will cause one of her activities to be scheduled while she is out of the office for her maternity leave, so she will be unable to work on the activity. How should you handle this situation?
   A. Add the issue to the issue log
   B. Notify the project sponsor
   C. Update the project status report with this information
   D. Recommend corrective action

103. Consider the following estimate information:

Phase	Low	Most Likely	High
Design	$6,000	$12,000	$17,000
Development	$5,000	$8,000	$12,000
Testing	$7,000	$10,000	$11,000
TOTAL	$18,000	$30,000	$40,000

Which phase of the project has a mean estimate closest to the most likely estimate?
   A. Both design and development
   B. All phases are equal
   C. Development
   D. Both design and testing

104. **Mitigation is to threats as _____ is to opportunities.**
    A. Enhancement
    B. Exploitation
    C. Acceptance
    D. Tolerance

105. **The project team has identified 76 risks to the implementation project. With the risk register complete, the team needs to perform an analysis of the risks. Qualitative risk analysis differs from quantitative analysis in that quantitative analysis:**
    A. Is quick and easy to perform
    B. Is usually conducted at the individual risk level
    C. Is usually conducted to get an understanding of the impact to the project cost and schedule objectives
    D. Is a subjective evaluation of likelihood and impact

106. **Risk management has never been fully recognized or implemented within your organization. The new director of the PMO, recently hired, feels that risk management should be conducted on all projects within the portfolio. It can be said that project risk management aims to do all of the following except:**
    A. Increase the probability and impact of positive events
    B. Identify and prioritize risks in advance of their occurrence
    C. Ensure that resources are being used appropriately
    D. Decrease the probability and impact of negative events

107. **Your project team has been selected for the implementation of the new human resource management system. As one of your first steps in evaluating the project, you conduct a brainstorming session with your team members. The benefits of using a brainstorming session to identify risks include of the following except:**
    A. Participants have increased buy-in.
    B. Brainstorming sessions provide a forum for stakeholder involvement and team building.
    C. Brainstorming allows for the creative generation of new ideas.
    D. Brainstorming sessions prevent "group think" from dominant personalities.

108. **Your project team and stakeholders have documented the risk management approach in the risk management plan, identified risks, and performed a qualitative analysis. You would like to conduct a quantitative risk analysis on a subset of the identified risks. In order to perform a quantitative risk analysis, all of the following components are needed except:**
    A. High-quality data
    B. A prioritized list of risks
    C. An appropriate project model
    D. A dedicated risk owner for each risk

109. Karen's project has been underway for seven months and has moved from the analysis phase into development. Unfortunately, due to changing economic conditions, the organization has undergone a restructuring, and layoffs have affected Karen's project team structure. Three of her management leads have been replaced with individuals who have significantly less experience. The risks associated with the project have been closely scrutinized, as there is very little funding available for contingent responses. What would be the most effective technique for monitoring and controlling the risks on her project?

    A. Highlighting the key risks to the sponsor on a monthly basis
    B. Incorporating a review of the highest-priority open risks in every team status meeting
    C. Establishing a weekly meeting with the organization's HR representative
    D. Including the risk register in her status report

110. As part of your risk management efforts, you and your team have developed a risk breakdown structure (RBS). A risk breakdown structure provides team members and stakeholders with all of the following except:

    A. The root causes of risk
    B. Resources assigned to manage the risks
    C. The most significant sources of risk to the project
    D. Areas of dependency or correlation between risks

111. You are performing an AHP analysis of various risks. The schedule objective has a weighting of .35. For scheduling implications, risk 1 has an average score of .72, risk 2 has an average score of .31, and risk 3 has an average score of .15. What is risk 3's overall score against the scheduling objective?

    A. .15
    B. .05
    C. .35
    D. .5

112. You have been assigned to work on the new marketing campaign project. The project has been progressing very well despite a few shifts in the organization's priorities. Your team has been working well together, and most of the milestones for the project have been met. Which of the following techniques would be least appropriate to employ at this point in your project?

    A. An analysis of your contingency reserve
    B. A reassessment of the identified risks
    C. A Delphi session
    D. An audit of risk management effectiveness

113. In evaluating the internal capabilities of the organization, you decide to leverage the use of a vendor for one of the project components to best capture an opportunity. This is an example of:

    A. Risk transference
    B. Risk partnership
    C. Risk sharing
    D. Risk enhancement

114. Residual risks are:

    A. The same as secondary risks
    B. A direct result of implementing a risk response
    C. Risks that remain after risk responses have been taken
    D. Risks that have no impact on the project budget or schedule

115. An uncertain event that may impact the project in the future, either positively or negatively, is called a(n):
    A. Risk factor
    B. Risk-opportunity dichotomy
    C. Project risk
    D. Expected value

116. As you evaluate a vendor bid of $350,000, you take into consideration the probability and impact of any delays. You determine that there is a 65% probability that the vendor will come in behind schedule at a cost of $125,000 and there is a 35% probability that the vendor will come in early for a savings of $50,000. What is the total value of the bid?
    A. $286,250
    B. $63,750
    C. $448,750
    D. $413,750

117. The risk response that can be categorized as either passive or active is:
    A. Risk avoidance
    B. Risk mitigation
    C. Risk transference
    D. Risk acceptance

118. Used in modeling and simulation, these represent the uncertainty in values, such as durations of schedule activities and costs of project components.
    A. Sensitivity analyses
    B. Risk analyses
    C. Earned value analyses
    D. Probability distributions

119. This analysis technique is a statistical concept that calculates the average outcome when the future includes scenarios that may or may not happen.
    A. Earned value analysis
    B. Delphi technique
    C. Qualitative risk analysis
    D. Expected monetary value analysis

120. You are the project manager for a construction project. A risk has been identified that the installation of the electrical components presents a safety hazard to the workers. You decide to make the area impassable to all workers during the installation. What type of risk response is this?
    A. Risk avoidance
    B. Risk mitigation
    C. Risk acceptance
    D. Risk transference

121. You are the project manager for the development of the new community park. The residents of the community have requested that a portion of the area be used for a dog park. If implemented, the dog park would require the use of a two-gate system in order to reduce the risk of a dog escaping the defined area. What is the most accurate statement regarding the double-gate system?

    A. It is an example of risk avoidance.

    B. It is an example of a fallback plan.

    C. It is an example of risk mitigation.

    D. It is an example of contingent response planning.

122. Your product development project is creating a new children's toy. There has been extensive component testing of the parts for the toy. While most of the components tested were satisfactory, piece B has been determined to be a significant choking risk to the target age group. What would be the most appropriate risk response to piece B?

    A. Determining a fallback plan to implement if the beta testing identifies the choking risk as well

    B. Identifying a risk avoidance response

    C. Developing a contingent response strategy for dealing with customer complaints

    D. Identifying a risk mitigation response

123. Exploitation is to opportunities as _____ is to threats.

    A. Acceptance

    B. Mitigation

    C. Avoidance

    D. Transference

124. Which statement is most accurate regarding contingency and fallback plans?

    A. A contingency plan is used when a fallback plan is not effective.

    B. A fallback plan is another name for a contingency plan.

    C. A contingency plan is defined in advance of a risk event, whereas a fallback plan is reactive in nature.

    D. A fallback plan is used when a contingency plan is not effective.

125. You are evaluating the following information to understand the implications of risk on the estimate. There is 40% chance it will take 12 days, a 25% chance it will take 18 days, and a 35% chance it will take 10 days. What is the best estimate?

    A. 11.8 days

    B. 13 days

    C. 12.4 days

    D. 14 days

126. A workaround is considered:

    A. A contingency plan

    B. Implementation of the contingency plan for a positive risk event

    C. A response to a negative risk that has occurred but was not planned in advance

    D. Using global sourcing to continue project development around the clock

127. An employee performing consistently with Maslow's self-actualization concept would most likely fall in line with McGregor's theory on:

    A. X people
    B. Y people
    C. High need for achievement
    D. Hygiene-driven people

128. One of your team members recently lost their spouse, and his performance on the project has suffered as a result. His inability to perform his job is based on his current focus on his social needs according to which theory?

    A. Vroom's expectancy
    B. Maslow's hierarchy of needs
    C. McClelland's achievement
    D. Herzberg's motivation and hygiene

129. Which contract type places increased risk on the seller?

    A. Cost-reimbursable
    B. Time and material
    C. Fixed-price
    D. Negotiated

130. You have been presented with three options for purchasing materials for your project. Option A will cost $40,000. With Option A, there is a 30% probability that additional support will cost $12,000 and 70% probability that additional support will cost $18,000. Option B will cost $38,000. With Option B, there is a 60% probability that additional support will cost $15,000 and a 40% probability that additional support will cost $30,000. Option C will cost $25,000. With Option C, there is a 75% probability that additional support will cost $18,000 and a 25% probability that additional support will cost $40,000. There is a 30% probability the organization will pursue Option A and a 40% probability the organization will pursue Option C. Based on the probability of the selection process, what is the value of Option B?

    A. $21,000
    B. $11,400
    C. $59,000
    D. $17,700

131. Risk data can be used for all of the following except:

    A. To decrease costs and frustration
    B. To justify pursuing a particular project
    C. To guarantee success of the project
    D. To assist with building an appropriate project portfolio

132. Which statement is most accurate regarding risk management?

    A. Risk management should be defined organizationally and applied universally to all projects conducted within the organization.
    B. While related to project management, risk management is a separate and unique approach.
    C. Risk management requires upper management commitment, as many risk responses will require support and approval.
    D. If an organization has a strong risk management commitment, the commitment of the individual project manager is less important.

133. The kitchen remodel project for the Jones family appears to be running behind. As the project manager, you evaluate the construction team's work performance information. Based on the information you received, the $30,000 project appears to be about 40% complete. Work billed to date was $10,000, although the project budget indicates that anticipated costs were to be $12,000 by this date. When you follow-up with the construction team lead, he estimates that there will be approximately $15,000 in remaining costs. The status of the project is:

    A. Ahead of schedule and under budget
    B. On schedule and under budget
    C. Behind schedule and over budget
    D. Behind schedule and on budget

134. Project risk can best be defined as:

    A. An unplanned event that, if it occurs, will have an impact on project objectives
    B. The occurrence of a problem that will potentially delay the project or cause additional costs
    C. An uncertain event that, if it occurs, will have a positive or negative impact on project objectives
    D. An uncertain event that, if it occurs, will cause problems for the project team

135. All of the following statements about risk management are true except:

    A. As a result of risk monitoring and controlling, the risk management plan may need to be updated.
    B. Risk identification is completed when the project is initiated.
    C. Risk management planning defines the risk management approach for the project.
    D. Risk analysis may include both qualitative and quantitative analysis of the risks.

136. Why is risk identification an iterative process?

    A. Because it only needs to be done once on the project, during the planning process
    B. Because project risks evolve or may become known as the project progresses through its life cycle
    C. Because new team members will have their own personal risks
    D. Because the risks will need to be proven legitimate by the project team

137. Purchasing insurance is best considered an example of risk:

    A. Mitigation
    B. Acceptance
    C. Avoidance
    D. Transfer

138. Which of the following is a true statement regarding negative risks?

    A. They are also called threats.
    B. They are not present on well-defined projects.
    C. For every negative risk, there is a positive risk.
    D. They are usually all originating from one cause.

139. All of the following statements are accurate about project risk except:

    A. Because projects are temporary, there are likely risks associated with the project schedule.
    B. Because projects are a mechanism to achieve something that cannot be done within normal operations, there can be risks associated with the level of experience in the organization.
    C. Because projects usually compete with operations for resources, there are likely risks associated with scarce resources.
    D. Because projects are managed by individuals who have experience, there are rarely any human-resource-related risks.

140. Along with your sponsor, you are working with your key stakeholders regarding the approach to risk management on a construction project. After extended discussion, one of your key stakeholders approaches you to discuss her concerns. She states that renovating the work area of her team will be extremely disruptive, and she is concerned that if the work is not completed on time, it will have a negative impact on her team during the busy holiday season. What should you do next?

    A. Escalate the situation to the project sponsor to determine if the project can be rescheduled
    B. Provide the stakeholder with a copy of the risk register
    C. Communicate to the other key stakeholders that the risk threshold is any schedule delay
    D. Document that the stakeholder has minimal risk tolerance for any schedule delays

141. In order to ensure that your team receives the incentive offered for completing the project early, you decide to fast-track a number of activities that are on the critical path. This is an example of what risk response strategy?

    A. Enhance
    B. Exploit
    C. Share
    D. Accept

142. Your project team and key stakeholders have identified over 100 risks for your current project. Those risks have been analyzed and prioritized. Proactive risk responses have been validated and approved. For the remaining risks, without a proactive response, you may:

    A. Do something if the risk happens, which will be implementing a fallback plan
    B. Do something if the risk happens, which will be implementing the contingency plan
    C. Do something if the contingency plans are not effective, which will be implementing the workaround plan
    D. Do something if the fallback plans are not effective, which will be implementing the contingency plans

143. If a risk event has a 90% chance of occurring and the consequence would be $10,000, what does $9,000 represent?

    A. The contingency budget
    B. The expected monetary value
    C. The present value
    D. The risk value

144. Commonly used with a decision tree, this is calculated by multiplying the value of each possible outcome by its probability of its occurrence and adding the products together.

    A. Risk likelihood
    B. Earned value
    C. Planned value
    D. Expected monetary value

145. Your $85,000 project is estimated to take 12 weeks, and you are 30% complete. What will the planned value (PV) be at the end of the project?

    A. Unable to determine until the project is 100% complete
    B. $59,500
    C. $85,000
    D. $7,083

146. You are gathering the cost estimates for a renovation project. Upon reviewing cost data on previous projects, you find that for 20-member teams, the average equipment cost was $3,800. You anticipate a 15-person team. Which statement is most accurate?

    A. A parametric estimate would be $2,850
    B. An analogous estimate would be $2,850
    C. The estimate cannot be determined due to pricing increases
    D. A budgetary estimate would be $2850

147. What is the benefit of involving stakeholders outside of the project team in identifying risks?

    A. They may provide additional objective information.
    B. They will have shared responsibility in mitigating the risks.
    C. They have more availability than the project team.
    D. They are at a more senior level than the project team and thus have more insight into potential risks.

148. Which contract type places increased risk on the buyer?

    A. Fixed-price
    B. Cost-reimbursable
    C. Fixed-price with incentive fee
    D. Time and material

149. One of your stakeholders is very resistant to adding a new feature to the existing software. To validate her resistance, she continually brings up data she has found through her research showing that the feature can cause issues in existing systems. This is an example of:

    A. Planning fallacy
    B. Ostrich effect
    C. Framing effect
    D. Confirmation bias

150. A black swan risk is:

    A. A risk that is highly likely to occur
    B. A risk that is considered impossible to occur
    C. A risk that has been previously unidentified until late in the project
    D. A risk that has been quantified as being especially dangerous

151. Also known as a rectangular distribution, this is a distribution that has constant probability.

    A. Continuous distribution
    B. Gaussian distribution
    C. Normal distribution
    D. Uniform distribution

152. This is a risk funding allocation for unknown-unknown risks that is controlled by the project sponsor.

    A. Buffer
    B. Contingency reserve
    C. Sponsor reserve
    D. Management reserve

153. **An emergent risk is:**

    A. A risk that is identified later in the project that could not have been identified earlier
    B. A risk that is considered impossible to occur
    C. A risk that arises as a result of implementing a risk response
    D. A risk that remains after an action has been taken

154. **This is a computerized simulation that applies a stratified approach, selecting a limited set of values from each strata or segment rather than pulling all random variables.**

    A. Monte Carlo simulation
    B. Latin Hypercube sampling
    C. Probability distribution
    D. System dynamics

155. **The critical path is:**

    A. The most important tasks that are developed in a precedence diagram
    B. The longest path through the schedule network with zero or negative total float
    C. The schedule network with the most float
    D. The sequence of activities that have mandatory dependencies

156. **This is a diagram that provides a graphical representation of situations showing causal influences, time ordering of events, and other relationships among variables and outcomes.**

    A. Influence diagram
    B. Decision flow chart
    C. System diagram
    D. Ishikawa diagram

157. **PESTLE, TECOP, and SPECTRUM are all**

    A. Qualitative risk analysis approaches
    B. Prompt lists for risk identification
    C. Risk categories
    D. System dynamics

158. **Using earned value to evaluate risk exposure is an example of leveraging _____.**

    A. Diagnostic metrics
    B. Retrospective metrics
    C. Predictive metrics
    D. System metrics

159. **This is a particular application of influence diagrams used to identify risks within a project situation by using feedback and feed-forward loops.**

    A. Decision flow charts
    B. Control charts
    C. System dynamics model
    D. Fishbone diagram

160. **A bowtie analysis:**

   A. Facilitates the discovery of predecessors to project problems by incorporating both what comes before and what comes after a specific risk event
   B. Analyzes the feedback and feed-forward loops in a complex risk management scenario
   C. Provides feedback on the performance of the various risk owners on the project
   D. Analyzes the root cause of risk events and quantitatively analyzes the impacts of the risk events

161. **Consider the following data set:**

   8, 9, 11, 11, 14, 14, 14, 15, 15, 17, 19, 20, 22

   What is the mean?

   A. 14
   B. 15
   C. 14.5
   D. Unable to determine

162. **This is the planned, systematic distortion or misstatement of facts in response to incentives. It can include deliberately underestimating costs and overestimating benefits in order to get project approval.**

   A. Strategic misrepresentation
   B. Planning fallacy
   C. Confirmation bias
   D. Loss aversion

163. **Consider the following data set:**

   8, 9, 11, 11, 14, 14, 14, 15, 15, 17, 19, 20, 22

   What is the median?

   A. 14
   B. 15
   C. 14.5
   D. Unable to determine

164. Your project is estimated to cost $32,000. After conducting a Monte Carlo simulation, you have the following information:

Probability %	Forecast
P0	$29,000
P10	$32,000
P20	$34,000
P30	$37,000
P40	$40,000
P50	$43,000
P60	$44,000
P70	$47,000
P80	$51,000
P90	$55,000
P100	$57,000

The maximum contingency to be allowed is 20%. With that contingency, what is the approximate confidence level?

A. P30
B. P40
C. P35
D. P20

165. This is a detailed, computer-intensive simulation approach to determining the value and probability of possible outcomes of a project objective such as a project schedule or cost estimate.

A. Monte Carlo simulation
B. Latin Hypercube sampling
C. Probability distribution
D. System dynamics

166. This is the action of misremembering predictions and exaggerating in hindsight what was known in foresight. This happens when people see past events as being more predictable than they were before they took place.

A. Framing effect
B. Confirmation trap heuristic
C. Hindsight bias
D. Anchoring and adjustment heuristic

167. A function that represents the distribution of many random variables as a symmetrical bell-shaped graph is a:

A. Uniform distribution
B. Bowtie distribution
C. Triangular distribution
D. Gaussian distribution

168. **An organization's risk taxonomy may define all of the following except:**

    A. Risk tolerance
    B. Risk rating scales
    C. Risk categories
    D. Risk responsibilities

169. **The element of the sample that occurs most often in a set of values is the:**

    A. Mean
    B. Mode
    C. Median
    D. Multiplier

170. **A probability distribution with a negative skew:**

    A. Has more values below the mean
    B. Is a typical project financial distribution
    C. Has more values above the mean
    D. Indicates the costs will exceed the budget

Appendix B

Answer Key

1. **Answer: B**

   Because taking actions to respond to risk involves work (effort), the WBS must be updated to include the work involved.

2. **Answer: A**

   The first area to consider is scope. Ultimately, if the organization is unable to deliver on the scope of the project, the cost and schedule do not matter.

3. **Answer: B**

   Penalty clauses within a contract are a form of transference. They may also serve to mitigate the risk, but ultimately, they are considered a transfer of the risk. Avoidance would be not using the writing, and acceptance would be taking no action.

4. **Answer: A**

   Risk monitoring and controlling are done throughout the project, regardless of the type of project. David will also rely on other team members to monitor and control risks.

5. **Answer: C**

   All high-priority risks should be addressed in detail and not be limited to a certain number.

6. **Answer: A**

   The project manager is ultimately responsible for ensuring that the appropriate risk response strategy has been selected and implemented.

7. **Answer: B**

   Risk avoidance eliminates the probability and/or impact of the risk

8. **Answer: D**

   Because the SPI indicates that the project is 28% behind schedule, the schedule is of most concern.

9. **Answer: B**

   Risks that are no longer applicable to the project should be marked as closed. Risks should never be deleted, as the archived record of them will be valuable for future projects.

10. Answer: C

Because you are responding to a risk that was not previously identified, the first thing you need to do is implement a workaround. There is no contingency plan, given that the risk was not previously identified.

11. Answer: C

This describes the contingency plan. A fallback plan is used if the original risk response does not work as intended. A workaround is an action taken in response to the occurrence of an unidentified risk.

12. Answer: B

A reserve analysis is be the most useful technique for providing an early warning threshold, as it is a comparison of the remaining reserve available to the relative uncertainty still remaining on the project. Nominal group technique is a brainstorming technique that is enhanced with a voting mechanism. Neither interviews nor a qualitative risk analysis would be a means for tracking the spending and release of contingency.

13. Answer: A

Risk enhancement increases the probability and/or positive impacts of an opportunity.

14. Answer: D

Analogous estimating is essentially a combination of historical information from a previous, similar project and expert judgment. A three-point estimate uses optimistic, pessimistic and most likely durations to come up with a weighted average. Parametric estimating is different than analogous estimating in that it uses a relation between variables to develop a unit cost or unit duration. Analogous estimating is not time-consuming; it is actually the quickest technique to perform.

15. Answer: A

Because there is not a physical or contractual limitation (a mandatory dependency), this would be considered a discretionary dependency.

16. Answer: C

A contingency plan would not determine the need for a workaround, as a workaround is an action taken in response to an unidentified, unplanned-for risk event.

17. Answer: C

Reducing the probability or impact of a threat is risk mitigation. Avoidance would completely eliminate the risk. Risk enhancement would increase the probability or impact of an opportunity. Risk management itself is not considered a response.

18. Answer: B

Because the risk event has a 30% probability for a given month, regardless of the month, it will still be a 30% probability.

19. Answer: C

Risk management roles and responsibilities are documented to ensure that the team members are aware of the expectations prior to the risk event occurring. This way, the team can focus directly on the risk event.

20. Answer: D

A workaround is a response to a previously unidentified threat that has occurred. A contingent response strategy would be appropriate if the risk event had been previously identified. A corrective action is a type of change request.

21. **Answer: B**

Risk communication involves all of the team members and stakeholders and is not limited to just communication of the risks analyzed through qualitative analysis.

22. **Answer: C**

Exploitation changes the plan to ensure the capture of opportunities. Risk avoidance changes the plan to ensure that the threat does not occur.

23. **Answer: C**

The CPI reveals that the project is over budget. Analogous estimating is top-down, and while it is quick, it is not as accurate as a bottom-up estimate. Given the status of this project, a bottom-up estimate would be helpful in verifying the accuracy of the estimates.

24. **Answer: B**

The frequency and depth of reviews and updates are dependent upon the nature of the project and the volatility of the environment. Stakeholder availability and team member commitments and roles do not dictate the frequency of risk assessments or ongoing risk evaluation.

25. **Answer: B**

The schedule planning technique that accounts for limited resources is the critical chain method.

26. **Answer: B**

Organizational restructuring, a change to the project objectives, or the use of all contingency reserves would dictate the need to revisit the risk management plan and the risk planning processes. Additional risk response development would be appropriate if the original risk response were not working as expected.

27. **Answer: D**

Because training the team on conflict resolution strategies will decrease the probability or impact of team conflicts, it is considered risk mitigation.

28. **Answer: D**

During the status meetings, it is important to focus on risk actions taken or needed. An evaluation of risk and trigger conditions, responses taken, and lessons learned are important to promote real-time discussion and evaluation. However, project management plan changes are not directly related to risk, nor do they necessarily need to be discussed interactively during a status meeting.

29. **Answer: A**

Entering into a partnership, specifically through a contractual relationship, is an example of positive risk sharing.

30. **Answer: B**

Risk-neutral individuals will take risks if there is an anticipated future pay-off relative to the level of risk taken. They are not particularly sensitive to opportunities or highly reactive to threats.

31. **Answer: C**

Delivering under budget is an opportunity. In order to enhance the opportunity, you would begin negotiation for the equipment earlier to attempt to secure a lower price. Cost-reimbursable contracts have increased risk to the buyer, and developing an "extensive" in-house training program could be very costly. Eliminating a requirement is usually not the first or best action to take.

32. **Answer: C**

The most effective setting for risk monitoring and controlling is the team status meetings. These keep everyone involved, informed, and engaged in risk management. Neither change control nor steering committee meetings generally include the project team members who are responsible for risk management activities.

33. **Answer: B**

To mitigate the risks (decrease the probability), it would be best to assign a team member to evaluate the vendor's results on a pre-determined schedule. A cost-reimbursable contract places increased risk on the buyer. A workaround is not planned in advance. Generally, only questions/issues surrounding scope should be escalated to the sponsor.

34. **Answer: B**

This describes the quantitative risk analysis process. "Numerically analyzing" means incorporating an analysis of the risk impacts on the project schedule and budget.

35. **Answer: A**

Risk-seeking individuals are primarily focused on opportunities, but as project manager, you must set realistic expectations with them regarding threats to the project.

36. **Answer: A**

Prototyping the component will allow the end-users to "touch and feel" the part and test it out to ensure that it meets the requirements. This will mitigate the risk associated with unsatisfactory results.

37. **Answer: A**

Risk audits are the responsibility of the project manager, not of a "project risk sponsor."

38. **Answer: D**

Risk avoidance means that you are eliminating the probability/impact of a negative risk. Removing the QA analyst is an example of risk avoidance.

39. **Answer: A**

A Pareto diagram is a histogram that ranks the causes or complaints by frequency of occurrence.

40. **Answer: D**

Because every project is different, project risk management must be scalable and applied as appropriate to a particular project. Risk management is not a one-size-fits-all solution.

41. **Answer: B**

Individuals who are risk-averse feel uncomfortable with uncertainty and ambiguity. As PM, you should provide them with clear, detailed information regarding the overall risk status and the responses that are planned.

42. **Answer: B**

Because there will be additional effort required in association with the mentoring, the schedule will need to be updated. The baselines should not be updated, as this is not a scope change.

43. Answer: C

To determine EMV:

0.2 x $180k = $36K

0.5 x $40k = $20k

0.3 x ($140k) = ($42k)

$36k + $20k + ($42k) = $14k

44. Answer: B

The overall project budget includes management reserve, whereas the cost baseline does not. Therefore, the difference between the baseline and the budget is the management reserve.

45. Answer: D

Cancelling the project is an example of risk avoidance. Mitigating the risk would be taking steps to decrease the probability or impact of the risks. Transferring the risk would involve some type of insurance policy or penalty clause.

46. Answer: C

A Pareto diagram is a histogram that ranks risks by frequency of occurrence or relative impact.

47. Answer: D

Individuals who are risk-tolerant have a casual approach toward risk. It is important to set realistic expectations of both the threats and opportunities identified for the project.

48. Answer: A

After planning or implementing risk responses, the next step is to identify the residual risks (the risks remaining) and the secondary risks (the risks that arise from implementing a risk response) to ensure that the residual and secondary risks are within the project risk threshold.

49. Answer: B

Float, or total float, is the amount of time that an activity can be delayed without delaying the project. Lag is different from float, because lag is a delay in the successor activity. Slack, synonymous with float, is not the time between the activities but rather the amount of time an activity can be delayed without impact.

50. Answer: C

Because the cash flow problems are a result of implementing a risk response (the transfer of risk via the insurance policy), they are considered a secondary risk. Had the organization not purchased the insurance policy, the cash flow problems would not exist.

51. Answer: C

Because multiple critical paths increase the possibility of a delay in the project, the fact that there are three critical paths will increase the risk associated with the project. However, multiple critical paths will not make the project more expensive or necessarily increase the need for additional resources.

52. Answer: A

Contingency can be used at the discretion of the project manager, but management reserve requires the authorization of the project sponsor. Contingency reserve is part of the baseline and is used for "known-unknowns." Management reserve is used for "unknown-unknowns"

53. **Answer: D**

The three-point (or PERT) estimating formula is (O+4M+P)/6. The most likely estimate is weighted by four in order to create a weighted average.

54. **Answer: B**

Expected monetary value (EMV) is not a tool that is used to monitor and control risks. EMV is a technique used when conducting a quantitative risk analysis.

55. **Answer: B**

Cost estimates generally do not include contingency reserve, but the cost performance baseline does include contingency reserve. Management reserve would be above and beyond the cost performance baseline.

56. **Answer: C**

The risk management plan does not request the human resources for the team, but it does document risk-related roles and responsibilities. The risk owners are assigned during risk analysis and response planning.

57. **Answer: C**

To determine the project budget:

$795k + $79.5k (contingency) = $874.5k

15% reserve would be an additional $131,175

$874,500 + $131,175 = $1,005,675

58. **Answer: B**

In a fixed-price contract, the buyer does not know what the profit is, as there is just one set price for the work. The price is not overtly broken up into costs and profit.

59. **Answer: A**

Risk management plays a role in providing realistic expectations for the completion dates and cost of the project. Risk management should be considered alongside project management, not separately. Risk management occurs throughout the entire project life cycle and it does not decrease in value contribution as the project progresses.

60. **Answer: B**

Because the request is a change to the scope, the best option, once approved, would be to utilize the management reserve to cover the costs.

61. **Answer: B**

The $2,700 represents the expected monetary value (EMV) of the risk.

62. **Answer: A**

To calculate the communication channels, you need to add yourself into the formula: 63 x (63-1) = 3,906 / 2 = 1953

63. **Answer: D**

Risk-related contract decisions are most likely the result of transferring threats or sharing opportunities.

64. **Answer: D**

Trend analysis is used to forecast future performance, allowing the team to take preventive or corrective actions as needed.

65. **Answer: C**

The critical chain method may not be adequate in dealing with special causes of variances.

66. **Answer: A**

The Identify Risks process determines which risks may affect the project and documents information such as the risks' characteristics.

67. **Answer: C**

Project risk management must include other stakeholders outside of the project management team.

68. **Answer: A**

Scenario analysis is based on assumptions, so there is a possibility that the analysis is inaccurate because of the quality of the underlying scenarios.

69. **Answer: B**

The best technique is the reserve analysis, which evaluates the amount of contingency time and money as compared to the amount of relative risk or uncertainty remaining on the project.

70. **Answer: C**

Contingency plans are established for moderate risks. The actions are planned in advance but only used when the trigger or risk event occurs. Therefore, it is not possible to have a contingency plan for "unforeseen" risk events.

71. **Answer: A**

The negative risk in this scenario is that the team managers may receive smaller bonuses. The calibration being different is a cause.

72. **Answer: C**

The cause of the threat is the difference in the calibration mechanism.

73. **Answer: B**

The potentially most dangerous risk attitude is risk-tolerant, because individuals with this attitude tend not to take proactive actions toward risk.

74. **Answer: D**

Along with the identification of the appropriate risk responses, a risk owner must be identified and assigned to the risks.

75. **Answer: B**

Based on the information provided, it appears as though you did not engage the project team in the risk identification process.

76. **Answer: D**

Because you do not have access to the probability and impact scale, you cannot determine if the project is low- or high-risk. To determine the overall project risk score, the individual risk scores are added and then divided by the number of risks: $8.8 / 4 = 2.2$

77. **Answer: C**

Risk responses generally require some type of action and therefore lead to modifications in the project budget and schedule. Risk response planning is the responsibility of the project manager, not the project sponsor. The qualitative risk analysis must be completed prior to determining responses.

78. **Answer: D**

Individual risks are those specific events or conditions that could affect the objectives, whereas overall risks are based upon the project's ability to achieve the set objectives.

79. **Answer: B**

Because he is comfortable with risk and does not want to do any additional work regarding risk assessment and evaluation, he is risk-tolerant.

80. **Answer: A**

Because you are not taking proactive steps but have designated a contingent response strategy should the risk occur, this is active acceptance.

81. **Answer: D**

This is considered parametric estimating, as a statistical relationship between variables is being used to determine a cost.

82. **Answer: D**

A Pareto chart will depict risks in order of greatest impact or influence.

83. **Answer: C**

Because their response will "ensure" that the project will be delivered, this is an example of risk exploitation. Sharing would involve some type of a contract or partnership agreement. Transferring is used for threats, not opportunities. Acceptance would be not taking any action.

84. **Answer: B**

Analogous estimating is a top-down estimating technique that uses the actual cost or duration of a previous similar project. Analogous estimating is usually used early in the project before there is a lot of detailed information.

85. **Answer: B**

The risk register would include the risk ID number, the description of the risk, and the risk owner. The risk schedule is not included in the risk register but is in the risk management plan.

86. **Answer: B**

Passive risk acceptance means that no action will be taken. However, that decision must still be documented. Active risk acceptance would set aside contingency funding.

87. **Answer: B**

This is describing a Monte Carlo simulation.

88. **Answer: A**

A decision tree allows you to compare alternatives and the implications of the alternatives. Earned value analysis is used to understand the implications of any cost or schedule variances. A sensitivity analysis evaluates the potential impact of different variables. A probability distribution is a common output of a Monte Carlo simulation.

89. **Answer: C**

The Delphi technique uses anonymous feedback from multiple experts.

90. **Answer: D**

A tornado diagram is a sensitivity chart that places the risk with the highest impact at the top of the chart with the remaining variables in descending order of impact.

91. **Answer: C**

During interviews, additional information that is not pertinent to the project or the project risks could surface and take the attention away from what is most important to discuss.

92. **Answer: B**

For each option, multiply the rating by the weighting of that criterion. Add the scores together for each option to determine which option has the highest score: A = 138, B = 140, C = 139. Therefore, B is the best option.

93. **Answer: D**

A sensitivity analysis would illustrate which risks have the most potential impact.

94. **Answer: A**

Multiple critical paths increase the risk of the project. To address this risk, an appropriate response would be to add time buffers within those critical paths.

95. **Answer: B**

RPN is calculated by multiplying severity by occurrence by detection. For failure mode C: 3 x 7 x 8 = 168.

96. **Answer: D**

Risk responses are planned strategically, at a high level, and then are validated tactically, ensuring that actions are documented to properly respond to the risk.

97. **Answer: D**

Criticality is calculated as severity multiplied by occurrence. For failure mode B, the criticality score is 18.

98. **Answer: A**

A workaround is a response to a previously unidentified threat that has occurred. Therefore, a workaround would be determined during risk monitoring and controlling.

99. **Answer: B**

Criticality is calculated as severity multiplied by occurrence. A = 24, B = 18, C = 21, D = 28. Therefore, D has the highest criticality score.

100. **Answer: A**

This is the nominal group technique. Brainstorming does not use a tallying process. The Delphi technique gathers anonymous feedback. The category of group decision-making techniques includes brainstorming, nominal group, and Delphi techniques.

101. **Answer: C**

The mean of the project is $29,333. Therefore, the sponsor would actually allocate $670 less than the most likely estimate.

102. **Answer: D**

Because the project is already running behind schedule, you need to determine and recommend corrective action to bring the project back on schedule.

103. **Answer: A**

The mean of the design estimates is $11,667, $333 less than the most likely estimate. The mean of the development is $8,333, $333 more than the most likely estimate. The mean of the testing phase is $9,333, $667 less than the most likely estimate. Therefore, the development and the design phases' mean are both closest to the most likely estimate.

104. **Answer: A**

Both mitigation and enhancement change the plan to change the probability or impact of the identified risk.

105. **Answer: C**

Quantitative risk analysis is generally conducted at the project level, whereas qualitative risk analysis is conducted at the individual risk level. Quantitative risk analysis leads to a probabilistic determination of the project objectives.

106. **Answer: C**

Project risk management does not ensure that resources are being used appropriately.

107. **Answer: D**

Brainstorming increases participant buy-in, provides a forum for stakeholder involvement and team-building, and allows for the creative generation of new ideas. However, there is the chance that if there are dominant personalities involved in the brainstorming session, the group may tend toward "group think."

108. **Answer: D**

To perform a quantitative risk analysis, you need to have a prioritized list of risks, high-quality data, and an accurate and appropriate model of the project. You do not need a dedicated risk owner, as the risk owners are identified as part of the risk response planning process. Risk response planning follows qualitative and quantitative analysis.

109. **Answer: B**

The most effective setting for risk monitoring and controlling is the team status meetings. These would help keep everyone involved, informed, and engaged in risk management.

110. **Answer: B**

The RBS can illustrate the root cause of the risk, the most significant sources of risk, and any areas or dependencies between the risks. The RBS does not show the resources assigned to manage the risks. Risk owners are documented on the risk register.

111. **Answer: B**

To determine the overall score for risk three, multiply the average score of .15 by the weighting of the schedule objective (.35).

0.15 x .35 = 0.0525

112. **Answer: C**

All of the listed techniques are used for risk monitoring and controlling, with the exception of the Delphi technique. The Delphi technique is used when you want to capture anonymous feedback, such as during risk identification or requirements gathering.

113. **Answer: C**

Partnering up to maximize an opportunity is risk sharing. Transferring is a risk strategy for threats, not opportunities.

114. **Answer: C**

Residual risks are the risks that remain after mitigating response is taken. Secondary risks are risks that arise directly as an outcome of implementing a risk response. Residual risks may impact the budget and the schedule.

115. **Answer: C**

This describes a project risk.

116. **Answer: D**

To calculate the total value of the bid, first calculate the expected monetary value of the risk scenario:

0.65 x $125,000 = $81,250

0.35 x -$50,000 = -$17,500

EMV = $63,750

Total value = initial bid + EMV
Total value = $413,750

117. **Answer: D**

Risk acceptance for threats can be categorized as either passive or active. Passive acceptance involves only documenting the risk. Active acceptance implies identifying or allocating contingent response strategies, reserves, etc.

118. **Answer: D**

Probability distributions are the output of modeling and simulation and represent the uncertainty in values.

119. **Answer: D**

The expected monetary value (EMV) analysis calculates the average financial outcome of a risk situation, using the probability of an outcome and the value of that outcome.

120. **Answer: A**

Because the area is made "impassable," meaning that none of their team workers can get near the hazard, this is considered risk avoidance.

121. **Answer: C**

The two-gate system reduces the chance of a dog escaping. Risk reduction is known as risk mitigation.

122. **Answer: B**

Given that the piece can result in choking and possibly death, the most appropriate risk response would be risk avoidance, to eliminate the risk.

123. Answer: C

Both risk exploitation and risk avoidance change the plan to remove the uncertainty. With exploitation, the opportunity will definitely happen. With avoidance, the threat is eliminated.

124. Answer: D

A fallback plan is used when the original response is not effective. Both fallback plans and contingency plans are planned in advance.

125. Answer: B

To calculate the best estimate, use a decision tree:

0.4 x 12 = 4.8

0.25 x 18 = 4.25

0.35 x 10 = 3.5

SUM = 12.55 days

The closes estimate provided is 13 days, using standard rules of rounding.

126. Answer: C

A workaround is a response to a negative risk event that has occurred.

127. Answer: B

People who are self-actualized are all about giving back, being productive, and contributing. McGregor's Y people are self-directed and motivated, like Maslow's self-actualized people.

128. Answer: B

The team member is dealing with his social needs and therefore is not focused on his higher level needs. This is consistent with Maslow's hierarchy of needs.

129. Answer: C

Fixed-price contracts place the most risk on the seller, as the seller is being paid one set price regardless of his or her expenses.

130. Answer: C

To calculate the value of Option B, use a decision tree. First calculate the expected monetary value of the risks associated with Option B:

0.6 x $15,000 = $9,000

0.4 x $30,000 = $12,000

EMV = $21,000

Then calculate the total value: original estimate + EMV

Total value = $59,000

131. Answer: C

There is nothing that can "guarantee" the success of a project, including risk data.

132. **Answer: B**

Risk management cannot be applied universally to all projects within an organization, as each project and all project stakeholders have varying requirements, etc. Risk management and project management are inextricably linked and cannot be considered separate approaches. The commitment of the project manager is always important. Risk management requires upper management commitment, as many risk responses require support and approval.

133. **Answer: B**

Earned value (EV) is calculated as: budget at completion (BAC) x % complete

EV = $30,000 x 40% = $12,000

Planned value (PV) = $12,000

Schedule variance (SV) = EV – PV = $12,000 - $12,000 = 0 (on schedule)

Actual costs (AC) = $10,000

Cost variance (CV) = EV – AC = $12,000 - $10,000 = $2,000 (positive variance, under budget)

134. **Answer: C**

A project risk is an uncertain event that, if it occurs, will have an impact on the project. The impact can be positive (opportunities) or negative (threats).

135. **Answer: B**

Risk identification occurs throughout all phases of the project so is therefore not complete after initiation.

136. **Answer: B**

Risk identification is iterative and repeated throughout the project, as risks may evolve as the project progresses. Changes in the project progress, the project environment, stakeholder tolerances, etc., can all drive, modify, or eliminate risks.

137. **Answer: D**

Purchasing insurance is risk transference. While the risk event may still occur, a third party will be responsible for handling some, if not all, of the impact.

138. **Answer: A**

Negative risks are also known as threats.

139. **Answer: D**

Human resources are unpredictable, their experiences vary, and availability may be a challenge, etc., so there are typically a number of human-resource-related risks.

140. **Answer: D**

The stakeholder has a concern about a risk, an uncertain event. Because it is a risk and not an issue, it would not be appropriate to escalate to the sponsor. Providing her with a copy of the risk register would also not do anything to help with the situation. There is nothing in the question to indicate that "any" schedule delay would be the risk threshold, or the point at which an action is taken. Therefore, the only appropriate answer is to document that the stakeholder has minimal risk tolerance for schedule delays.

141. **Answer: B**

Because fast-tracking "ensures" that the opportunity will be realized, this is considered risk exploitation.

142. **Answer: B**

A fallback plan would only be appropriate for risks for which the original response was not effective. There is no such thing as a workaround plan, as workarounds are not planned in advance. A contingency plan would come before a fallback plan.

143. **Answer: B**

$9,000 (0.9 x $10,000) is the expected monetary value.

144. **Answer: D**

Multiplying the value by the probability calculates the expected monetary value.

145. **Answer: C**

Planned value (PV) is the expected amount of spending for the project, cumulative from the start date through the status date. At the end of the project, PV is equal to the budget at completion (BAC), because that is the planned value of the project overall.

146. **Answer: A**

This is a parametric estimate using a statistical relationship between variables to calculate an estimate. If the average equipment cost is $3,800 for 20 team members, that is $190 per person. For a 15 person team, the estimate would be $2,850.

147. **Answer: A**

Involving stakeholders outside of the project team will provide additional objective information.

148. **Answer: B**

A cost-reimbursable contract places the most risk on the buyer, as the buyer cannot know what the final costs will be.

149. **Answer: D**

Because the stakeholder is validating her position by finding data to support it, this is considered a confirmation bias.

150. **Answer: B**

A black swan risk is a risk that is considered impossible to occur.

151. **Answer: D**

A uniform distribution is also known as a rectangular distribution, as it has a constant probability. No one value is any more likely than any other value.

152. **Answer: D**

Management reserve is a risk allocation for unknown-unknown risks.

153. **Answer: A**

An emergent risk is a risk that is identified later in the project and could not have been identified earlier.

154. **Answer: B**

Latin Hypercube sampling pulls data from a stratified approach.

155. **Answer: B**

The critical path is the longest path through the schedule network with zero or negative total float.

156. **Answer: A**

An influence diagram provides a graphical representation of situations showing causal influences, time ordering of events, and other relationships.

157. **Answer: B**

PESTLE, TECOP, and SPECTRUM are all examples of prompt lists used to identify risks.

158. **Answer: A**

Using earned value is an example of leveraging diagnostic metrics.

159. **Answer: C**

A systems dynamics model is a particular application of influence diagrams used to identify risks within a project situation by using feedback and feed-forward loops.

160. **Answer: A**

A bowtie analysis facilitates the discovery of predecessors to project problems by incorporating both what comes before and what comes after a specific risk event.

161. **Answer: C**

The mean is calculated by summing the values and dividing the result by the number of values: 189 / 13 = 14. 5

162. **Answer: A**

This describes strategic misrepresentation.

163. **Answer: A**

The median is the value separating the lower values from the higher values. In this data set, that value is 14.

164. **Answer: C**

Based on the information provided, a P30 estimate would be 15% contingency and a P40 estimate would be 25% contingency. A 20% contingency allocation would be approximately a P35 confidence level.

165. **Answer: A**

A Monte Carlo simulation is a computer-intensive simulation that provides confidence levels of achieving cost and schedule objectives.

166. **Answer: C**

Hindsight bias occurs when an individual misremembers their predictions or position.

167. **Answer: D**

A Gaussian distribution, also known as a normal distribution, is a symmetrical, bell-shaped graph.

168. **Answer: D**

An organization's risk taxonomy would not define risk responsibilities, as that would be determined on an individual project basis.

169. Answer: B

The mode is the value within the sample that occurs most frequently.

170. Answer: A

A probability distribution with a negative skew would have more values below the mean, which is the opposite of the typical project's financial distribution.

Actual Cost (AC). Total costs actually incurred and recorded in accomplishing work performed during a given time period for a schedule activity or work breakdown structure component. Actual cost can sometimes be direct labor hours alone, direct costs alone, or all costs, including indirect costs. See also *earned value management* and *earned value technique.*

Analogous Estimating [Technique]. An estimating technique that uses the values of parameters, such as scope, cost, budget, and duration, or measures of scale such as size, weight, and complexity from a previous, similar activity as the basis for estimating the same parameter or measure for a future activity.

Assumptions. Assumptions are factors that, for planning purposes, are considered to be true, real, or certain without proof or demonstration.

Assumptions Analysis [Technique]. A technique that explores the accuracy of assumptions and identifies risks to the project from inaccuracy, inconsistency, or incompleteness of assumptions.

Baseline. An approved plan for a project, plus or minus approved changes. It is compared to actual performance to determine if performance is within acceptable variance thresholds. Generally refers to the current baseline, but may refer to the original or some other baseline. Usually used with a modifier (e.g., cost performance baseline, schedule baseline, performance measurement baseline, technical baseline).

Bottom-Up Estimating [Technique]. A method of estimating a component of work. The work is decomposed into more detail. An estimate is prepared of what is needed to meet the requirements of each of the lower, more detailed pieces of work, and these estimates are then aggregated into a total quantity for the component of work. The accuracy of bottom-up estimating is driven by the size and complexity of the work identified at the lower levels.

Brainstorming [Technique]. A general data-gathering and creativity technique that can be used to identify risks, ideas, or solutions to issues among a group of team members or subject-matter experts.

Budget at Completion (BAC). The sum of all the budgets established for the work to be performed on a project, a work breakdown structure component, or a schedule activity. The total planned value for the project.

Change Request. Requests to expand or reduce the project scope; modify policies, processes, plans, or procedures; modify costs or budgets; or revise schedules.

Closing Processes [Process Group]. Those processes performed to finalize all activities across all Project Management Process Groups in order to formally close the project or phase.

Constraint [Input]. The state, quality, or sense of being restricted to a given course of action or inaction. An applicable restriction or limitation, either internal or external to a project, which will affect the performance of the project or a process. For example, a schedule constraint is any limitation or restraint placed on the project schedule that affects when a schedule activity can be scheduled and is usually in the form of fixed imposed dates.

Contingency Reserve [Output/Input]. The amount of funds, budget, or time needed above the estimate to reduce the risk of overruns of project objectives to a level acceptable to the organization.

Control Chart [Tool]. A graphic display of process data over time and against established control limits, which has a centerline that assists in detecting a trend of plotted values toward either control limit.

Control Limits. The area composed of three standard deviations on either side of the centerline, or mean, of a normal distribution of data plotted on a control chart that reflects the expected variation in the data. See also *specification limits*.

Corrective Action. Documented direction for executing the project work to bring expected future performance of the project work in line with the project management plan.

Cost Management Plan [Output/Input]. The document that sets out the format and establishes the activities and criteria for planning, structuring, and controlling the project costs. The cost management plan is contained in, or is a subsidiary plan of, the project management plan.

Cost Performance Baseline. A specific version of the time-phased budget used to compare actual expenditures to planned expenditures to determine if preventive or corrective action is needed to meet the project objectives.

Cost Performance Index (CPI). A measure of cost efficiency on a project. It is the ratio of earned value (EV) to actual costs (AC). CPI = EV divided by AC.

Cost-Plus-Fixed-Fee (CPFF) Contract. A type of cost-reimbursable contract where the buyer reimburses the seller for the seller's allowable costs (allowable costs are defined by the contract) plus a fixed amount of profit (fee).

Cost-Plus-Incentive-Fee (CPIF) Contract. A type of cost-reimbursable contract where the buyer reimburses the seller for the seller's allowable costs (allowable costs are defined by the contract), and the seller earns its profit if it meets defined performance criteria.

Cost-Reimbursable Contract. A type of contract involving payment to the seller for the seller's actual costs, plus a fee typically representing seller's profit. Cost-reimbursable contracts often include incentive clauses where, if the seller meets or exceeds selected project objectives, such as schedule targets or total cost, then the seller receives from the buyer an incentive or bonus payment.

Cost Variance (CV). A measure of cost performance on a project. It is the difference between earned value (EV) and actual cost (AC). CV = EV minus AC.

Crashing [Technique]. A specific type of project schedule compression technique performed by taking action to decrease the total project schedule duration after analyzing a number of alternatives to determine how to get the maximum schedule duration compression for the least additional cost. Typical approaches for crashing a schedule include reducing schedule activity durations and increasing the assignment of resources on schedule activities. See also *fast tracking* and *schedule compression*.

Critical Activity. Any schedule activity on a critical path in a project schedule. Most commonly determined by using the critical path method. Although some activities are "critical" in the dictionary sense without being on the critical path, the dictionary meaning is seldom used in the project context.

Critical Chain Method [Technique]. A schedule network analysis technique that modifies the project schedule to account for limited resources.

Critical Path. Generally, but not always, the sequence of schedule activities that determines the duration of the project. It is the longest path through the project. See also *critical path methodology*.

Critical Path Methodology (CPM) [Technique]. A schedule network analysis technique used to determine the amount of scheduling flexibility (the amount of float) on various logical network paths in the project schedule network and to determine the minimum total project duration. Early start and finish dates are calculated by means of a forward pass using a specified start date. Late start and finish dates are calculated by means of a backward pass starting from a specified completion date, which is sometimes the project's early finish date as determined during the forward pass calculation. See also *critical path*.

Decision Tree Analysis [Technique]. The decision tree is a diagram that describes a decision under consideration and the implications of choosing one or another of the available alternatives. It is used when some future scenarios or outcomes of actions are uncertain. It incorporates probabilities and the costs or rewards of each logical path of events and future decision, and it uses expected monetary value analysis to help the organization identify the relative values of alternate actions. See also *expected monetary value analysis*.

Defect Repair. The formally documented identification of a defect in a project component with a recommendation to either repair the defect or completely replace the component.

Delphi Technique [Technique]. An information-gathering technique used as a way to reach the consensus of a group of experts on a subject. Experts on the subject participate in this technique anonymously. A facilitator uses a questionnaire to solicit ideas about important project points related to the subject. The responses are summarized and are then recirculated to the experts for further comment. Consensus may be reached in a few rounds of this process. The Delphi technique helps reduce bias in the data and keeps any one person from having undue influence on the outcome.

Early Finish Date (EF). In the critical path method, the earliest possible point in time on which the uncompleted portions of a schedule activity (or the project) can finish, based on the schedule network logic, the data date, and any schedule constraints. Early finish dates can change as the project progresses and as changes are made to the project management plan.

Early Start Date (ES). In the critical path method, the earliest possible point in time on which the uncompleted portions of a schedule activity (or the project) can start, based on the schedule network logic, the data date, and any schedule constraints. Early start dates can change as the project progresses and as changes are made to the project management plan.

Earned Value (EV). The value of work performed expressed in terms of the approved budget assigned to that work for a schedule activity or work breakdown structure component.

Earned Value Technique (EVT) [Technique]. A specific technique for measuring the performance of work. Used to establish the performance measurement baseline (PMB).

Enterprise Environmental Factors [Output/Input]. Any or all external environmental factors and internal organizational environmental factors that surround or influence the project's success. These factors are from any or all of the enterprises involved in the project and include organizational culture and structure, infrastructure, existing resources, commercial databases, market conditions, and project management software.

Executing Processes [Process Group]. Those processes performed to complete the work defined in the project management plan to satisfy the project objectives.

Expected Monetary Value (EMV) Analysis. A statistical technique that calculates the average outcome when the future includes scenarios that may or may not happen. A common use of this technique is within decision tree analysis.

Fast Tracking [Technique]. A specific project schedule compression technique that changes network logic to overlap phases that would normally be done in sequence, such as the design phase and construction phase, or to perform schedule activities in parallel. See also *crashing* and *schedule compression.*

Firm-Fixed-Price (FFP) Contract. A type of fixed-price contract where the buyer pays the seller a set amount (as defined by the contract), regardless of the seller's costs.

Fixed-Price-Incentive-Fee (FPIF) Contract. A type of contract where the buyer pays the seller a set amount (as defined by the contract), and the seller can earn an additional amount if the seller meets defined performance criteria.

Float. Also called slack. See *total float* and *free float.*

Flowcharting [Technique]. The depiction in a diagram format of the inputs, process actions, and outputs of one or more processes within a system.

Forecast. An estimate or prediction of conditions and events in the project's future based on information and knowledge available at the time of the forecast. The information is based on the project's past performance and expected future performance and includes information that could impact the project in the future, such as estimate at completion and estimate to complete.

Forward Pass. The calculation of the early start and early finish dates for the uncompleted portions of all network activities. See also *schedule network analysis* and *backward pass.*

Free Float. The amount of time that a schedule activity can be delayed without delaying the early start date of any schedule activities immediately following. See also *total float.*

Identify Risks [Process]. The process of determining which risks may affect the project and documenting their characteristics.

Initiating Processes [Process Group]. Those processes performed to define a new project or a new phase of an existing project by obtaining authorization to start the project or phase.

Input [Process Input]. Any item, whether internal or external to the project, that is required by a process before that process proceeds. May be an output from a predecessor process.

Issue. A point or matter in question or in dispute, or a point or matter that is not settled and is under discussion or over which there are opposing views or disagreements.

Lag [Technique]. A modification of a logical relationship that directs a delay in the successor activity. For example, in a finish-to-start dependency with a ten-day lag, the successor activity cannot start until ten days after the predecessor activity has finished. See also *lead.*

Late Finish Date (LF). In the critical path method, the latest possible point in time that a schedule activity may be completed, based upon the schedule network logic, the project completion date, and any constraints assigned to the schedule activities, without violating a schedule constraint or delaying the project completion date. The late finish dates are determined during the backward pass calculation of the project schedule network.

Late Start Date (LS). In the critical path method, the latest possible point in time that a schedule activity may begin, based upon the schedule network logic, the project completion date, and any constraints assigned to the schedule activities, without violating a schedule constraint or delaying the project completion date. The late start dates are determined during the backward pass calculation of the project schedule network.

Lead [Technique]. A modification of a logical relationship that allows an acceleration of the successor activity. For example, in a finish-to-start dependency with a ten-day lead, the successor activity can start ten days before the predecessor activity has finished. A negative lead is equivalent to a positive lag. See also *lag*.

Lessons Learned [Output/Input]. The knowledge gained from the process of performing the project. Lessons learned may be identified at any point. Also considered a project record to be included in the lessons learned knowledge base.

Methodology. A system of practices, techniques, procedures, and rules used by those who work in a discipline.

Control Risks [Process]. The process of implementing risk response plans, tracking identified risks, monitoring residual risks, identifying new risks, and evaluating risk processes throughout the project.

Monitoring and Controlling Processes [Process Group]. Those processes required to track, review, and regulate the progress and performance of the project, identify any areas in which changes to the plan are required, and initiate the corresponding changes.

Monte Carlo Simulation. A process that generates hundreds or thousands of probable performance outcomes based on probability distributions for cost and schedule on individual tasks. The outcomes are then used to generate a probability distribution for the project as a whole.

Near-Critical Activity. A schedule activity that has low total float. The concept of near-critical is equally applicable to a schedule activity or schedule network path. The limit below which total float is considered near-critical is subject to expert judgment and varies from project to project.

Network Path. Any continuous series of schedule activities connected with logical relationships in a project schedule network diagram.

Opportunity. A condition or situation favorable to the project, a positive set of circumstances, a positive set of events, a risk that will have a positive impact on project objectives, or a possibility for positive changes. Contrast with *threat*.

Organizational Process Assets [Output/Input]. Any or all process-related assets from any or all of the organizations involved in the project that are or can be used to influence the project's success. These process assets include formal and informal plans, policies, procedures, and guidelines. The process assets also include the organizations' knowledge bases, such as lessons learned and historical information.

Output [Process Output]. A product, result, or service generated by a process. May be an input to a successor process.

Parametric Estimating [Technique]. An estimating technique that uses a statistical relationship between historical data and other variables (e.g., square footage in construction, lines of code in software development) to calculate an estimate for activity parameters, such as scope, cost, budget, and duration. An example for the cost parameter is multiplying the planned quantity of work to be performed by the historical cost per unit to obtain the estimated cost.

Pareto Chart [Tool]. A histogram, ordered by frequency of occurrence, that shows how many results were generated by each identified cause.

Path Convergence. The merging or joining of parallel schedule network paths into the same node in a project schedule network diagram. Path convergence is characterized by a schedule activity with more than one predecessor activity.

Path Divergence. Extending or generating parallel schedule network paths from the same node in a project schedule network diagram. Path divergence is characterized by a schedule activity with more than one successor activity.

Percent Complete. An estimate, expressed as a percent, of the amount of work that has been completed on an activity or a work breakdown structure component.

Performance Measurement Baseline. An approved, integrated scope-schedule-cost plan for the project work, against which project execution is compared to measure and manage performance. Technical and quality parameters may also be included.

Work Performance Reports [Output/Input]. Documents and presentations that provide organized and summarized work performance information, earned value management parameters and calculations, and analyses of project work progress and status.

Perform Qualitative Risk Analysis [Process]. The process of prioritizing risks for further analysis or action by assessing and combining their probability of occurrence and impact.

Perform Quantitative Risk Analysis [Process]. The process of numerically analyzing the effect of identified risks on overall project objectives.

Plan Risk Management [Process]. The process of defining how to conduct risk management activities for a project.

Plan Risk Responses [Process]. The process of developing options and actions to enhance opportunities and reduce threats to project objectives.

Planned Value (PV). The authorized budget assigned to the scheduled work to be accomplished for a schedule activity or work breakdown structure component. Also referred to as the budgeted cost of work scheduled (BCWS).

Planning Processes [Process Group]. Those processes performed to establish the total scope of the effort, define and refine the objectives, and develop the course of action required to attain those objectives.

Precedence Diagramming Method (PDM) [Technique]. A schedule network diagramming technique in which schedule activities are represented by boxes (or nodes). Schedule activities are graphically linked by one or more logical relationships to show the sequence in which the activities are to be performed.

Predecessor Activity. The schedule activity that determines when the logical successor activity can begin or end.

Preventive Action. A documented direction to perform an activity that can reduce the probability of negative consequences associated with project risks.

Probability and Impact Matrix [Tool]. A common way to determine whether a risk is considered low, moderate, or high by combining the two dimensions of a risk: its probability of occurrence and its impact on objectives if it were to occur.

Program Evaluation and Review Technique (PERT). A technique for estimating that applies a weighted average of optimistic, pessimistic, and most likely estimates when there is uncertainty about the individual activity estimates.

Project Management. The application of knowledge, skills, tools, and techniques to project activities to meet the project requirements.

Project Management Body of Knowledge. An inclusive term that describes the sum of knowledge within the profession of project management. As with other professions, such as law, medicine, and accounting, the body of knowledge rests with the practitioners and academics that apply and advance it. The complete project management body of knowledge includes proven traditional practices that are widely applied and innovative practices that are emerging in the profession. The body of knowledge includes both published and unpublished materials. This body of knowledge is constantly evolving. PMI's *PMBOK® Guide* identifies that subset of the project management body of knowledge that is generally recognized as good practice.

Project Management Knowledge Area. An identified area of project management defined by its knowledge requirements and described in terms of its component processes, practices, inputs, outputs, tools, and techniques.

Project Management Office (PMO). An organizational body or entity assigned various responsibilities related to the centralized and coordinated management of those projects under its domain. The responsibilities of a PMO can range from providing project management support functions to actually being responsible for the direct management of a project.

Project Management Plan [Output/Input]. A formal, approved document that defines how the project is executed, monitored, and controlled. It may be a summary or detailed and may be composed of one or more subsidiary management plans and other planning documents.

Project Management Process Group. A logical grouping of project management inputs, tools and techniques, and outputs. The Project Management Process Groups include initiating processes, planning processes, executing processes, monitoring and controlling processes, and closing processes. Project Management Process Groups are not project phases.

Project Management Team. The members of the project team who are directly involved in project management activities. On some smaller projects, the project management team may include virtually all of the project team members.

Project Manager (PM). The person assigned by the performing organization to achieve the project objectives.

Project Risk Management [Knowledge Area]. Project Risk Management includes the processes concerned with conducting risk management planning, identification, analysis, responses, and monitoring and control on a project.

Project Schedule Network Diagram [Output/Input]. Any schematic display of the logical relationships among the project schedule activities. Always drawn from left to right to reflect project work chronology.

Reserve. A provision in the project management plan to mitigate cost and/or schedule risk. Often used with a modifier (e.g., management reserve, contingency reserve) to provide further detail on what types of risk are meant to be mitigated.

Reserve Analysis [Technique]. An analytical technique to determine the essential features and relationships of components in the project management plan to establish a reserve for the schedule duration, budget, estimated cost, or funds for a project.

Residual Risk. A risk that remains after risk responses have been implemented.

Resource Leveling [Technique]. Any form of schedule network analysis in which scheduling decisions (start and finish dates) are driven by resource constraints (e.g., limited resource availability or difficult-to-manage changes in resource availability levels).

Responsibility Assignment Matrix (RAM) [Tool]. A structure that relates the project organizational breakdown structure to the work breakdown structure to help ensure that each component of the project's scope of work is assigned to a person or team.

Risk. An uncertain event or condition that, if it occurs, will have a positive or negative effect on a project's objectives.

Risk Acceptance [Technique]. A risk response planning technique that indicates that the project team has decided not to change the project management plan to deal with a risk or is unable to identify any other suitable response strategy.

Risk Avoidance [Technique]. A risk response planning technique for a threat that creates changes to the project management plan that are meant to either eliminate the risk or to protect the project objectives from its impact.

Risk Breakdown Structure (RBS) [Tool]. A hierarchically organized depiction of the identified project risks arranged by risk category and subcategory that identifies the various areas and causes of potential risks. The risk breakdown structure is often tailored to specific project types.

Risk Category. A group of potential causes of risk. Risk causes may be grouped into categories such as technical, external, organizational, environmental, or project management. A category may include subcategories such as technical maturity, weather, or aggressive estimating.

Risk Management Plan [Output/Input]. The document describing how project risk management will be structured and performed on the project. It is contained in or is a subsidiary plan of the project management plan. Information in the risk management plan varies by application area and project size. The risk management plan is different from the risk register that contains the list of project risks, the results of risk analysis, and the risk responses.

Risk Mitigation [Technique]. A risk response planning technique associated with threats that seek to reduce the probability of occurrence or impact of a risk to below an acceptable threshold.

Risk Register [Output/Input]. The document containing the results of the qualitative risk analysis, quantitative risk analysis, and risk response planning. The risk register details all identified risks, including description, category, cause, probability of occurring, impact(s) on objectives, proposed responses, owners, and current status.

Risk Tolerance. The degree, amount, or volume of risk that an organization or individual will withstand.

Risk Transference [Technique]. A risk response planning technique that shifts the impact of a threat to a third party, along with ownership of the response.

Root Cause Analysis [Technique]. An analytical technique used to determine the basic underlying reason for a variance, defect, or risk. A root cause may underlie more than one variance, defect, or risk.

Schedule Baseline. A specific version of the schedule model used to compare actual results to the plan to determine whether preventive or corrective action is needed to meet the project objectives.

Schedule Compression [Technique]. Shortening the project schedule duration without reducing the project scope. See also *crashing* and *fast tracking.*

Schedule Model [Tool]. A model used in conjunction with manual methods or project management software to perform schedule network analysis to generate the project schedule for use in managing the execution of a project. See also *project schedule.*

Schedule Performance Index (SPI). A measure of schedule efficiency on a project. It is the ratio of earned value (EV) to planned value (PV). The SPI = EV divided by PV.

Schedule Variance (SV). A measure of schedule performance on a project. It is the difference between the earned value (EV) and the planned value (PV). SV = EV minus PV.

Scope Baseline. An approved, specific version of the detailed scope statement, work breakdown structure (WBS), and associated WBS dictionary.

Scope Change. Any change to the project scope. A scope change almost always requires an adjustment to the project cost or schedule.

Scope Creep. Adding features and functionality (project scope) without addressing the effects on time, costs, and resources or without customer approval.

S-Curve. Graphic display of cumulative costs, labor hours, percentage of work, or other quantities plotted against time. Used to depict planned value, earned value, and actual cost of project work. The name derives from the S-like shape of the curve (flatter at the beginning and end, steeper in the middle) produced on a project that starts slowly, accelerates, and then tails off. Also a term used to express the cumulative likelihood distribution that is a result of a simulation, a tool of quantitative risk analysis.

Secondary Risk. A risk that arises as a direct result of implementing a risk response.

Sensitivity Analysis. A quantitative risk analysis and modeling technique used to help determine which risks have the most potential impact on the project. It examines the extent to which the uncertainty of each project element affects the objective being examined when all other uncertain elements are held at their baseline values. The typical display of the results is in the form of a tornado diagram.

Simulation. A simulation uses a project model that translates the uncertainties specified at a detailed level into their potential impact on objectives that are expressed at the level of the total project. Project simulations use computer models and estimates of risk, usually expressed as a probability distribution of possible costs or durations at a detailed work level, and are typically performed using Monte Carlo analysis.

Sponsor. The person or group that provides the financial resources, in cash or in kind, for the project.

Stakeholder. The person or organization (e.g., customer, sponsor, performing organization, or the public) that is actively involved in the project or whose interests may be positively or negatively affected by execution or completion of the project. A stakeholder may also exert influence over the project and its deliverables.

Start-to-Finish (SF). The logical relationship in which completion of the successor schedule activity is dependent upon the initiation of the predecessor schedule activity. See also *logical relationship.*

Start-to-Start (SS). The logical relationship in which initiation of the work of the successor schedule activity depends upon the initiation of the work of the predecessor schedule activity. See also *logical relationship.*

Strengths, Weaknesses, Opportunities, and Threats (SWOT) Analysis. This information-gathering technique examines the project from the perspective of its strengths, weaknesses, opportunities, and threats to increase the breadth of the risks considered by risk management.

Successor Activity. The schedule activity that follows a predecessor activity as determined by their logical relationship.

Technical Performance Measurement [Technique]. A performance measurement technique that compares technical accomplishments during project execution to the project management plan's schedule of planned technical achievements. It may use key technical parameters of the product produced by the project as a quality metric. The achieved metric values are part of the work performance information.

Technique. A defined systematic procedure employed by a human resource to perform an activity to produce a product or result or deliver a service. It may employ one or more tools.

Template. A partially complete document in a predefined format that provides a defined structure for collecting, organizing, and presenting information and data.

Threat. A condition or situation unfavorable to the project, a negative set of circumstances, a negative set of events, a risk that will have a negative impact on a project objective if it occurs, or a possibility for negative changes. Contrast with *opportunity*.

Three-Point Estimate [Technique]. An analytical technique that uses three cost or duration estimates to represent the optimistic, most likely, and pessimistic scenarios. This technique is applied to improve the accuracy of the estimates of cost or duration when the underlying activity or cost component is uncertain.

Threshold. A cost, time, quality, technical value, or resource value which is used as a parameter and may be included in product specifications. Crossing the threshold should trigger some action, such as generating an exception report.

Tool. Something tangible, such as a template or software program, used in performing an activity to produce a product or result.

Total Float. The total amount of time that a schedule activity may be delayed from its early start date without delaying the project finish date or violating a schedule constraint. Calculated using the critical path method technique and determining the difference between the early finish dates and late finish dates. See also *free float*.

Trend Analysis [Technique]. An analytical technique that uses mathematical models to forecast future outcomes based on historical results. It is a method of determining the variance from a baseline of a budget, cost, schedule, or scope parameter by using prior progress reporting periods' data and projecting how far that parameter's variance might be from baseline at some future point in the project if no changes are made in executing the project.

Triggers. Indications that a risk has occurred or is about to occur. Triggers may be discovered in the risk identification process and watched in the risk monitoring and control process. Triggers are sometimes called risk symptoms or warning signs.

Variance. A quantifiable deviation, departure, or divergence from a known baseline or expected value.

Variance Analysis [Technique]. A method for resolving the total variance in the set of scope, cost, and schedule variables into specific component variances that are associated with defined factors affecting the scope, cost, and schedule variables.

Work Breakdown Structure (WBS) [Output/Input]. A deliverable-oriented hierarchical decomposition of the work to be executed by the project team to accomplish the project objectives and create the required deliverables. It organizes and defines the total scope of the project.

Work Breakdown Structure Dictionary [Output/Input]. A document that describes each component in the work breakdown structure (WBS). For each WBS component, the WBS dictionary includes a brief definition of the scope or statement of work, defined deliverable(s), a list of associated activities, and a list of milestones. Other information may include: responsible organization, start and end dates, resources required, an estimate of cost, a charge number, contract information, quality requirements, and technical references to facilitate performance of the work.

Work Package. A deliverable or project work component at the lowest level of any branch of the work breakdown structure. See also *control account.*

Work Performance Information [Output/Input]. Information and data on the status of the project schedule activities being performed to accomplish the project work, collected as part of the Direct and Manage Project Work processes. Information includes: status of deliverables; implementation status for change requests, corrective actions, preventive actions, and defect repairs; forecasted estimates to complete; reported percent of work physically completed; achieved value of technical performance measures; and start and finish dates of schedule activities.

Workaround [Technique]. A response to a negative risk that has occurred. Distinguished from a contingency plan in that a workaround is not planned in advance of the occurrence of the risk event.

Appendix D

Index

Made in the USA
Middletown, DE
14 May 2022

65770099R00170